Researching Schools

Stories from a schools–university
partnership for educational research

Colleen McLaughlin,
Kristine Black-Hawkins,
Sue Brindley, Donald McIntyre
and Keith S. Taber

 Routledge
Taylor & Francis Group

LONDON AND NEW YORK

First published 2006
by Routledge
2 Park Square, Milton Park, Abingdon, Oxon OX14 4RN

Simultaneously published in the USA and Canada
by Routledge
270 Madison Ave, New York, NY 10016

Routledge is an imprint of the Taylor & Francis Group, an informa business

Typeset in Galliard by
Book Now Ltd
Printed and bound in Great Britain by
The Cromwell Press, Trowbridge, Wiltshire

British Library Cataloguing in Publication Data
A catalogue record for this book is available
from the British Library

Library of Congress Cataloging in Publication Data
Researching schools: stories from a schools–university partnership for
educational research/Colleen McLaughlin, [...] et al. – 1st ed.
　　p. cm.
Includes bibliographical references and index.
1. College–school cooperation–England–Cambridge–Case studies.
2. Education–Research–England–Cambridge–Case studies. I. McLaughlin, Colleen.

LB2331.53.R47 2006
378.1′03–dc22　　　　　　　　　　　　　　　　2006006742

ISBN10: 0–415–38841–4 (hbk)
ISBN10: 0–415–38842–2 (pbk)
ISBN10: 0–203–08610–4 (ebk)

ISBN13: 978–0–415–38841–2 (hbk)
ISBN13: 978–0–415–38842–9 (pbk)
ISBN13: 978–0–203–08610–0 (ebk)

Contents

Researching Schools

There has been a debate in both academic and educational policy arenas around the generation and use of educational knowledge. In the United Kingdom this has led to many recent and far-reaching initiatives which aim to enhance the relationship between universities and schools and which also aim to develop new ways of supporting practitioner research and inquiry. Internationally there are similar trends particularly in the United States, Australia and Norway, which are about to invest considerable sums of money in generating new partnerships between universities and schools focused on educational research.

This book presents the work of a highly innovative partnership between the University of Cambridge Faculty of Education and eight secondary schools, over six years. The focus of this networked learning community has helped to define the use and production of educational knowledge and research both within and between various partners.

This book explores the central questions and gives examples of the outcomes of the development that will assist any researchers, especially teachers undertaking research, to develop school–university research. Stories and examples from practitioners and others who worked directly in and with schools are presented throughout the book.

This book will appeal to a wide audience of practitioners and academics: to all who are interested in how research and inquiry can be used to support the development of practice in schools.

Colleen McLaughlin, Kristine Black-Hawkins, Sue Brindley, Donald McIntyre and **Keith S. Taber** are all at the University of Cambridge.

Illustrations

Figures

Tables

Boxes

Contributors

Vivienne Baumfield, University of Newcastle

Chris Clayton, Arthur Mellows Village College

John Clemence, Sharnbrook Upper School

Peter Garbett, Sharnbrook Upper School

Howard Gilbert, Soham Village College

Alison Gill, Sharnbrook Upper School

Mary Martin, Comberton Village College

Rolf Purvis, Chesterton Community College

Jennie Richards, Sharnbrook Upper School

Chris Tooley, Soham Village College

Dan Wilson, St Ivo School

Diana Wilson, St Ivo School

Acknowledgements

We are grateful to all the members of the SUPER partnership, both staff and students, within the schools and the university, for their time and collaboration in producing this book. In addition many thanks must go to Lyndsay Upex for her efforts and diligence in producing the manuscript and to Alison Craig for her work as communications and administrative secretary to SUPER from 2002 to 2005. Thanks too to the Wallenberg Centre for Research on the Improvement of Education for providing the initial funding for SUPER and to the National College of School Leadership (Networked Learning Communities) for its funding of SUPER as a Networked Learning Community. Thanks to Dave Ebbutt, who worked so hard to lay the foundations of SUPER in the first three years, and to David Hargreaves for his inspirational thinking.

Introduction
Structure of the book

> If the purpose of educational research is to inform educational decisions and educational actions, then our overall conclusion is that the actions and decisions of policy-makers and practitioners are insufficiently informed by research.
>
> (Hillage *et al*. 1998: 46)

This quotation exemplifies the national debate about the quality and usefulness of educational research taking place in the United Kingdom in the late 1990s. At the same time a more local debate was occurring in Cambridge, both within local schools and in the Faculty of Education – most clearly identified in the writings of two professors, David Hargreaves (1999) and Donald McIntyre (1998; McIntyre and McIntyre 1999). Out of these debates emerged the Schools–University Partnership in Educational Research (SUPER). This partnership has aimed to develop and research a partnership between eight schools and the University of Cambridge Faculty of Education which has focused on the development of educational research in all these settings, and has been in existence since 1998.

This book is the story of the partnership and the research undertaken on and within it. In Chapter 1 the local and national context are outlined, including the debates about the nature and usefulness of educational research. Ten case studies follow, comprising the eight schools, the university and the partnership as a whole. The final two chapters are a reflection on 'researching schools' and on schools–university research partnerships.

The Schools–University Partnership in Educational Research

Roots and branches

Colleen McLaughlin and Kristine Black-Hawkins

This chapter aims to explore the background to the Schools–University Partnership in Educational Research (SUPER) and in particular to explore the reasons for SUPER and for a research project in this area. The second half of the chapter provides a brief description of SUPER so that the reader can understand the context of the case studies that follow. A more detailed case study of the partnership can be found in Chapter 11.

Locating the Schools–University Partnership in Educational Research

The work described in this book and the questions that drive SUPER are rooted in debates and ideas that have driven those working in education and educational research for the past one hundred years. First, it is rooted in the tradition of thinking about and supporting practitioner research. Second, it is rooted in debates about the nature and usefulness of educational research or knowledge. Third, it emerged from some very local interests and concerns.

The tradition of teacher research

The argument that teachers should be more engaged in the production and use of educational knowledge is not a new one. It was in 1929 that Dewey wrote that teachers' contributions to educational research were 'an unworked mine'. Much work has been undertaken on the development of teachers as researchers since then and there have been traditions that have emphasised different purposes and aspects of the work. Zeichner and Noffke (2001) identified five major traditions.

> First is the action research tradition in the United States that developed out of the work of Collier, Lewin and Stephen Corey. Second is the British teacher-as-researcher movement that evolved in the 1960s and 1970s out of the curriculum reform work of British teachers and the supports provided by several academics, such as Lawrence Stenhouse and John Elliott, and the participatory action research movement in Australia that has many direct links

to the British movement. Third is the contemporary teacher researcher movement in North America that has been developed primarily by teachers, often with the support of their university colleagues and subject-matter associations. Fourth is the recent growth of selfstudy research by college and university educators who – as teachers and teacher educators – study their own practice. Finally is the tradition of participatory research that (a) evolved out of work in Asia, Africa, and Latin America with oppressed groups and (b) was then adapted to community-wide research in North America that included, but went beyond, the educational sphere.

(Zeichner and Noffke 2001: 301)

In the United Kingdom Lawrence Stenhouse's major contribution to this work still influences the debate. He argued strongly for a 'research model' of curriculum development and one that had teachers as researchers at its centre.

All well founded curriculum research and development, whether the work of an individual teacher, of a school, of a group working in a teachers' centre or of a group working within the coordination framework of a national project, is based on the study of classrooms. It thus rests on the work of teachers. It is not enough that teachers' work should be studied: they need to study it themselves.

(Stenhouse 1975: 143)

Stenhouse argued that there could not be any significant improvement in education without the creation of 'a research tradition which is accessible to teachers and which feeds teaching' (Stenhouse 1975: 165). Teachers needed to adopt a research stance to their teaching and this involved examining 'One's own practice critically and systematically' (1975: 156). Teachers would engage with research by conducting research. He acknowledged that this alone would not bring about change since 'the power of the individual teacher is limited' and so he argued both for collaboration between teachers and for coordination and support within schools. John Elliott (1991) and others built on Stenhouse's work and argued that the goal of teacher action research was to transform practice.

This tradition of academics working with teachers to support individual teacher research has a history within the now Faculty of Education at Cambridge and this has informed and shaped the work (e.g. Bradley *et al.* 1994; Dadds 1995).[1] Up until the 1990s this tradition was largely of working with individuals in schools or within courses. It is hard to make the distinction between individuals and schools in this way but it would be fair to say that mostly the focus was on the work of an individual or a small group of enthusiasts.

1 The current Faculty of Education is the result of a merger between the University of Cambridge Department of Education, the Cambridge Institute of Education and the teaching colleagues of Homerton College.

In the 1990s there were initiatives within the faculty that aimed to expand the work and to focus on working with schools rather than individuals. Examples of this were initiatives that built the links between research, schools and teachers' professional development (Bradley *et al.* 1994); the 'Improving the Quality of Education for All' project (Hopkins *et al.* 1994), which had a focus on school improvement informed by school-based research; and a Masters degree planned jointly with Hertfordshire Local Authority (Frost *et al.* 2003), which focused on research and teacher leadership within schools.

So one of the roots of SUPER was within this evolution within the Institute of Education (now the Faculty of Education) from focusing on individual teacher research to a focus on the school level. SUPER aimed to develop and interrogate the practical and theoretical aspects of a vision that had been in existence for some time.

Debates about the nature and usefulness of educational research

The second area of debate in which SUPER is rooted is concerned with the nature and usefulness of educational research. It is almost a decade since key documents were published that exemplified a concern about and criticism of educational research. These were David Hargreaves' (1996, 1999) papers on teaching as a research-based profession and the knowledge-creating school and the report by Hillage *et al.* (1998). These authors were critical of the quality of educational research and its use by practitioners. They raised issues related to the dissemination of educational research, the nature of the research undertaken and the gap between research and practice. Hargreaves (1996: 1) lamented that 'teaching is not at present a research-based profession. I have no doubt that if it were it would be more effective and more satisfying.' He went further in his 1999 article, where he offered a cogent argument for better professional knowledge about the management of schools and effective teaching and learning. He drew on models of knowledge creation in industry and in particular that of Nonaka and Takeuchi (1995) to argue that schools should learn from industry and become knowledge creating. This would involve four key tasks: auditing the professional knowledge in the school, managing the process of knowledge creation, validating the professional knowledge created and disseminating the professional knowledge created (Hargreaves 1999: 124). There already existed, he suggested, four key 'seeds' of knowledge creation.

> In short, educational knowledge creation is likely to be particularly explicit and effective when schools are engaged in school-based initial teacher training and school-based research, where middle managers become knowledge engineers and professional tinkering of various kinds is encouraged and supported, since these demand and then strengthen the processes that are central to the dynamics of professional knowledge creation and dissemination.
>
> (Hargreaves 1999: 133)

At the end of his 1999 article, Hargreaves set out an agenda for action, including six recommendations for action, one of which was that 'Schools of Education should establish formal partnerships with designated "research schools" either singly or in consortia' (1999: 142). Some of the policy responses to these debates will be considered next and other debates within this field will be returned to in a later section.

Policy responses and initiatives around school-based research

While many academic educational researchers have responded sceptically to Hargreaves' suggestions, government agencies have been more supportive, although often only hesitantly through short-lived initiatives. There were many initiatives in response to these debates and they were often around the support for school-based research but were also related to strengthening the links between research and policy and practice. Furlong and Oancea (2005) chart a range of initiatives in the UK which had different emphases and characteristics but which focused on strengthening the links between research and policy and practice. These included the Research Unit for Research Utilisation at the University of St Andrews (not focused on education alone); the Centre for the Use of Research and Evidence in Education (CUREE); the establishment of the National Educational Research Forum, which has engaged in bulletins to disseminate research findings as well as initiatives which bring practitioners, users and researchers together; the Teacher Training Agency (TTA) Research Consortia. Codifying and communicating accredited knowledge was another category e.g. the development of research reviews through the EPPI-Centre (at the University of London); and also those focused on the dissemination of research in different forms, e.g. the TTA Effective Practice and Research Dissemination Team; the Professional User Reviews of the British Educational Research Association, the establishment of the National Teacher Research Panel and the Research of the Month Website at the General Teaching Council for England. There were also some significant developments to support teacher research on practice and education as well as applied research. The Best Practice Research Scholarships (BPRSs) were established by the Department for Education and Skills (DfES) (www.teachernet.gov.uk) and inquiry was developed as a key strand within the Networked Learning Communities (NLCs) programme of the National College of School Leadership (NCSL). In addition a major research programme, the Teaching and Learning Research Programme (TLRP) was established by the Economic and Social Research Council (ESRC) to develop applied research partnerships, although these partnerships tended to keep policy-makers and practitioners firmly in the role of users in contrast to researchers. As can be seen there have been a raft of initiatives aimed at rising to the challenge of developing 'teaching as a research-based profession' (Hargreaves 1999). But whether and how this may be possible, and what part school–university partnerships might play in realising such an aspiration, remain matters for debate.

The debates, challenges and questions for the partnership

Many of those who have explored the notion of schools as researching organisations or teachers as researchers have been clear that the work provides many challenges. Stenhouse (1975: 142) was clear that 'it will require a generation of work, and if majority of teachers – rather than only the enthusiastic few – are to possess this field of research, [then] the teacher's professional self-image and conditions of work will have to change'. The need for schools to change and adapt organisationally has been identified by many as one of the key areas for investigation (Hargreaves 1999; McIntyre 2005). The question of how schools should adapt is one that is open for research. McIntyre (2004: 372) noted 'a striking resemblance between the picture that Elliott paints of the innovative secondary modern schools of the 1960s and the characteristics of schools identified in the 1990s as those in which staff have operated as "professional learning communities"'. The characteristics he identified from current research are:

> Inclusiveness: all teaching staff should understand the proposed mission for change and should be involved in deciding about change. School principals in such schools work supportively as peers and colleagues with teachers, engaging with them in professional development, being in the middle of things, easily accessible and making opportunities to stimulate conversation about teaching and learning. Active support is given by leaders for teachers seeking to develop their teaching strategies and skills. A culture of inquiry and questioning, searching for new ideas, critical thinking, dialogue, debate and collective problem-solving is deliberately fostered. Partly this is done by creating conditions for teachers to work together, protected time and space being crucial resources, and partly through policies which prioritise effective communication, collaboration and an undeviating focus on meaningful student learning. Emphasis is placed too on fostering community solidarity within the staff and the development of trust and mutual respect among colleagues. Conflicts are not avoided but are actively addressed and resolved through discussion and debate. Fullan (1991: 353) is quoted approvingly as recommending 'a redesign of the workplace so that innovation and improvement are built into the daily activities of teachers'. These then are the suggested characteristics of schools in which staff are committed to learning and to changing their practices in the light of that learning. These might then be necessary but probably not sufficient conditions for schools to become research institutions.
>
> McIntyre (2004: 22)

Stenhouse (1975) saw barriers in terms of the social and psychological climate of teaching since close examination of practice is threatening and therefore requires support. He saw these as major issues in the development of research in schools. 'I conclude that the main barriers to teachers assuming the role of researchers studying their own teaching in order to improve it are psychological and social' (1975: 159). The conditions under which schools can create knowledge from research and the concomitant social, psychological, organisational and managerial issues have been identified by many as a central challenge and clearly an area for further research and development.

The second key area for debate is in the field of research methodology and the implications for school-based research, in particular the issues of knowledge validation and dissemination. Both Stenhouse and Hargreaves identified these as key challenges. Stenhouse (1975: 157) commented that there were two set of problems: 'First, there is the problem of objectivity. Second, there is the problem of securing data'. Hargreaves (1999) was critical of the self-validation of teacher research. Although it seems to be widely believed that the findings of teacher research do not have to be as rigorously validated as those of academic research, nobody has yet offered a coherent rationale for such a belief. And the problems of disseminating the findings of school-based research so that they have a practical impact beyond where the research is done seem to be at least as great as they are for academic research.

The third major area for research and development is the nature of school–university partnerships which are focused on the use and production of educational research. There are many examples of school-university partnerships and the extent to which they focus on or use research varies. Many do use research but it may not be the primary focus. One example, part of the Professional Development Schools networking project in the United States, comprised teachers from four elementary schools, plus academic staff from Ohio University (see Darling-Hammond 1994). The primary purpose of this network has been to improve teachers' day-to-day classroom practices through engaging in practitioner inquiry, supported by university staff. Among school–university partnerships that did focus primarily on research were the TTA's four consortia (e.g. Baumfield 2001) is another example. The development of research has been a particular focus of the SUPER partnership. Miller (2001: 116) noted that 'a school/university partnership is a precarious organisation. Bridging two cultures, it remains marginal to each. This marginalisation, though difficult to manage, is essential for survival'. So a key thrust behind SUPER was the desire to research and share what could be learned about a research-focused schools–university partnership.

Introducing SUPER: the Schools–University Partnership for Educational Research

The purpose of this section is to give a brief description of the Schools-University Partnership for Educational Research (SUPER). This is intended to provide some background context to SUPER and also to Chapters 2 to 11 which comprise case studies of its members (eight schools and the Faculty of Education) plus a case study of the partnership as a whole. A brief chronological outline of the partnership is shown in Box 1.1.

Box 1.1 Outline of key stages in SUPER

1997 • Discussions take place within the faculty, resulting in the formation of the schools–university partnership

1999 • Three years' funding received from the faculty's Wallenberg Centre
     • Faculty research officer appointed to the project
     • Teacher research coordinator (TRC) appointed in each school

2001 • Faculty research officer retires and a new research officer appointed
     • Member of the faculty academic staff joins SUPER to oversee its management and to support the research of the project

2002 • Wallenberg funding ends
     • SUPER becomes a Networked Learning Community and receives three years' funding
     • Each school is allocated a critical friend from the faculty
     • Student voice coordinator (SVC) is appointed in each school

2005 • Funding from NLC ends
     • New stage in SUPER begins

The who, how and why of SUPER

Like all partnerships, SUPER comprises three elements which are closely related to each other: people (*who*), organised so as to engage in activities (*how*) that have shared purposes (*why*). For SUPER, these interconnections have been largely shaped by the diverse and shifting understandings held by members, within the schools and the university, concerning the nature and intentions of educational research. These concern:

* *Who* participates in the research (the researchers and the researched plus the doers and the users of research).
* *How* research is conducted and subsequently used.
* *Why* members chose to engage in and/or with research.

Furthermore, because partnerships necessarily involve real people engaging in real activities, SUPER has never been static in its composition, activities and intentions (*who*, *how* and *why*). Indeed, SUPER has existed in various forms and even now continues to adapt to the shifting needs and expectations of its membership. Such evolutions can partly be traced through existing literature; for example, the description of the partnership, as it was organised in 1999, is both similar to and different from its incarnation some four years later (see Ebbutt 2002; Black-Hawkins 2003; McLaughlin and Black-Hawkins 2004). Some schools have left, others have joined; key participants have been replaced in schools and the university;

purposes have been developed; new structures have been introduced; changes have been made in funding arrangements. Yet even this does not tell a complete story. Although the research partnership was first established in 1997, it grew out of a variety of school–university relationships (see, for example, James and Worrall 2000). This history is important because it continues to shape the partnership's current activities as well as its future possibilities. Indeed, as Stronach and McNamara (2002: 155) note, any institutional partnership, including that between schools and a university, is 'never a stable or final achievement, always a work in progress'.

Finally, however explicit the stated aims of a schools–university partnership may be, individuals within it may interpret them, and how they might be fulfilled, in a variety of ways. Richmond (1996: 215), a lecturer at the University of Michigan, noted 'the particular challenges' posed by tensions between herself and the science teachers with whom she set out to collaborate. Somekh (1994) not only experienced similar concerns *between* university and school staff, but also commented on the potential for comparable pressures *within* individual schools as well as *within* a university research team. Such concerns and influences are also part of SUPER's overall story. The following sections therefore should be read with the understanding that across the partnership and even within its composite institutions, there is not, and has never been, uniformity, in terms of *who*, *how* and *why*.

Who are the members of SUPER? Institutions and individuals

This book provides case studies of nine institutions, comprising eight secondary/upper schools and the Faculty of Education, all based in East Anglia, England. In terms of the schools, this constitutes a population of approximately eight hundred teachers and ten thousand students, all of whom potentially could be both the researchers and the researched. However, the selection of these eight represents the membership of SUPER only over a particular slice of its history, during a three-year period of 2002 to 2005. Since then two of those schools have withdrawn from the partnership (Queen Elizabeth's Girls' School and Netherhall School) and the involvement of another is temporarily reduced (St Ivo School). Of the seven schools in the original partnership, established in 1999, five remain (Arthur Mellows Village College, Chesterton Community College, Comberton Village College, Sharnbrook Upper School and St Ivo) and, of course, the university is a constant factor. Between 2002 and 2005, SUPER was also part of the national initiative of Networked Learning Communities, established by the government (National College for School Leadership 2002). This provided some opportunities for members of SUPER to collaborate with colleagues in other NLCs.

There are also key individuals in each of the SUPER schools who are expected to fulfil particular responsibilities that support both research and partnership activities. These are teacher research coordinators, student voice coordinators and head-teachers. As might be expected, the nature and purposes of these roles vary between the schools and have also evolved since 1999. Similarly, members of the faculty have also held key roles in the partnership, including the project director, the researcher to the project, the partnership coordinator and the critical friends to the schools. These roles too have changed and developed over time.

Teacher research coordinators

Since 1999, a condition of membership for each school has been a clear commitment to establish and maintain the post of a TRC. This position has been pivotal to all SUPER research activities, both within individual schools and across the partnership: without their support, SUPER would not be able to function as it has. Teachers appointed to be TRCs are expected to be a member of their school's senior management team (SMT) so that they have access to decision-making processes. Furthermore, they should be considered by their teaching colleagues to be highly competent classroom practitioners, and so likely to exert influence across the staff. Each school is expected to fund the TRC to be released from teaching duties for the equivalent of one day a week. In practice, the amount of time allocated by schools has varied, although all have fulfilled some of this commitment; for example, the attendance of TRCs at partnership meetings has been consistently high. However, in general terms, TRCs have been particularly effective in those schools where their time is consistently protected. The primary purposes of a TRC are to coordinate and support research generally within their own school and to collaborative with other TRCs and members of the faculty. This involves activities such as providing research training to school colleagues, participating in SUPER meetings and disseminating information about the partnership to members of their school. In the descriptions of the eight schools provided in this book, three of the TRCs have been in post since SUPER was established in 1999, others have taken over from colleagues at different points since that date.

Student voice coordinators

The idea of establishing one SVC in each of the SUPER schools was introduced in 2002. Therefore, compared to the position of TRC, this has been a relatively recent development in the partnership. SVCs are responsible, within their own schools, for coordinating and supporting research around issues of student voice. For some, this has involved training and encouraging students to engage in their own research activities. For others, the focus has been on consulting students so as to inform research undertaken by teachers. SVCs also attend and contribute to meetings and other activities across the partnership. Unlike their TRC colleagues, SVCs are not guaranteed any non-teaching time in which to undertake SUPER work. However, they are usually released from timetable to attend partnership meetings and, in some of the schools, additional time has been given. The extent and the effect of the research undertaken by individual SVCs has therefore been partly determined by the time and other resources they have been allocated.

Headteachers

Headteachers have always had the potential to play an important role in the partnership. Indeed, when SUPER was formally established, the schools which were first invited to join were chosen largely because of existing associations between their headteachers and members of the faculty. Their primary role has been to support the management of the research in their schools; they have also been encouraged to collaborate with each other as a group and with members of the faculty. Of particular importance is the extent to which individual headteachers have been able to provide opportunities and resources, including time, to enable research and partnership activities to take place, most crucially by ensuring that TRCs are able to fulfil their role. Their influence is also significant in terms of how far they are able to establish the status of practitioner research in their schools. For example, by building research into the school development/improvement plan; by engaging in research themselves; by responding positively to the research findings of members of their school.

Members of the project steering group

From the beginning SUPER has had a steering group consisting of a small number of elected representatives of the schools and an equal number of faculty researchers, including the partnership researcher and its director or coordinator. The steering group has had responsibility for maintaining the overall strategy of the partnership on behalf of all its members as well as accountability for the partnership and its members to its financial sponsors.

Project director

Professor Donald McIntyre was the project director from 1997 to 2002, with responsibility for week-by-week direction of the project on behalf of the steering group. Since 2002, when the direction of the partnership was reorganised, he has remained an active member of the project and of the steering group, seeking especially to ensure continuity in the partnership's work and to be an advocate for its work, both within and beyond its partnership members.

Researcher to the SUPER project

The role of the faculty research officer has been important throughout, as indicated by the funding costs of maintaining such a post. This position was first held by Dave Ebbutt, until he retired some two years later in 2001. During this period his primary concern was to research the processes of establishing a partnership for research between the schools and the university and, crucially, how such a partnership might effectively serve the research interests of all its members. However, and perhaps unsurprisingly, teachers in the schools, and notably the newly established TRCs, expected him to fulfil three other key roles. First, to manage the overall running of the project; second, to provide teachers with practical research support and training; third, to act as a critical friend to each of the schools. It became clear that one person could not accomplish all four responsibilities. Therefore, when Kristine Black-Hawkins was appointed as the researcher in 2001, her work was supported by the additional appointment of a partnership coordinator. A year later their work was further augmented by three more colleagues from the faculty joining SUPER so as to form together a team of five critical friends.

Partnership coordinator

As Dave Ebbutt had recognised from the beginning, there was a need for somebody to manage and coordinate the work of the partnership, a role for which Donald McIntyre did not have time and which he himself was therefore obliged to fulfil, thus distracting him from his proper research role. It was not until his retirement that this problem was resolved, however, with the appointment of Colleen McLaughlin as partnership coordinator. In 2002, with the move to a new funding regime, this new role also replaced that of project director. Her role includes coordinating and managing the work of SUPER on behalf of the steering group; providing research training and support to individual teachers and the schools; engaging in her own research into the nature of the research partnership. A key aspect of her work has involved developing and maintaining communication strategies for the partnership, for example, through meetings. She has also encouraged debate among key members around issues such as partnership relationships and roles.

Critical friends

The role of critical friend to the schools was part of David Ebbutt's responsibilities as the original researcher to the project. However, as noted above, it was not possible for one person to provide the amount of support required across the schools. Even when both a researcher and a partnership coordinator were established, the level of support was still spread too thinly. Therefore, in 2002, a faculty team of five critical friends (including the project researcher and the partnership coordinator) was formed, with members supporting either one or two schools each. The role of critical friends has been twofold. First, to undertake their own investigations into the nature and development of the school's research activity and the part played by the partnership in facilitating it; their findings are presented as the case studies in this book. Second, to support the research taking place in the schools by offering practical help and information. This has included mentoring practitioner researchers to conduct, write and disseminate research; training students as researchers; supporting practitioners' access to faculty facilities (for example, library services and specialist knowledge of academic colleagues). Critical friends have also provided an outside perspective about the school with which they are paired: asking questions and providing feedback on what they have observed.

How does SUPER work? Key strategies for partnership activities

Identifying the conditions, structures, processes and activities, which have supported the work of SUPER over its history, is complex. Understanding how the partnership has worked must take into account shifts over time as well as variations between its institutional members. There have been significant differences between how (and how much) members of each school have set out to engage in research and how (and how far) they have chosen to research in partnership with other members including the faculty. Nevertheless, the following two characteristics of SUPER have been crucial to its development and sustainability: the role of key individuals (as examined in the section above), and the nature and purposes of strategies for cross-partnership meetings and other activities, which are considered in this section. They are, of course, closely connected: key partnership individuals are likely to engage in partnership activities.

Since 1999, a range of meetings have taken place regularly within the SUPER partnership, organised and supported by the project coordinator and researcher from the faculty. Their primary purposes are

- to develop and sustain research activities in the schools
- to develop and sustain research activities across the partnership
- to support and strengthen relationships between key members
- to encourage effective communication across the partnership as a whole.

However, none of these objectives is achievable merely by either organising or attending a meeting per se. Their value is in the opportunity they provide for people to get together, talk to one another and share their concerns and enthusiasms. Meetings which focus on the exchange of ideas rather than giving out of information have been the most fruitful.

Since 2002, such meetings have been more diversified, with the intention of supporting, developing and sustaining the different roles of key people in SUPER. The following partnership-wide meetings take place about once or twice a term:

- teacher research coordinators
- student voice coordinators
- headteachers
- research critical friends.

In addition the following meetings also occur:

- External (partnership) steering group: comprises representatives from each of the other groups noted above, who meet once a term to report on and monitor the activities in the partnership.
- Internal (school) steering groups: organised by each school and usually attended by TRC, SVC, headteacher, faculty critical friend, plus others.

- Overnight conference: includes all TRCs, SVCs, headteachers and critical friends, who meet once a year to evaluate the progress of the partnership and to discuss its future intentions.
- Research training and support sessions: for any staff and/or students from the schools who wish to attend; for example, 'teaching and learning days' to share research activities with others in the partnership.

Why be in SUPER? A partnership for educational research

As already examined in the first half of chapter, there had been much debate during the 1990s, in the United Kingdom and beyond, about the usefulness of educational research, whether undertaken by members of university departments or by practitioners in schools (see Hargreaves 1996; Hillage *et al.* 1998). One emerging consideration had been how far this problem might be resolved by academics working in partnership with teachers in schools, so as to produce educational research which was not only robust in academic terms but also useful to practitioners. Similar discussions took place at the faculty between David Hargreaves and Donald McIntyre. Their interest and support led them, in 1997, to approach a small number of local headteachers with the idea of setting up a schools–university partnership concerned with doing and using educational research. Later, Donald McIntyre and David Ebbutt successfully applied for funding from the faculty's Wallenberg Centre to support an associated research project and, in 1999, SUPER was formally launched. From its inception its primary purpose was, therefore, to examine whether, and if so how, the faculty and a group of schools could work effectively as a partnership so as to serve the research interests of all members. SUPER was concerned with practitioner research and with the development of schools as researching institutions, but only in so far as these matters were relevant to the project overall aim of understanding the nature of a research based partnership.

From the perspective of the faculty, at least, SUPER was, and still is, fundamentally a research project. This is highlighted in the following extract from the proposal to the Wallenberg Foundation, written by Donald McIntyre and David Ebbutt.

> It is the challenge to seek to understand how [university] staff and school staff within the partnership find ways and means of working together on research issues and questions of mutual interest in order to create a systemic research culture within and across the partnership schools. One problem (of perhaps many) posed by this challenge will be to find ways in which the research process and outcomes can have utility for teachers in terms of their front-line accountabilities, at the same time as meeting the different accountability pressures upon [university] personnel.

From this the following research aim was established: 'To observe, describe and document, analyse, interpret, conceptualise, understand and report on the processes and outcomes of the work within the evolving partnership'. A number of key research questions were also formulated at the same time:

1   Within the partnership what kinds of research knowledge do schools and teachers value and find useful, in what ways and why?
2   What mechanisms can be found to make research knowledge from one school in the partnership readily and attractively accessible to another?
3   How, within the partnership, can the conduct and findings of practice-based research be both rigorous and at the same time couched in a language that is meaningful and accessible to practitioners?
4   What claims and justifications are made for research within the partnership contributing to the enhanced learning of students?
5   How, within the partnership, can the different rhythms and pacing of academic research, and those of a busy school life be productively combined?
6   How, within the partnership schools, can full time teachers be, and feel themselves to be, full partners in the research processes?
7   How, within the partnership, can research *with* teachers best be facilitated from within and without schools?
8   How, within the partnership, does useful research-based knowledge combine with other sorts of professional knowledge?

Since 1999 these broad research aims and questions have continued to direct the work of the project. They have also, necessarily, shaped the debates and issues presented here in this book as well as in each of its composite case studies. However, as would be expected, at different times in its history, the project has concentrated more closely on some questions than on others. Furthermore, some partners have chosen to focus on particular aspects of the project because they perceive them to be of greater relevance to their specific needs, interests and circumstances. And, even within the same institutions, priorities may vary. For example, teachers have often been motivated by the immediate practical application and usefulness of research in their classrooms to support the learning of their students, while headteachers are especially interested in the overall effects of research on their schools more generally. Meanwhile, members of the faculty are likely to be more concerned than either of these groups to undertake research which will, through its publication, contribute useful knowledge and understanding to a broader audience. Such discrepancies are probably inevitable in any partnership and the recognition and reconciliation of these differences form a critical theme which runs throughout the subsequent chapters of this book and the story of SUPER overall.

Chapter 2

Arthur Mellows Village College
A SUPER case study

Donald McIntyre, with Chris Clayton

> Arthur Mellows Village College is a mixed comprehensive college for students aged 11 to 19. It has 1,386 students, making it above average size. The college is heavily oversubscribed and numbers have been increasing steadily in recent years. There are equal numbers of girls and boys. Students are predominantly of white British heritage. ...
>
> Arthur Mellows Village College maintains above average standards ... provides a safe caring environment in which positive relationships are formed and high standards of behaviour are maintained ... offers a wide range of high quality learning opportunities which enables the individual needs of all students to be met effectively.
>
> (Office for Standards in Education (Ofsted) 2003a: Part A, p. 7)

Arthur Mellows Village College (AMVC) was one of the original seven schools that formed the SUPER partnership with the Faculty of Education in 1999. It was not one of those that had already been actively engaged in research with the university, nor was it one of those that actively sought a research relationship with the university. It had however been very active in the university's initial teacher education and training (ITET) partnership with secondary schools; and its headteacher, who soon afterwards became co-chairman of that partnership's steering group, had been suggesting that that partnership might take on a wider remit. AMVC was therefore invited, and enthusiastically agreed, to become part of this new research partnership.

AMVC was pretty much a beginner as a school engaged with research when it joined the partnership. Much has therefore depended on the headteacher, Fred Mann, and on the teacher research coordinator, Chris Clayton, the two people with specific responsibilities for the school's part in the partnership. It has been to the advantage of AMVC that Fred and Chris have both remained in these roles since 1999, thus providing important continuity, and also that Chris has been able to bring to her TRC role her authority and whole-school perspective as a deputy head.

Our account here of AMVC as a partnership school will be simply structured. First we will offer an appraisal of where the school had got to in 2002, together with Fred's and Chris's vision at that time of what they wanted for the school and how that vision might be realised. This will be based primarily on two interviews with Fred in that year by two different university members of the partnership, but will take account also of the reflections at the time of the two authors of this chapter.

The core of the chapter will then be concerned with various strategies attempted, primarily by Chris, to develop AMVC's engagement with research, and with assessments of the value and limitations of each of these strategies. And finally, we shall briefly reflect on any general lessons that might be learned by other schools from the AMVC story thus far.

AMVC and research in 2002

By 2002, AMVC had been engaged in the research partnership for three years. Chris especially, but also Fred and other members of the school staff, had had multiple opportunities to meet with colleagues from the other partnership schools and from the university, and to learn of their ambitions, their approaches, a lot about their achievements and a little about their problems. Within the school, it had been possible to explore teachers' varying attitudes to research, including their readiness to get involved and the considerations that encouraged or constrained such involvement. Two teachers had taken advantage of TTA scholarships to do research on thinking skills, and had reported on their research findings both in writing and in presentations to the school staff. There had thus been not only time but also various kinds of information and stimuli to aid Fred's and Chris's reflection on what the school wanted from research and what might be necessary and possible in working for these ends.

We have no record of Fred or Chris or anyone at AMVC at any time saying that they wanted it to be a 'researching school'. By 2002, they were in no doubt of the value of 'research' or 'inquiry', but they were equally sure that the value of research was as a means towards realising Fred's ambition for AMVC to be 'a thinking school'. Nor was being 'a thinking school' an end in itself, but only a necessary means towards improving the learning opportunities offered to students.

Furthermore, research was not at all a straightforward key with which to open problematic locks. Fred talked of his hope that research might 'cast light on real uncertainties' in the school, but they had already discovered in the previous three years that research didn't always lead tidily towards desired developments; it was just as likely to reveal false assumptions and the need to think again. Nonetheless, involvement in SUPER had in Fred's view been an important catalyst influencing the senior management team's thinking. In particular, it had led the SMT to think beyond the disparate things that needed to be done and towards more explicit and fundamental thinking about questions that needed to be asked about the school and its distinctive context in order to foster a range of developments.

As yet, however, involvement in SUPER had not had a significant impact on the thinking and practice of most members of the teaching staff. It had provided opportunities and support for individual teacher enthusiasts for their own class-room research, but research had not become institutionalised as an element of the school's way of working. The institutionalisation of research, or rather of 'inquiry', was what was needed, and the central question was 'how?' The central answer was to find ways of connecting inquiry effectively with other aspects of the school's work, starting from the school development plan, but also professional develop-ment planning and the school's initial teacher education work. For example, in the school's recently developed performance management scheme, all staff had been asked to engage actively with one aspect of the school development plan, and doing this through inquiry had been suggested as one exemplary way of doing this. A second answer was that Fred, as headteacher, should use every opportunity to emphasise the centrality of inquiry in his thinking, for example when talking to governors, parents or students, and most fundamentally when talking with teach-ing staff. More generally, the presentation to staff of findings and of opportunities for inquiry had to be carefully managed, to ensure that engagement with inquiry was always presented in attractive and credible ways. A third answer, but a difficult one to put into practice, was the provision of resources: time was of course the most precious resource, and non-teaching time was an especially scarce resource, but at least it was possible to ensure that cover arrangements prioritised protection of active researchers' non-teaching time. A fourth answer was that, in parallel with the development of inquiry by teachers, student inquiry should be developed, thus making inquiry, and the questioning and thinking that it can promote, more pervasive in the ethos of the school.

There was a clear acceptance in 2002 that the influence of research on the school's way of doing things could come only gradually. The school's engagement in the partnership had led to a clear recognition of how fundamental a change would be involved in research-based thinking becoming an important facet of the school's way of doing things. Given that the school was already doing a good job, and that all teachers were very busy indeed doing that good job, there was neither a need nor a possibility for an urgent and dramatic introduction of such fundamen-tal change. Initially, inquiries would be undertaken by those teachers who were enthusiasts or who were in the most senior roles. Initially, it would be those students who were academically successful, articulate and confident that would engage in inquiry. Initially, inquiries would be focused on a limited range of issues, and would involve relatively short investigations. And initially, research done elsewhere would impinge only on some areas of the school's work. None of this should cause concern, since only gradual change was possible, and only gradual change was needed; but there was a need for deliberate planning, so that these initial activities would be actively used as springboards for further developments so that eventually research would play a larger part in the work of the school.

To an outside observer in 2002, it seemed that the headteacher and the TRC had a very realistic understanding of how far the school had by then engaged with research. Their view of research as one potentially useful way of promoting critical thinking within the school, itself a means towards improving the quality of students' education, also seemed to be a very balanced assessment of what research could offer. The emphasis on gradualism, and the reliance on such approaches as 'talking up inquiry', connecting it to other elements in the school's work, creating opportunities for staff to engage in inquiry, and a very modest provision of resources for such inquiry, seemed to fit well with this assessment of what research could offer. But, given the unambiguously non-research nature of the school's culture, and given how busy teachers evidently were with other things, it did seem doubtful whether such strategies would be adequate to make research more useful to the school or to give it a more central place in the school's life.

Strategies for developing research at AMVC

At an operational level, the task of developing research as part of the life of AMVC has been consistently placed on the shoulders of Chris Clayton as teacher research coordinator. This has of course been true to varying degrees for all TRCs, but members of other institutions in the partnership have not only observed the active and reliable part Chris plays in partnership activities but also been aware that it is she who carries the load for AMVC. Internally in AMVC, it is clear that all the responsibility for making research significant belongs to Chris. For example, when all the schools agreed to appoint student voice coordinators, it was predictably Chris who, at least in the SUPER context, took on that role in AMVC for the first three years. Fred Mann as headteacher led the school into the partnership and he has supported Chris's efforts; in the wider partnership, he has consistently made AMVC's commitment clear; and in the school, he has pursued the general philosophy that we have outlined above. But it has been Chris's task to make research a significant element of AMVC's life and, in particular, to encourage teachers (and students) to engage in research.

In approaching that task, Chris has pursued the philosophy that she shares with Fred, that research in the school is useful only in so far as it improves students' learning opportunities. Therefore, the point of involving colleagues in research is to enhance the quality of teaching in the school. Three important propositions follow from that:

1   'To make it the very best for the child,' Chris says, 'I as a teacher have to continue to be a learner, and so an inquirer. Each individual teacher has to be an inquirer, to develop the quality of their own distinctive teaching.'
2   'It isn't just an acceptance of the need to learn that's necessary: we need to equip ourselves to know how to learn, and so how to inquire.'
3   'The important thing, therefore, is involving colleagues in inquiry, and in an improved quality of inquiry, about their teaching. The important thing is not to do "research" or to obtain research findings. It is to help us, individually and jointly, to think well about our teaching.'

Therefore it isn't 'traditional research' that she has been concerned to promote in the school, it is 'inquiry-based teaching'. Such teaching has to depend on many non-research-based judgements. So using the term 'research' would have been seriously counter-productive: it would needlessly have turned people off by implying demanding things that were no part of Chris's intention. Instead, she has attempted to start from an opposite emphasis, suggesting that the inquiry she is seeking to promote is 'what we do anyway', but that it might perhaps be done more deliberately, more self-critically and sometimes be shared.

As noted above, Chris has been a very active and reliable participant in the research partnership's activities. Why has she done that? From the beginning, Chris was in no doubt that the school needed to be involved in the partnership in order to get itself involved in inquiry. Having recently come from London, she found the school to be very traditional and very cautious about taking new initiatives, and she felt that it needed the stimulus that the partnership could give. The school, she thought, owed it to the staff and to the students to seize the opportunity to get involved. Despite having mixed feelings about being the TRC herself, because of her already busy role, she recognised that someone in her position and with her commitment to inquiry was needed in this role.

In practice she has not been disappointed by what the partnership has offered. 'The school', she says, 'has been given a fantastic opportunity to reflect and to inquire and to learn from its own practice as well as the practice of the other schools. ... Every meeting there was something to take back and use, one way or another, to develop the school for the benefit of students.' The university has played a central role in all of this, providing ideas, learning resources and questions and 'holding the group together'.

What strategies has Chris used in the school to pursue her agenda? She has been very conscious that the school's culture is a traditional one, with teachers seeing the teaching of their subjects as the serious part of their work, and being very busy in recent years responding to the many innovations involved in that core job. The gradualist approach that she and Fred have pursued, and her own emphasis on starting from 'what we do anyway', were not intended to challenge that traditional culture in any kind of frontal way. It has been more a question of chipping away at that culture, with the support of other members of the SMT.

Given that overall perspective, an important breakthrough in the early years of SUPER came through the school's engagement with the partnership's Thinking Skills agenda. Chris exploited the partnership's enthusiasm for this, as well as being able to provide her own internal evidence, to persuade both governors and SMT to commit themselves to it. This agenda was ideal in that it was classroom-focused, cross-curricular, directly relevant to improving students' learning, and gently challenging to the subject-dominated culture.

Two teachers with TTA scholarships joined Chris in pursuing that agenda within the school. The focus was on the generic need for students to be helped in thinking about how to set about first analysing and then solving problems, and also how to set about writing reports. Although the question was formulated and addressed in generic terms, the solutions that were suggested were differentiated across subjects. The project's thinking and recommendations were disseminated through the school both through a whole-school professional development day and through a series of quarterly papers. In Chris's view, it didn't matter that the research didn't 'prove' anything. What was important was that it exemplified to the whole school the need and the possibility for teachers to engage seriously in inquiry into issues of undeniable importance for the effectiveness of classroom teaching and learning.

It was true that not all teachers had been impressed; indeed, the eagerness of the enthusiasts had been counterproductive with some. But the SMT had been sufficiently impressed to introduce a new Thinking Skills teaching programme for Key Stages 3 and 4, and so a research initiative had had an impact that everyone could see. Chris is confident, furthermore, that students' problem-solving and writing abilities, and their General Certificate of Secondary Education (GCSE) results, have improved as a result of this programme (but there are no research findings to demonstrate that this is so!).

What was disappointing about the Thinking Skills work was that it did not stimulate a wider enthusiasm among the teaching staff to engage in inquiry projects of their own. So, when the 2002 opportunity to bid for BPRS scholarships arose, Chris had to think of a new strategy for encouraging teachers to become engaged. The opportunity to bid for these scholarships was of course widely publicised within the school, but Chris had by then come to recognise that opportunity was not enough. More than opportunity was needed to persuade busy teachers to engage in such challenging extra work. (Sure enough, only one subject teacher in the school – Andrew Barrett, a geography teacher – responded spontaneously to the BPRS opportunity.) Taking the long view, Chris embarked on a strategy of influencing teachers' attitudes through first changing the practice of leaders within the school. She successfully persuaded and helped four of her SMT colleagues to join her in bidding for, and being awarded, BPRS scholarships, in the hope that, if it came to be seen as normal for senior members of staff to engage in such inquiry, other teachers – especially dynamic, ambitious teachers – would 'get the message'.

These BPRS studies had a considerable impact. Three members of the SMT each looked at complementary aspects of how the school could make even fuller use of the large amounts of data it holds about individual students, especially through thoughtful sharing of that data with students and their parents. For example, one of them, having already established procedures for predicting GCSE grades from Cognitive Ability Tests (CATs), Standard Assessment Tasks (SATs) and internal assessment data, explored the hypothesis that sharing these predictions with students and their parents would lead to an enhancement of GCSE performance. The others adopted more qualitative action research approaches, exploring the impact of ways of getting parents to understand and reflect on information provided by the school from its regular monitoring of students' progress.

As a result of these studies, meetings of staff and then of governors had led to significant changes in whole-school policy for communicating with parents.

A fourth member of the SMT, responsible for behaviour policy in the school, had investigated different groups' perspectives on an innovative programme he had developed for 'at-risk' students in Key Stage 4. The positive findings of this study helped the further development of the programme within the school and also contributed to dissemination and celebration of the programme through the local education authority (LEA). Andrew Barrett's research on the use of information and communication technology (ICT) in geography teaching also had a significant impact on school policy, in this case on its ICT provision. So once again, serious engagement in inquiry had a very evident impact on school policy and practice.

Again, however, it was less clear that this strategy for encouraging more teachers to engage in inquiry had worked. Several factors might be relevant here. The whole-school focuses of research which had engaged the interest of SMT members were interesting enough to other teachers, but did not offer them a model of classroom inquiry relevant to their own work and concerns. Furthermore, it was obvious that SMT members spent much of their time doing things that ordinary teachers didn't have time for, and if research was one of these things, so what? The dominant factor, however, was certainly the news that a school Ofsted inspection was on its way in a few months' time: concern with inquiry therefore had to be put on a back burner, even for Chris herself. One simple but striking manifestation of this was that there were no bids for BPRS scholarships from the school for the following year – the last year, as it turned out, that they would be available.

The goal throughout has been to make inquiry seem a normal part of established or unavoidable aspects of the school's work, and so the performance management scheme was deliberately used to try to promote inquiry. Initially, as noted earlier, the strategy was to ask all staff to set themselves a target that involved active engagement with one aspect of the school development plan, and to suggest that it would be very good to do so through inquiry. However, this individualised approach depended on each teacher having the necessary combination of know-how, confidence and commitment to be able to set up such inquiries on their own, or else on them all having individual mentors to guide and encourage them. There was no possibility of either of these conditions being met: hardly any teachers had the necessary expertise, confidence and motivation, and the only person available to provide support was Chris. That version of the scheme was therefore unworkable, but the central principle of the scheme seemed so important that a more manageable version had to be found, less demanding on leadership resources and closer to 'what we do anyway'.

The solution that seemed to meet these criteria, and is now being trialled, was to make use of teachers' accustomed ways of working in subject faculties. Each head of faculty was charged with the task of negotiating with Chris three appropriate practical areas of inquiry – reflecting both the school development plan and the concerns of that faculty – and then the task of coordinating staff involvement in inquiries on one or more of these areas of inquiry. Chris has the task not only of supporting Heads of Faculty but also of monitoring and reviewing this strategy. No doubt further modifications will be made in the light of experience.

A further strategy, introduced in 2003, is that of requiring all new staff to undertake inquiry tasks as part of their induction into the school. Already in 2002 Fred was pointing out that he emphasised the importance of the school's engagement in inquiry to new members of staff, and that he found newly qualified teachers (NQTs) in particular accepted involvement in inquiry as a proper and quite attractive continuation of their university-based studies. The new strategy of requiring new staff to undertake inquiry tasks is clearly a powerful way of communicating to potential recruits what a significant part inquiry is intended to play in their work at the school. The earlier perception that such a message was more attractive to younger staff has now been confirmed by the finding that NQTs tend to find this aspect of their induction very exciting and stimulating, while the experienced teachers are more inclined to see it as just extra work.

Some of the NQTs' inquiry work has been very impressive, one inquiry into the teaching of citizenship, for example, having had an important impact on the school's developing policy in that area. It is notable, however, that NQTs have not yet been persuaded to make presentations to their more experienced colleagues about their inquiries. Perhaps they sense that their own enthusiasm for inquiry is not generally shared. Another problem, with this strategy as with others, is that more monitoring and support for the new teachers' inquiries is needed, but that there is a lack of people with time and expertise to fulfil this need.

The ending of the BPRS scheme, coming on top of the disruption by Ofsted of AMVC's use of it, was a significant disappointment to the school. However, the school's own commitment to inquiry is reflected in that it has found the resources from its own budget to be able to offer small sums to support teacher inquiries. However, pursuing the same agenda of 'what we do anyway' here as elsewhere, Chris has required that all bids for these scholarships should come from faculties, not just from individual teachers. While initially little interest was expressed in this opportunity, several very promising bids have now been received from faculties for scholarships for 2005–2006.

It will be remembered that, from 2002 to 2005, Chris felt obliged to take on the role of student voice coordinator as well as all her duties as teacher research coordinator. She managed to be remarkably active in that SVC role, initially working with the student council, listening to the students' concerns and then investigating with the students the issues raised to get a clearer view of them before action was planned. One important issue, for example, was about 'feeling safe' when moving around the school building. Since 2003 Chris has, with students from the council, surveyed student opinion throughout the school using an annual questionnaire, each year identifying new things for the SMT's attention. One issue identified recently and now being explored more fully is that of 'respect' between staff and students. In 2005–2006, Chris will be working with a group of Year 9 students who have had some research training for inquiring into teaching and learning issues. Now, however, she has been able to recruit a colleague who, having been an active NQT researcher in 2004–2005, is eagerly taking on the SVC role.

The above developments seem to reflect a recent widening of enthusiasm for inquiry in AMVC, and perhaps a growing confidence in the inquiry agenda. One further development points in a similar direction. AMVC's own lack of resources of staff time and expertise for leading and supporting inquiry has been exacerbated throughout by having a critical friend who has played only a minimal support role, not extending much beyond mentoring the school's BPRS scholars. Among several factors behind this, one has been an uncertainty shared by the school and the critical friend about how he could be useful. Chris for example has suggested that until recently the school was not perhaps ready for a critical friend's help. Since 2005, however, there has been some change in this respect, in that the critical friend has been actively involved by Chris in the training of the team of Year 9 students for the inquiries that they will undertake with her support in 2005–2006.

Reflections on the story thus far of AMVC as an inquiring school

We believe that this story of one school over a period of a few years, inevitably told from the limited perspective of those who were seeking to change it, if only a little and only slowly, exemplifies a number of generally significant themes. Arthur Mellows Village College, like every other school, is unique. It is, we believe, a good school and a successful school. But in many respects it is not an unusual school. And in many respects, what has been happening there could easily happen elsewhere.

First, then, the culture of teaching in the United Kingdom is not generally, we believe, a culture of inquiry. AMVC is not unusual in that most of the teachers who work there have quite enough to do without engaging in any kind of disciplined inquiry about their teaching, their students' learning or anything that impinges on these. Inquiry is not near the core of how most of them learned to teach; nor is it at all near the core of what a very demanding government requires of them if they are to succeed and prosper in their chosen profession. So teachers need very good reasons for adding inquiry to their already considerable workloads. For the great majority of them, opportunity is not enough.

So if one has given oneself the task, as a school leader, of trying to persuade teachers to approach their work in an inquiring way, one has to accept that it will not be an easy task. The story of Chris's efforts at AMVC is a little like that of Robert Bruce and the spider, the moral of which is that if one strategy fails, try another, and then another. But it is more complicated than that. From each of Chris's strategies there was always something useful to salvage, and even more important, there was always something useful to learn. The impressive thing about this story of trying to promote inquiry is the inquiring way in which inquiry was promoted.

The story at AMVC is far from its conclusion. For example, just as continuity so far has been important, so the problem of succession is one that has properly worried both Fred and Chris. If either of them were to leave, would the culture of inquiry be strong enough to survive that? Nothing yet seems so strongly developed as to be secure. Their successes are fragile and vulnerable, and have been slow in coming, but they do seem to be successes. To what can these successes be attributed? Imaginative, sympathetic and persevering leadership would seem the most plausible answer. And why have these successes been so difficult to achieve, and in the end so tentative? Here the answer seems simpler: almost certainly the main constraint has been lack of resources, especially human resources, and most especially available, expert, committed support and guidance. What could have been done with twice as much of Chris's time, to say nothing of several others like her?

Finally, two particular merits of the leadership at AMVC should not be overlooked, but easily could be, especially since they could easily be viewed in negative terms. One has been the clarity of the shared vision. The vision shared by Fred and Chris has been of a school committed to nothing more than its job of facilitating learning as effectively as possible, but therefore of a school with thinking, inquiring teachers working out how to do that. It has not been a radical vision, concerned with changing the functions of schools. If the teachers at AMVC have been rather slow to buy into the vision of inquiry-led teaching, just think how put off they might have been by a vision of a knowledge-generating school!

The other similar merit has been that the leadership has been content to see the path towards AMVC becoming an inquiry-led school as being a gradual one. Not for them any great leap forward! It has sometimes seemed so gradual that one wondered whether there was sufficient momentum to make any progress. Yet what has been achieved looks a good deal more hopeful in 2006 than at any previous time. Gradualism, it seems, can work.

Chapter 3

Chesterton Community College
A SUPER case study

Sue Brindley, with Rolf Purvis

Context

Chesterton is an 11–16 community college, based in the heart of Cambridge. The college has an intellectually and ethnically diverse student population with both highly able and less able students, some with behavioural issues. It is perceived as a challenging school at which to teach by staff and by local residents. In recent times the school has sought to address the behavioural issues problem with the appointment of one of the assistant heads, Rolf Purvis, who had also been responsible for coordinating research in the school for over ten years, to lead a behaviour management strategy. The school has a highly stable core staff population but also has a number of staff changes at the end of each year. In September 2004 Chesterton appointed a new headteacher, Mark Patterson, who not only continued with the previous head's positive policy in terms of supporting research but also developed this further through reforming management structures to enhance and extend the place of research in the school.

With a relatively newly appointed headteacher, it is accurate to say that the development of research in Chesterton has remained as delegated entirely to Rolf Purvis. At the time of writing, Rolf had just been promoted to deputy head, still with responsibility for coordinating research in the school, and a research-active Head of English, Lee Ling, had been appointed to assistant head position. The appointment of the new headteacher will, over time, inevitably impact on the development of research at Chesterton but Rolf remains responsible for both the direction of research and related policy development at Chesterton. Howard Gilbert, who was the head of the college in 1997 (succeeded by Beverley Jones and more recently Mark Patterson), was one of the original instigators of the SUPER project.

In this chapter we want to explore the factors that have emerged as significant in developing a research culture within the school, and in particular the ways in which the SUPER project has impacted on that process.

The data informing this chapter has been collected over several years (1999–2005) and draws on interviews over time with the deputy head, Rolf Purvis, and researching staff, records of research development kept by myself as the SUPER project critical friend to the school and additional recorded observations of patterns of involvement in school based research and beyond.

Early stories 1997–2002

Research in Chesterton has an interesting development story to tell. Chesterton was part of the SUPER project from 1997 and over the next two years became involved with two major projects located within SUPER: Thinking Skills and Technology Integrated Pedagogic Strategies (TIPS). The person chosen to work with the university with these two projects was Rolf Purvis, because he had both an interest in and experience of research.

The perspective that Rolf brought to the place of research was filtered through a particular personal lens: his father was an academic at the University of Durham and undertook research into education as part of his academic professional life. Rolf observed:

> He very much involved research in his practice so I was aware from a young age that as a teacher one could do research ... Like him, I did an MEd although mine was here at Cambridge, that was about ten years ago, and it really sparked a very keen interest in research. Ever since then I've been doing research of some sort.

In terms of the school context, however, Rolf's own early involvement in research was fairly isolated:

> When I did my MEd ten years ago here, I was the only person doing any research. Nobody took a particular interest in what I was doing. I was quite happy to work in an isolated way. I didn't really share much of what I did. So in many ways I was the only one benefiting plus the children I was teaching. Whilst that was fine, I just think it was very limiting.

The advent of SUPER meant that Rolf's research interest had a particular importance for the school and his appointment in 1999 was an opportunity to consolidate and shape that interest. As TRC, Rolf in conjunction with the then headteacher, Beverley Jones, had constructed the SUPER research within the school in the Stenhouse (1975) 'teacher researcher' model, with one person effectively undertaking research on various school practices. Rolf recalls: 'Initially I was the one doing research ... '

However, late in 1999 the Faculty of Education at Cambridge had invited Chesterton, with a number of other schools, to be involved with a research project on the use of ICT in the classroom, Technology Integrated Pedagogic Strategies, coordinated by Professor Kenneth Ruthven, and involving myself as one of the research team. This research project contributed significantly to Chesterton's whole-school strategic planning when the college was awarded specialist technology college status. The coincidence of these two events proved a catalyst for rooting research into the wider school context, as Rolf explained:

> Broadly speaking, a number of colleagues have undertaken research into the role of ICT ... this was initiated by the TIPS team – of course you were part of that team as well – and this coincided with us becoming a specialist technology college and so that really gave us further impetus to explore the whole field.

Teacher research coordinator

SUPER, in creating the TRC role, left open the ways in which a school could respond to this demand, beyond an agreed set of parameters relating to meetings and in house organisation. Chesterton took a critical step in committing to the concept of TRC wholeheartedly and the appointment of Rolf was significant in the vision he brought to this role:

> So I think what's been pivotal in what I think is quite a rich research school is the role of teacher research coordinator [in SUPER]. I've had dedicated time one day a week to coordinate this research and that has really given me the opportunity to develop things at Chesterton ... my role is much more about helping colleagues doing research, giving them time and money to do it, putting them in contact with a mentor from the university, encouraging and providing opportunities for dissemination as well.

Over the next three years, the way in which Rolf interpreted the TRC role was particularly significant in that he moved quickly into thinking about the ways in which *structures* in the school could be instituted to support research: he saw the TRC role as the opportunity to create an infrastructure to support research on a long-term basis:

> I really would like to see something which lasts beyond my existence at this college so were I to leave ... I would love to see research carrying on, something that is valued so much not only by the senior management but by most colleagues ... I really would love to see Chesterton becoming a leading learning school.

Much of the focus in these early days was on securing a BPRS grant, because of the opportunity the funding gave to the college to support research in very practical terms:

> When BPRS was first announced we applied for six research grants and we got all six, and then the subsequent year, with you, we applied for twelve and got

ten and we're currently now applying for a further twelve grants and that's been instrumental in giving us time and space and a very clear link with the university to support the work at the college.

The BPRS grants enabled Rolf to begin to think about making research practicable within Chesterton, and in parallel to begin to build a critical mass of teachers participating in research in the school:

> Had it not been for BPRS I would not be sitting here talking about all the different research projects we've done. It would be unreasonable to expect colleagues to undertake quite a significant time commitment without giving them something, giving them space, giving them time and the mentoring opportunity and I think that without that generous funding we would have been very limited and I would have ended up doing a lot more of the research – I and perhaps a few other colleagues but certainly not the numbers we are taking about so I think that has been pivotal.

Critical friendship and building the 'critical mass'

Developing a research-focused school is a demanding and complex undertaking. A key part of my role as critical friend to Chesterton was to work with Rolf to help develop that part of the strategy. We decided that one-to-one mentoring at regular and fairly frequent intervals (three or four times a term with meetings lasting about 40 minutes – one lesson – with teachers given supply cover to enable them to meet without giving up their own free time) would be one element. During these sessions I worked with the teachers to identify and develop a 'research area' which did not necessarily have to relate to their classroom teaching, nor to the 'raising of standards' agenda. I devised a pro forma for use during these sessions which allowed me to make full records of these discussions and, with the teacher's per-mission, I copied these to Rolf, to the teacher and to myself so that we all had a clear idea about what had been agreed. Where I had given advice on methodology, I noted that down in some detail. In between my meetings with the teachers, Rolf met with them again, and using the records produced, supported the teachers further as appropriate to their research needs at that time. As budget holder he was able, where appropriate, to offer some further time to allow teachers to pursue their research. At Chesterton, the involvement of a significant number of teachers – a 'critical mass' which acted as a dynamic in positioning research in the college – emerged quite quickly. Important, therefore, though not articulated in these terms, was Rolf's insistence in an interview in 2002 that the infrastructure he was building had to be seen as belonging to all:

> Well, we've not really created anything new in terms of a teaching and learn-ing group or a research group. I was very keen to avoid creating an elite within

the college ... therefore we've used existing structures ... the heads of department meetings, the staff meetings and department meetings to try and encourage teachers to talk about research.

It was a strategy which even then could be seen to be productive, as Rolf explained:

I don't think there is a subject within the college where there hasn't been at least one member of staff involved in some sort of research ... and therefore I've noticed that teachers are much more willing to talk about research and use research to back up their arguments when they're creating a case and that's been quite noticeable, certainly in the last year and a half and with you as critical friend.

The critical mass did not simply exist in terms of active researchers, however. There emerged an important group within the staff who were to prove central to the development from Chesterton having individual researchers to Chesterton having a research culture:

And the other thing is that within those structures that colleagues who haven't necessarily, you know, haven't done the research themselves but have heard a colleague talking about their research, they will often refer to that and that's quite flattering as a teacher researcher.

The shift from research as an individual activity to research as part of the language of teacher discourse is of great importance. It marks the change from an 'out there' experience to one which demonstrates teacher involvement with the ideas, with the data collected and with the perceived validity of the activity of research itself. Acceptance of and indeed accolades about research, such as that quoted above, are the foundation stones of research becoming an integrated part of teaching thinking.

Networks and limitations

One advantage which had been hoped for by the school in relation to the SUPER project was the opportunity to work with other schools. In that the schools met regularly every half term, a good basis for networking was established:

It's been very important to share, to talk to colleagues from other schools, to learn about research that is going on there and also to explore possibilities of working in partnership.

However, interviewed in 2003, Rolf presented networking as sharing of research practice rather than joint projects:

although this is four years down the line and I can't cite one project ... where we have worked in collaboration with another school. We've talked about it but we haven't actually done it ... I wouldn't say I am particularly working with other schools ... apart from Comberton I haven't actually visited other schools.

In seeking to address this at school level, Rolf had been very successful in using dissemination strategies to develop networking:

> For example, in November we held a research symposium here which was open to the whole [SUPER] community and several did attend, including pretty much all our staff at Chesterton.

This first attempt at networking was successful and met the stated intention of providing a shared forum for research exchange. The research symposium included Chesterton and faculty staff presenting on their joint research projects undertaken at the school. The symposium had unexpected spin-offs too for Chesterton:

> [The symposium] was a wonderful chance for colleagues to talk about the work that they had been doing for their BPRS. It was a full term's work and it really was very encouraging to see the quality of the work that had been undertaken, but also the enthusiasm with which they were talking about research and the level of interest for colleagues who had never done any research before and that was really gratifying, particularly when so many who I thought might not be interested in research ... then submitted their BPRS application a couple of months later ... so I feel that was very positive.

Other plans were in the offing for extending networking, at least between two schools:

> To date, however, since you became the SUPER critical friend to Comberton and Chesterton, you know this has led to more collaboration than we have ever had ... when we were submitting BPRS applications, you, Mary [Martin] and myself got together and discussed how some of these could be joint projects and we have submitted some projects [to BPRS] where collaboration has been at the forefront.

The extent to which networking featured in later developments is, however, best explored in the next section, along with the research stories of those teachers who had become part of the Chesterton approach to research.

Evolving stories 2002–2005

The reliance placed on BPRS funding by all schools (including Chesterton) and the subsequent withdrawal, with very little notice, of that grant by the government might have been expected to sound the death knell of research at the college. But the structures put in place at Chesterton by Rolf have proved robust and resilient and current evidence seems to be that, far from disappearing, research is now moving into a new stage of collaboration. Before we investigate this aspect, however, I want to return to Rolf to see whether his thinking changed at all on research in Chesterton and then explore the research stories of the teachers and the ways in which they experienced being teacher researchers at Chesterton Community College.

The range of research projects which had been undertaken in 2002–2003 was wide: developing effective learning in mathematics; working with low ability students in history; enhancing high ability students' learning through Internet use in humanities; fast tracking English GCSE students; Year 7 pupil perspectives on learning and the use of laptops; enhancing the learning experience of refugee pupils, and so on. The full research profile of projects can be found on the school website. Over time these developed further still. Research in the college expanded to explore the ways in which students could lead their own research. By 2004, for example, five Year 9 students were receiving weekly training sessions on research methods with a view to these students leading their own research over the next year. This was constructed as a cascade model so that these students in turn would train others.

Interviewed in late 2004, what was striking in Rolf's responses was the consistency of the approach towards research in Chesterton following on from his early plans and intentions. However, what we see is also an expansion of early ideas as Rolf developed his role as TRC. In particular, the place of structure, of ownership, and of collaboration and networking all re-emerged as central to his strategic planning, and all now associated with research realities at Chesterton.

Structure

Cochran-Smith and Lytle (1993) comment on the ways in which a lack of supportive structures impact on the development of research in schools:

> formal/informal support for research: inflexible workloads and teaching schedules, little monetary support or release time and few local or national forums for dissemination/publication [are issues.]
>
> (Cochran-Smith and Lytle 1993: 12)

Rolf's early concentration on structure therefore seems to have been particularly prescient in forestalling some of the difficulties associated with building a teacher research community. In interview in 2004, he reiterated:

> I think structure is important. ... A lot of research that we've been doing here has been instigated by individual members of staff who are interested in a

particular field and they need help … [my TRC role means that] I'm identified as the person they can come to if they need some help on say research
methods or they need to find a particular article they are looking for … So I
am the link between them and the university and particularly you as critical
friend and that serves a very useful purpose.

In turn, all of the teachers interviewed in 2004 made reference to the structures
within Chesterton:

ANDY: I think it's very important for there to be a structure within a school … if
you've been out of the research loop for a few years, it's really good to have
somebody who will support you, who will put you in contact with other
people. You can research alone, but it's difficult. One of the really positive
parts of research is not just the improvement you might find within the
classroom but also the links you can make, which can be very inspirational

MARK: We've got a research coordinator who's made sure we are all on track and
has kept us going with other links [with the university and other teachers].

LLOYD: There's a lot of help available. One of the really useful things about this
research is that you do get time to actually undertake some of the activities …
[you as critical friend] have mentored me through all of the research projects
that I have been involved in and that's been excellent.

The structures were thus not simply administrative events (though this played a
part), but rather to do with regular interaction with individuals with specific
responsibility for supporting research. Rolf commented:

The role of the TRC is a multifaceted role. It is taking a lead on research issues
in the college; it's being knowledgeable not only about the place of research
in school but how it can benefit people in a wider context. I believe that
colleagues of all research experience and abilities can participate in some way
and my job is to make them believe that too. Recognising that colleagues need
space and time to do that work so, for example, as TRC I often stood in as
'supply' to allow teachers time to undertake their research – I have a
commitment to making it happen. Research has its time and place and it's
about balance in the school day. But of course none of this can happen without the role of critical friend. I saw that role as helping make research happen
in a sense. The critical friend similarly believing in all the colleagues who
expressed an interest – making colleagues believe in themselves. That we had
common goals and clear structures for communicating were key so, where
appropriate, I could follow it up effectively. The critical friend brings another
perspective – and that is valued by all because you have 'legitimacy' – you have
worked in a number of school contexts and in teacher training so brought a
viewpoint we could trust.

Ownership

The insistence we saw earlier in this chapter that research should be part of the way of thinking at Chesterton has borne fruit. Building the critical mass in Chesterton has been highly successful, with staff taking part in research each year from 2002 to 2005 and a total of one in three staff now in a position of having undertaken research within Chesterton. Rolf's approach to this again has been consistent:

> I would like to think everyone in the college ... research is no longer closed, it's open, it's something staff have access to. There's a more inclusive approach ... all staff are not actively involved in research, [but] at least they feel they could be if they wanted to. And I think that's important rather than seeing it as elite with whom they have nothing in common ... So I think all staff benefit.

The emphasis has been on integrating research via the day-to-day processes and procedures of the school – an approach which sought to make the use and production of research a usual facet of teaching. Perhaps interesting evidence of this integration into the day-to-day emerged when the teachers interviewed were asked to identify their first involvement with research. Unlike other teachers in other schools asked this question, those interviewed found it difficult to identify any specific point where they had become involved in research:

MARK: My research is just part of what I do anyway ... it is part of your monitoring, evaluation and review.

LLOYD: I think I got involved through interest in trying to do some different things with [students] and trying to see what impact those different approaches would have on their learning.

ANDY: I got involved because I've always been involved in research.

This is not vagueness on the part of the respondents but a revealing fuzziness of boundaries: research has become part of their professional thinking – as aspect, as we will see later, which has immense implications for research and Chesterton.

Ownership relates too to the perceived purposes of research. Rolf's position was an interestingly wide horizon:

> So many times we are asked how does it impact on our teaching. Whilst that's an important question I don't think that's all research is about. I feel it's a lot more that that. Personally speaking I feel it keeps me in the job really because it keeps my interest in teaching. It's not something which is static ... it's changing. Asking those questions or trying to find the right questions to ask is I think an important part of my job as a teacher.

This position – the ability to see the impact of research as reaching further than the 'raising standards' agenda of the government – is an extremely important factor in allowing Chesterton teachers to set the research agenda to meet their needs: in enhancing ownership, it is difficult to think of a more effective way of bringing about a teacher focused research strategy. For several teachers, the release from any set classroom agenda paradoxically enabled them to engage more fully with it:

LEE: It had to become a priority. I had to see it [research] had an impact on raising standards from a middle manager's point of view and to those above and below as to the achievements of our pupils.

LLOYD: I think a lot of people think teacher research ... isn't that meaningful ... not that meaningful because it doesn't impact on teaching. I think certainly for me it has done. It's made me think far more about my own teaching ... research with these challenging children has certainly made me teach these kids better.

ANDY: Research helps us to change our teaching, to try new ideas and if we find success or a formula that may be able to work somewhere else then we can not only use it for ourselves but also to help other people.

Other highly significant results emerged too in relation to ownership: being a teacher researcher brought about a fascinating expression of professional ownership of education:

LEE: We're part of a system, as you know, that is all about conforming to a national curriculum ... teacher autonomy was taken away. The point when research discovered me, because I don't think I discovered research, I was actually feeling very helpless. It's given me the opportunity to take on my own profession and to make things change.

MARK: I did some fairly major research ... partly because I was so angered by ... government policies [which] were damaging [to education]. ... Now it made absolutely no difference to the government policies which were being pursued. I had no power to do anything about those. But what I did have was the power to work it out personally and to express what I felt about that and to have an audience for that expression.

ANDY: Personally, it keeps me going ... it's something else you are doing in your professional life apart from the paperwork and teaching ... it helps self-esteem, feeling you've actually achieved something ... I think it enriches the profession and in some ways dignifies it ... we're not just teachers; we're people who can actually improve the systems and structures within which we work.

These statements, reclaiming the ownership of education through research, offer a small glimpse into a wider debate surrounding professionalism, not perhaps this issue for this chapter but one which nevertheless points to the significance of place of teacher research in the retention of the teaching force.

Collaboration and networking

One of the earlier plans for Rolf was to attempt to extend and exploit the networking opportunities afforded by the SUPER project. In the early days of SUPER, Rolf felt that the networking potential had not been fully exploited and had attempted to begin to address that through his dissemination strategies. The extent to which this has been successful within the context of Chesterton can be measured by the teacher researchers' responses to questions about dissemination. One of the structures set up by Rolf in the SUPER context was a series of in-school seminars with invitations to all SUPER project schools to attend. Some teachers were able to attend from partner research schools, university faculty staff attended and these seminars were seen by the teacher researchers as both successful and as providing potential infrastructures for networking:

LLOYD: We've had a couple of research symposiums at Chesterton which have been really useful ... I think what we've tried to do is disseminate what we've found out at the school. And again we've had some positive feedback from colleagues about the possibility of using the ideas I've come up with and perhaps taking them forward themselves.

LEE: We've had seminars and we've presented no matter what stage we are at, we present where we are at. It doesn't have to be the finished article, it just has to be a sharing of practice.

ROLF: [The seminars] are public recognition to the hard work staff have been doing but equally giving them some feedback as well as starting a dialogue with staff and touching on those staff who ... haven't been active researchers but are nevertheless interested in what their colleagues are up to.

So within Chesterton, the seminars gave structured opportunity to discuss research activity and to this extent a highly collaborative and successful network of researchers and research ideas were created within Chesterton. But part of Rolf's earlier plan had been to network externally, beginning with SUPER partner schools. Although the seminars certainly sought to include SUPER schools, not many were able to attend. There are, of course, practical problems for schools – meetings, travel (a number of SUPER schools were over an hour away), after-school commitments (clubs etc.) – it may well be that the realities of school life simply prohibited attendance.

Inter-school research had also been planned in the form of joint SUPER BPRS projects. It would be fair to say that these made little headway. In the end, the BPRS funding supported in-house research rather than inter-school research and without the funding, it was difficult to manufacture time to give to the teachers who wanted to be part of these projects. Some exchange visits were made but these did not develop into joint research projects. However, some joint research has emerged between Rolf and another TRC at Comberton and this is ongoing, so far involving the TRCs in interviewing staff in each other's schools on the impact of research on their work, though again this research activity is slow because it is unfunded and thus subject to time able to be freed from the numerous other commitments of these two TRCs: this remains an area to be developed further.

Rolf had planned for networking to take place more widely, however, than SUPER schools alone. He had hoped to make Chesterton a leading 'learning school' with a national and international reputation. To what extent can we say this ambition has been realised?

ANDY: My research impacts locally within my faculty, within my college ... [and through] journals ... I subscribe to list[servs] of teachers internationally ... I'm swapping ideas, making comparisons. I spoke about my methodology to people who are researching in America ... It would be nice to find some sort of wider forum.

LLOYD: We've had work published on the web, we've had contact with people as far away as Australia who have read our work and commented on it.

ROLF: We've taken part in research seminars which the university has organised so giving the opportunity for staff to reach a wider audience and there have been national and indeed one international conference [in Australia] as well to which a colleague was invited.

For Rolf, there was an added significance for these seminars: these were active networks.

[As TRC] I'm the person who ... set up research seminars or [gave] opportunities to meet researchers from, in some cases, around the world.

So to some extent, there has been an increase in networking activity and certainly plans exist to extend networking further still. But this is not an area which we can say with honesty has developed fully as we had hoped.

Future plans: a 'leading learning school'

What however we feel we can claim with confidence is that the bringing together over time the three major features of structure, ownership and networking has resulted in a school which has moved research on from a position of individual teacher researchers undertaking personal projects, to a position where research permeates and informs the wider thinking and teaching behaviours of the school. The degree of change was highlighted by a teacher who joined Chesterton midway through its current research journey:

LEE: When I first arrived ... people were actively engaging in reflecting and evaluating their own classroom practice and being open and fluid and fluent in discussing their own research ... this was something new to me coming from a school that didn't have that as one of their priorities. [Research] was part and parcel of the day-to-day running of the school and it was disseminated from the senior managers right down to the classroom assistants, who were actively engaged in reflective activities. There was a research buzz, if you like, about the place ... a research culture.

The recognition of Chesterton as having a 'research culture' is a hugely significant step forward in pursuing the learning school vision, significant in that teachers, in identifying it as a school culture, also identify themselves as belonging to that culture: it assures the preservation of the critical mass of teachers we saw as central to securing ongoing involvement with research in the school – in other words, sustainability. Sustainability is a particular concern for Rolf with funding from BPRS now withdrawn:

One of the issues is to find new sources of funding. I'd like to think we will still be doing research but I think it's very hard with all the other constraints that teachers face. So I think that it is quite key to my role now to try and find other sources of funding and if that's not possible to find other ways of sustaining it [research] for sufficiently long period of time before more funding does come through.

The existing teacher researchers at Chesterton, however, feel confident that research will continue, again referring to the research culture:

ANDY: Certainly as far as our school is concerned the research will carry on. ... I think we have such a strong culture of research here. I can't see it stopping because so many of us see the benefits not only within our own practice but benefits within faculties and also sharing it with other people in our school and outside.

LEE: Research can move schools forward. We need to enter into the age of research cultures and then we will improve education.

Chesterton is already consolidating its research experience and knowledge. The next stage of research activity is being planned as coordinated collaboration with research themes being identified and then taken forward by groups of teacher researchers in the school. Bursaries are being offered from within the school to support this work – not large sums, but sufficient for the collaborative research groups to generate some free time. Importantly these bursaries are also recognition from Chesterton of the importance of this work to the ongoing improvement of school practices. The research culture established within SUPER has been extended and Chesterton is involved in wider networks of research with other members of the Cambridge faculty and with other universities.

Perhaps the final word in this section should be given to Rolf:

> I would like to see more research activity by almost, well, not a *requirement*, but I would like to think all teachers would see it as an important part of their job ... seeing perhaps that research is as important to an educational institution as research is in the industrial sector. And nobody would have this conversation [about the place of research] in industry. Research is linked directly with a company's performance. I would like to think that perhaps we would see research in a similar light in five years' time. Something indispensable, not an optional extra.

And the problems?

Writing in 2005, funding has still not been resolved as a key concern and much of the time Rolf has given to SUPER (which now can no longer fund the TRC role in any SUPER school) has been personal time, beyond his teaching commitment and recently, alongside his new role in heading up a behaviour management strategy. The appointment of Lee Ling as assistant head will, in time, contribute to developing research within Chesterton as Mark Patterson (the headteacher), Rolf and Lee decide on Chesterton's research priorities and on sustainability within the college. Chesterton certainly has an impressive foundation of research and the shared vision by many staff of research as a worthwhile activity will be a great advantage to Chesterton in moving on. Commitment to research in Chesterton has been constructed by Rolf to allow great intellectual freedom and it may be that future developments will, in linking funding to research, want to re-evaluate the legitimacy of this freedom. Its power has been in capturing the imaginations of those teachers quoted earlier and reinvigorating for them the debates about professional autonomy. Whether Chesterton Community College can stand against the pressures of Ofsted, league tables and other external drivers to maintain this, in my view, admirable position on the place of research remains to be seen.

Chapter 4

Comberton Village College
A SUPER case study

Sue Brindley, with Mary Martin

Context

Comberton Village College is an 11–16 mixed comprehensive set in rural Cambridgeshire, six miles west of the city. In 2005 in a *Sunday Times* poll, Comberton came out as the best school in its category in Britain, based on its 2004 GCSE results, where 43 per cent of pupils achieved at least five A*–A grades. In 2004 in a PANDA (Ofsted's Performance and Assessment) report, Comberton is placed in the top 5 per cent of schools in England for value added results at Key Stage 2 to Key Stage 4. Comberton is a leading edge school, a sports college, a training school, part of a Networked Learning Community together with seven other schools and the University of Cambridge, and an ambassador school for gifted and talented education.

The question for this chapter is to explore how research has developed within this highly successful school and the ways in which SUPER has contributed to Comberton becoming a research focused school.

The data informing this chapter was collected over several years (2002–2006) and draws on interviews over time with the headteacher, deputy head and staff, records of research development kept by the SUPER project critical friend to the school and recorded observations by the critical friend of patterns of involvement in school-based research and beyond.

Early stories 1997–2002

The early story of SUPER for Comberton Village College began in 1997 when, as we shall see in Chapter 11, the initiative to engage schools and universities in research partnerships began to take shape at the University of Cambridge Faculty of Education as the SUPER project. Comberton participated from the beginning with the involvement of the then headteacher, Ros Clayton. Comberton was one of the schools taking part in a funded research project exploring the impact of ICT on teaching and learning, Technology Integrated Pedagogic Strategies (TIPS), which was a significant research project for some of the SUPER group of schools.

By 1999, part of the SUPER project infrastructure emerging was the establishment of a teacher research coordinator in each school, a role to be funded by the
SUPER project in the first instance and which gave the TRC one day a week off
timetable to develop and support research within the school. In the case of
Comberton the person appointed to the TRC role in 1999 was Mary Martin, now
deputy head but then Head of English. Mary recalls:

> In the early days of building the foundations for a research culture, the TRCs
> benefited greatly from the university direction given by Dave Ebbutt who led
> regular (often bi-weekly) sessions at Cambridge University where the TRCs
> effectively formed a college; here the debate was significantly influenced by
> Dave Ebbutt's academic input re research mechanisms and support struc-
> tures. At this stage the role of TRC as model researcher (often sole researcher)
> was significant.
>
> In education, if you want someone to do something you have to model it.
> There's no point in theorising in order to hook people into it. You need a
> research story they can understand. The role of TRC supplied the narrative
> others needed to hear and in my case it was the gender research which was
> the key. The academic guidance was of course crucial in bringing teacher
> researchers onto the continuum of research inquiry, a continuum which
> culminated for some in the pursuance of research-based higher degrees.

At this stage, research, SUPER and Mary's role as teacher research coordinator
remained within what was effectively a subculture of the school. As enthusiastic as
Mary was about research, the impact of SUPER in Comberton was localised and
small scale. We shall see later in the chapter how Mary's work as TRC developed
into the wider school context. It is clear however that the SUPER project's
construction of the role of TRC and the funding of that role in the first instance
was critical to allowing Mary time to work on developing research more widely in
Comberton.

Critical friend

Over the next three years (1999–2002) Comberton engaged with a range of
research projects in conjunction with the SUPER project. (The story of one of the
most successful, the TIPS project, is told in Chapter 11.) The research story
emerging was in itself impressive and interesting, but still resided in discrete (and
usually, however reluctantly, university led) initiatives. One of the moves from
SUPER, made in 2002, was to attempt to widen participation in the project
through the development of the role of critical friend, working with SUPER
schools in developing a research culture. The invitation to university lecturers
made it clear that the role was unfunded and additional to any existing workload.
The rationale for becoming involved was in the opportunity to develop or enhance
any research interests. The early story of SUPER for me, therefore, as a critical

friend, did not begin until 2002 when I joined the SUPER project as a university lecturer already researching into teachers as researchers and therefore with a particular interest in the SUPER development.

My association with Comberton was, however, already well established. Initially this was through my work as the English subject lecturer for the Postgraduate Certificate in Education (PGCE) at a time when Mary Martin was Head of English and a very effective subject mentor for English PGCE trainees. In 2000 I had established with English teachers in the Cambridge partnership schools a subject-focused (English) research group of some twenty teachers, two of whom were working in Comberton, and this group included Mary Martin. The shared values and beliefs of this group (and perhaps too shared ways of constructing the world) had established a strong working relationship between Mary and myself alongside the ITET work, and so when Comberton asked that I should work with them as the SUPER critical friend, I was delighted to accept. That this role was able to draw extensively on previous successful working relationships is perhaps important to note: Mary and I had established a position of mutual trust through previous ITET work and I had already been involved in developing research within the English Department. My working relationship with staff in other departments in the school was widened through my involvement as a researcher on the TIPS project and I therefore knew, and was known to, the school and many of the staff already. I was therefore fortunate to be a 'familiar face' in Comberton and found little difficulty in extending the roles I already had through ITET and English research and the TIPS project into the work of critical friend.

On being a critical friend to Comberton: a personal perspective

Much has been written elsewhere about this role, its purposes and functions (Costa and Killick 1993; MacBeath 1998). As a SUPER critical friend with Comberton, I sought to develop the role in response to the needs of Comberton, both those declared and those I observed. From my perspective the role was simultaneously straightforward and highly complex. The straightforward part for me was that in many ways being a critical friend was an extension of the English research group which in itself was an extension of the ITET English work. In my role as SUPER critical friend the value of these previous working relationships was without doubt. For example, there already existed ways of working which could allow for joint (and enthusiastic) explorations of possible ways the role might develop in Comberton, but because of the background of a well-established working relationship, vigorous disagreement could also exist without any concerns for this damaging a fragile or simply recently emerging professional relationship.

'Critical friendship', which we interpreted as a reciprocal act of establishing, examining and evaluating the place of research for Comberton staff and our roles within that, was intertwined with conversations about ITET, English teaching and school developments more widely. The procedures we established and honed over time, of my mentoring staff on a one-to-one basis relatively frequently (at least three times a term and sometimes more often), keeping detailed research records using a pro forma I devised with a copy kept by the teacher and myself and copied, with the teacher's permission, to Mary, so that we were all aware of progress and so that Mary could, when possible, meet with staff and discuss specific issues to do with that teacher's research; meeting with small groups for presentations and peer commentary (again straightforward in a school which had established opportunities for self and peer evaluation through a Teaching and Learning Forum), meeting with the steering committee (which included the headteacher, Stephen Munday, research staff and students) to take an overview of progress worked well. They gave us a raft of ways of working which in turn allowed us flexibility of response. The 'personalised response' of the critical friend role always received very good evaluations and the clear lines of responsibility in managing Comberton's research vision (and effective delegation of that responsibility to Mary) enhanced the straightforwardness of organisation and shared vision immeasurably.

The complexity of the role was the complexity of any teaching relationship: in constructing any learning relationship as one of shared negotiation with the teacher as *critical listener*, as is my personal view, the balance of encouragement, honesty of response (sometimes with difficult messages), scaffolding, standing back, praising, challenging (though always on a professional collegiate basis) in the right ratio for the person or group you are working with is a complexity all teachers will recognise. Added to this for the SUPER role was the opportunity to work with senior management in Comberton to develop the strategic positioning of research within the school. The negotiations here had to take into account other, and sometimes, conflicting priorities within Comberton which often represented the need of Comberton to respond to external agendas such as SATs, Ofsted and GCSE.

As we shall see, one way in which Comberton has tried to reconcile some of these differing agendas (and indeed to meet the equally important concerns of teachers) has been to construct the purpose of research in terms of the raising of standards of teaching and learning in the classroom. In that this also meets government priorities for school-based research (see, for example, DfES 2005: 37–41) this strategy is successful. If however the purposes of research can be said to reside within knowledge building which may not impact in any measurable way on the 'raising standards' agenda, Comberton can be said to still be exploring the legitimacy of this dimension although there are certainly examples of this bolder construction of research emerging.

Research in Comberton 2001–2005

When I began working as a SUPER critical friend with Comberton, the college did not have a formalised research strategy as part of the day-to-day workings of the school although it certainly had had wide involvement in a number of research projects within SUPER.

In this section, exploring development from 2001 to 2005, most of the evidence is drawn from interviews with the headteacher and deputy head simply because there were almost no other staff identified as involved in research in the school-specific context.

In 2001, Comberton appointed a new headteacher, Stephen Munday. His appointment at this time was significant for this story because he decided to give a structural recognition to the place of research in the school strategic plan. Both the powerful statement made about research by a new headteacher and its place in the plan, and the high profiling of this position by the appointment of Mary Martin as deputy head with a brief to develop research in Comberton were important factors in positioning research in Comberton.

Interviewed early in 2002, Stephen Munday readily acknowledged that research in Comberton was not highly structured; when asked about the research being undertaken at Comberton, he replied:

> Well, it's an interesting question. In so far as there's various versions of informal or small-scale research that probably don't get reported properly ... lots of research going on at all sorts of levels in a fairly informal way.

The deputy head, Mary Martin (then Head of English), saw research as less rooted in the school at that point:

> Well, I would say that there isn't that much taking place; there is a lot proposed.

Mary's appointment as the SUPER Comberton TRC was a natural development of her enthusiasm for and experience in school-focused research. The role of TRC brought additional challenges however, not least in translating her own interest into wider staff involvement. This was a substantial undertaking, with workload being seen as a real problem, as Mary explained:

> I have found it a bit of a wilderness over the last three years in trying to encourage people to do research because they are too busy, they think it is too much, it's too extra, it's too much work.

The headteacher saw this as problematic too:

> I think a possible problem that teaching staff will often quote ... for why they're not doing any formalised research is they couldn't possibly have the time and I think I might well agree with them.

Mary, however, and perhaps drawing on her own experiences of research beginning with an MEd at Cambridge Faculty of Education, had adopted the processes and procedures of research she had encountered on that course as a framework for thinking more deeply about her own teaching. So powerful had Mary found her experience of research that she sought to build a research culture in her department and established quite quickly agreed ways of working that were designed to help understanding of how students engaged with specific areas of the English agenda:

> I found that colleagues could be encouraged to attach investigative processes to the implementation of innovation so that research behaviours become embedded within departmental practices as natural evaluative mechanisms.

Stimulating, motivating and sustaining research

In stimulating interest in research in Comberton, the impetus had come from SUPER and the appointment of Mary as TRC. Although this in itself was a major step forward, that the research interests had not developed into a research *culture* in Comberton as yet indicated that thinking about research had yet to become systemic: as yet, the infrastructure was still to be developed which would allow research to become a way of thinking about teaching and learning and to bring with it a language which would enable that. A sense of where the school might act to bring about that position was given by Stephen Munday in speaking about the structures he perceived as needed to enable research to develop:

> The key staffing structure is to have Mary Martin on senior management with one of her major briefs as a research oversight, which I think actually fits in appropriately and importantly with the oversight of the Training School. A key area of the whole of her job now is really in a sense as director of training and research within the school and that the two should overlap and link into each other – and I think they appropriately do.

The formalisation of a research brief when Mary was appointed as TRC in 1999 was central for Comberton in bringing about a strategic position for the harnessing of the energies Mary had brought to SUPER and research into wider staff involvement. But she acknowledged that stimulating interest in and motivation to undertake research was a major task. Her approach to this position was entirely and appropriately pragmatic:

> I try to make it look like the minimal text production effort because that is what puts a lot of people off and try and stress all the value in, you know, its practice, its strategy to what you are already doing in preparing lessons anyway.

These commonly echoed perceptions of time and priorities (see for example Cochran-Smith and Lytle 1993) reveal again the significance of locating research, at least in the first place, in classroom activity. As we saw earlier, in constructing research as classroom focused and linked to classroom improvement, Comberton was recognising an imperative that was shaping much of research progression in the school. Teachers in Comberton at least were, by and large, driven by the immediacy of the classroom; any investment of energy which did not repay dividends in this arena was likely not to be well received. The congruence of this as a starting point and the constructions of research in Comberton therefore made perfect sense: teachers' research repertoires were shaped as a response to their own practice needs and in the first instance at least, that was the place of research for many teachers at the school. The central question for teachers in Comberton beginning research at this point was 'Does it make a difference to my classroom teaching and learning?' 'It may' was the answer which emerged to this pertinent but highly complex question, though not necessarily through the production of short-term strategies which many teachers initially saw as the expected 'product' of research – and often not to measurable effects in terms of 'raising standards'; but as we see later in the chapter, this question remained central for many teacher researchers at Comberton.

Part of the strategic development of research within the school was the intro-duction of a group designed to give structure to the sharing of research and a 'recognised' route for its dissemination within Comberton. The Teaching and Learning Group in Comberton was seen as essential in bringing about motivation through peer support and involvement. This strategy formed part of the move to sustain research through a not yet articulated but clearly understood need to create a *critical mass* of participants (a group which varies in size but which is significant in terms of its ability to affect school perceptions and discourses) which would be needed to embed research as a naturalised way of working in the school. Mary commented:

> [We've] established a new teaching and learning group within the school which we did from September. [Teachers] meet regularly to consider areas of interesting and possibly good practice and ideas that are being considered in different ways around the college, [and] use it as a forum for sharing those thoughts and ideas with others, to lead to further action and developments in other subject areas and to evaluate the possible effectiveness of those developments.

While the notion of developing a critical mass of research engaged teachers as a key for sustaining research in Comberton was not explicit at this point, neverthe-less it is implicit in discussions relating to the potential impact of research to offer opportunities for extended engagement with other teachers. Mary said:

> Well, I am hoping there is still quite a bit of scope for us to really connect on a school to school basis. I feel we have had fantastic connection on a colleague to colleague basis in the network learning community and I have learnt a tremendous amount from the people who, I would say, are more advanced in

encouraging research in their schools over the years I have been connected with it.

This was echoed by the headteacher, for whom extended networking was a key component of the development of research in Comberton:

> I just think it makes research massively more meaningful and stimulating and worthwhile if you're not just gazing at your own navel but looking at a few other ones instead.

In part, of course, all that research was doing here was offering a shared agenda. But shared agendas already existed in plenty from a range of other commonalities that all state schools encounter in day-to-day running, and networking of the type described here had not happened to any significant extent. The part that SUPER played in bringing about meaningful and purposeful networking sits within its 'hidden' impact: the provision of infrastructure, not simply organisational but also intellectual.

The gradual changes that took place in relation to perceptions about research in Comberton were reflected in the types of questions being asked of research by the teachers. One of the questions that seemed at this point to permeate the thinking of Comberton related to what research actually *looked like* in school – what was its purpose? Did it replicate some of the earlier university-based models, or was it distinctive in its construction? In an interview early in 2003, Stephen Munday was asked about the place of research in the school. He replied:

> [Staff are] all involved in research of some sort because they're all or should be reflecting on or evaluating the work and the development that they're doing as a school. We're doing that and we look at our development plan and we try to have thoughts about what's worked, and what hasn't in light of how we should move forward.

A view that Mary had also articulated:

> I have tried to encourage the management to think that the kind of activity involved in research are the very kinds of activity that are useful when you try to come up with evaluative evidence for these other processes that everybody already knows we have got to try and do or fulfil.

Research then is seen at this stage as an enhancement of a process which all effective teachers undertake in evaluating their own performance; as Mary put it, 'All you are doing is putting an investigative spin on what you are doing.' What we are beginning to encounter here is perhaps what we might refer to as a notion of a *repertoire* of teacher research. As we shall see later in the chapter, conceptualisations of research, its value and place in teaching become described more variously

and widely as research is more rooted in Comberton. However, in that its definition becomes extended, it is not to say that this position becomes of lesser value. It
is simply perhaps the first response to the notion of teacher research and the
imperative many teachers feel: that to engage with research is only a legitimate
activity if it has an immediate and (preferably) measurable impact on classroom
practices. Indeed, it is a position espoused by government policy at the time of
writing. But this is not, as it will be clear later in the chapter, at all the point where
teachers in a school such as Comberton stop in their thinking about research.

Other factors: BPRS

For Comberton, SUPER and BPRS were intertwined in exploring the development of research in the school. The funding that BPRS brought to some extent
allowed the development of SUPER within the school and encouraged a much
more extended involvement of teachers in research in schools. However, it was not
simply the funding for Comberton (important as this was) but the legitimisation of
schools-based research from the precise groups defining the external agendas: a
recognition and consolidation of the value of research, enabling an enhancement
of peer group working and indeed of wider networking, which was precisely the
SUPER agenda.

STEPHEN: I think that just a tremendous opportunity to do some extremely good,
    fairly rigorous decently funded forms of professional development ... that
    teachers don't have the funding to do normally. So it is a very useful means of
    pulling in resources to help with research and giving a framework for what a
    decent piece of research might be that ties back in ultimately as all these things
    should to good effective classroom practice. So everyone gains. I wouldn't
    mind if every single member of staff were on a BPRS.

MARY: I [think you can] almost map the kind of receptivity to research and the
    level of research culture in a school by the take up of BPRS. It's going to be
    sad if this all goes out the window next year because I think my school is an
    interesting example in that here we have people very dedicated to their jobs
    and very hard working, very interested in what they are doing ... for me where
    people have done the BPRS that that has always enabled me to have some-
    thing concrete to say about this bit of work that was going on here and then
    what were the outcomes and what was the effect on the person in the practice
    etc. So I am completely sold on it as an idea.

Moving on

In 2004 the BPRS funding was withdrawn by the government as part of a wider
funding consolidation exercise and teacher research in many places was either
halted or slowed down. However, at Comberton the trajectory for research

involvement continued upward. We might ask at this point what other factors contribute to this onward progression. Certainly the headteacher's position is pivotal in seeing the potential of SUPER and the role of the critical friend to support research at Comberton:

> I do think it's important and it's helpful that it isn't just the schools networking together but in a sense there are those who had perhaps more of a full research understanding and background were able to stand slightly to one side of the schools and offer some partial guidance and advice and ways of constructing and developing research which if you haven't got that critical friend role, it would be somewhat easy to sort of go down a certain path whilst having your blinkers on and not knowing you've got your blinkers on. I think it is very helpful having someone looking with a strong background, maybe saying you're not obeying one of the standard accepted pieces of good practice about how you should be going about research or you might not be aware that there's some very interesting research that was done over there five years ago or something, it would be sensible to take account of that because they did something similar and were led to these things that might help to guide ... So having someone in that position with an area of expertise, a guidance hat and the sort of critical friend role within this, means that the research, I would suggest likely to be much more meaningful and helpful and rigorous and produce worthwhile outcomes than if we narrowly plough our own furrows and missed some rather important points as a result of that.

We shall turn now to explore how far this vision was realised at Comberton.

Evolving stories 2002–2005

In looking at the impact of research within the context of SUPER at Comberton, we have sought to use the early stories as a background, but we move now to foreground the voices of staff involved in research: teacher researcher stories. Key organisational questions for us have been concerned with school structures, stimulation, motivation and sustaining of research-focused activity and the place of SUPER; but we have attempted too to bring together these responses with the expectations and aspirations of teachers involved in research at Comberton.

Over two years on, Comberton had become a school confident about the place of research in its overall plans. It would probably be accurate to say that Comberton's development of a research focus still *includes* the SUPER project but is not *only* the SUPER project. The extent to which SUPER played a significant role in supporting research development is best described by Mary:

> SUPER has been crucial in allowing Comberton to learn how to encourage inquiry and research into teaching and learning. In recent years the influences have become diversified as more staff have joined Comberton bringing

research backgrounds with them. In addition a very significant influence has been the ITET partnership with the Faculty of Education, Cambridge University. Teachers who also become mentors are inevitably reflective practitioners and often the road to research opened up through the academic subject link lecturer partnerships independently of the SUPER networkings.

Comberton and teacher research: what stimulates research?

At the beginning of Comberton's development of becoming a research-focused school, we explored what stimulated research and looked at the role of the TRC as central to that. Interviews in late 2004 demonstrated that Mary's influence as TRC continued to be key. She identified her work as concerned with encouragement:

> For so long now I have been trying to encourage other people to examine what they are doing ... I'm constantly trying to suggest how you might examine and turn over and gather some evidence.

Interviews with teacher researchers at Comberton confirm the significance of the TRC role in stimulating – indeed securing – research interest:

CLAIRE: Well, with coming to Comberton and being nagged about research by Mary (*laughs*) as most people are.

REBECCA: When I came to the school, Mary asked me if I was interested in research and it's something I hadn't really thought about before but was something I had been interested in finding out ... how children learn and how we can help them better in classrooms.

LORNA: It's having Mary as a professional tutor. Someone who is always there reminding me about what I am doing and there to discuss my ideas with so that's a big impact to have one person that's always there and focused on research.

But other factors began to weigh in too. Previous involvement in research seems to have been a critical factor in developing a research interest:

MARK: I originally got involved with some research with another case study being done ... I'd just become a head of department and I was very interested in getting some different views on the department was working and the quality of teaching and learning in the department ... The research project we're involved in was initially a pilot study on pupil voice with the university [Jean Rudduck] ... we had one of the university researchers come in and worked with myself and a colleague looking at pupils' feedback on lessons.

RACHEL: My first involvement with research was a very, very reluctant involvement
... When I arrived in 1999 there was already a project ongoing with the
university ... [we were] one of the schools involved in a project about how
students' [foreign] language improves if they go on exchange. .... I was invited
to a meeting where some of the results were disseminated ... and I went along
feeling like oh, you know, I suppose I should be polite really and then I was
absolutely fascinated ... seeing the results and actually talking through some
of the things that undoubtedly were true, and were true for some of my pupils
... I thought 'yep', and that, if you like, was the seed. And then the BPRS ...
and then I started doing the MEd course and that's got me completely hooked
now so that's where I am – a reluctant convert but now very, very converted.

For others it was the more recent experience of ITET: one NQT noted that she
wanted to build on her recent PGCE experience and that the opportunity to be
involved in research at Comberton was a contributory factor to her choice of post:

LORNA: Well, ... obviously there were research aspects of my PGCE which I felt I
thoroughly enjoyed ... I found it really quite interesting to be able to do
research in that depth so when I came to look for a job and I was looking here
it was discussed at interview what research I would be involved in because I am
just interested.

Another NQT wanted to capitalise on her PGCE experiences in a more formalised way and decided to take an MEd (Researching Practice) at the University of
Cambridge which, at the time, was a newly created route specifically for early
career teachers:

NICOLA: I was quite interested in [research] during my PGCE and that was where
I sort of got the flavour for it during the dissertation there. And then following on from that I decided to get involved in the Early Career Masters and I
decided to do it straight away because I thought I was enjoying it so much and
I didn't want to lose that straight away, I wanted it to automatically be there
all the time so that's why I did it in the first place through that MEd.

Other, more established, teachers talk about their research involvement as an
extension of their professional interest in teaching and learning, a perspective
which in the early stories section, both Stephen and Mary had been at pains to
emphasise as a key conceptual framework.
A recently appointed Head of English said:

CLAIRE: I'd certainly been doing – well, experimenting in my own classroom – for
my own benefit and that of the pupils I had been teaching in my last school
but I wouldn't have thought that was called research or, you know, had any
audience beyond myself ... whereas here it's obviously been given a far higher

profile and I think certainly the work in English using the data projectors has had an impact on the work of the department.

Others see it as an integral part of their teaching:

MARK: I think for me teaching and research have become an integrated way of working.

To what extent this is a perspective ingrained through the emphasis Comberton gave to the context and purpose of research and to what extent that perspective simply echoed teachers' prevailing views is hard to establish, as Mary commented:

> I think individuals and departments have varying levels of consciousness about the notion of embedded evaluative practices (nascent research behaviours). This is only to be expected. As practitioners recognise how valuable 'research style' practice is as evidence gathering mechanisms for internal and external audiences.

What motivates teachers to continue with their research?

As with any innovation, rates of take up and commitment were not consistent across the teaching population. At Comberton there was certainly a pattern of successful initial stimulus for research being taken up by some teachers but then a falling away of any translation of intent into action. However, a substantial number, twelve of the original cohort of sixteen, made the leap from promise to reality. The factors that brought this about varied with the individual but patterns also emerged.

For some, it was the ongoing individual support that counted and here the TRC role was critical:

NICOLA: Mary – someone who is always there reminding me about what I'm doing and where I am going and there to discuss ideas with.

For others, the Teaching and Learning Group was to be a key structure. This powerful opportunity not only to share research but also to be seen as belonging to a peer group of researchers. One teacher said:

LAURA: To have a Teaching and Learning Group I think is a fantastic opportunity within the school ... we discuss the research and we discuss issues ... that's a place I can report on the research I am doing and discuss it with other staff and I can hear what other staff are doing ... and then I think that just having other staff within the school that are motivated in that way ... and think in that way ... that certainly keeps me going as well.

Certainly some teachers reiterated their prime motivation as seeking improved classroom practice:

LEIGH: I think the motivation for my research comes from teaching on a daily basis … I want to present German to them in a modern and accessible way and the only way I can do that is by asking them what is modern and what is accessible for them.

Others found that as well as impacting on practice, additional dimensions emerged:

NICOLA: The research itself: the end justifies the means. It's so satisfying getting into the theory and … you feel you can see how it's going to improve your practice and how you can share the ideas with other people.

MARK: It's partly the intellectual challenge of it and it provides a different style and way of working … it provides a means of continually refreshing how I'm looking at lessons.

Powerfully, however, it is the theme of repositioning their own perspective: 'research by teachers is a significant way of knowing about teaching … inquiry by individual teachers … realigns their relationship to knowledge' (Cochran-Smith and Lytle 1993: 43)

LORNA: It's about me learning as well. I am a learner too. I think there's always ways you can improve and only through doing research and having evidence on why something works … can you hope to develop yourself and become a better teacher.

MARY: From my perspective it's once teachers see a connection between actually doing research, and understanding the emergence of a 'new voice' in the classroom from the observation and data collection being undertaking – then it's exciting and stimulating – it's feedback on your teaching and it's incredibly invigorating and you begin to want to be systematic about collecting that information and that's what's motivating.

What sustains the research?

Comberton is a particularly successful research-focused school in many ways, not least in that the research dimension has not simply been a 'one-off' event but has developed year on year. Different factors will be significant in different schools but in Comberton there is a clearly identified link between school management and sustainability of research:

MARK: You've got to have a SMT who are willing to recognise the fact that you are putting in extra effort, time or work into doing this and are wiling to support you. At middle management level you've got to support people both the time to encourage them with the thinking and providing opportunities to get involved.

NICOLA: It's good having a supportive line manager that can give you time or access to resources ... and an ethos in the school of research and a willingness to help you.

But the critical mass of supportive and likeminded colleagues featured strongly in many responses, with the Teaching and Learning Group being a major factor:

LORNA: To have a Teaching and Learning Group ... that certainly keeps me going.

Mary reports that, for Comberton, there were several key points that contributed to sustainability in the school with SUPER providing the context for those developments:

- *Research support in Comberton*: the teacher research coordinator role enabled an identified person to offer support for carrying out research activity. The TRC had both understanding of research methodology and the legitimacy of being grounded in the reality the school so this was a particularly important element.
- *Showcasing*: in the Teaching and Learning Group opportunities were given for people to describe research projects, discuss findings and explore whether the research area is one which should be developed further. Mary describes this as 'speculative mining' – where one person's findings can stimulate interest in the area for a much wider range of teachers. Emerging too from these research discussions might be implication for classroom practice.
- *Ofsted*: because inspection requirements now demand evidence, Comberton has found that products (e.g. questionnaires/interviews/surveys/statistical analysis) from research projects provide excellent materials to support knowledge about teaching and learning in the school. This in turn confers a status on research activity one.
- *Critical friend*: brings an overview of academic and inter-school knowledge. The critical friend role enabled support for research methodology, extending the school based understandings; with the experience that the critical friend brings they can offer a perspective on mapping the research activities of Comberton and thus identify commonalities across the college.
- *Management support*: pursuit of research has to be written into the school improvement plan (SIP) to enable the TRC to make legitimate claims on resources or staff time to support research activity.

- *Notions of professionalism*: Comberton believes that practitioners who are exposed to research activity or experiment with it are likely to recognise the benefits in terms of their understanding of their own professionalism. As Mary said:

At the heart of professionalism you are trying to justify what you do and you want to speak with authority. Research gives people professional confidence.

And has it made a difference to teaching and learning?

As we saw earlier, sustainability is also about the research having demonstrable outcomes which teachers can identify as desirable; for some this was still about having evidence relating to their own classroom practice:

JO: One of the big things that we felt over the last couple of years is that we haven't been able to properly assess [the Sports Skills course] – what difference we are making to children's learning ... so the idea is that we do some research so we can back up what we are saying because I mean I believe firmly that the programme works and I would like some evidence to back that up.

NICOLA: It's made me more aware of what is going on ... I've planned a lot better ... it's definitely given me the ability to improve pupils' learning ... giving them activities that are going to make them think and take on responsibility for finding out things and making decisions about where to go next. I can feel more confident because the things I'm doing are grounded in evidence rather than just something I might think works

For others, research has changed the ways in which they construct themselves as teachers:

MARK: It's the reflective element ... it's hard to pin down any one precise thing but it's made me go back and look at the way I'm planning and delivering lessons ... I think far more deeply about the range of pupils that are in that room ... being able to keep refreshing what you are doing and therefore maintaining the challenge.

RACHEL: [It has made] a very big difference ... there's a heightened awareness as a teacher ... there are just times when you just step to one side and watch a little bit more what's going on ... a built-in different perspective.

LEIGH: I think research has made a massive difference to my teaching ... it's meant a reminder that I'm still learning ... it really has brought excitement back into the classroom for me.

A happy ending?

The progression of research in Comberton from a vague conviction that 'lots of research [is] going on at all sorts of levels in a fairly informal way' to a recognised and identified group of staff involved in research activities now up to and including PhDs is proof of the possibility of building a research community, with research seen as relevant, achievable and professionally liberating. Asked 'Who benefits?' research-active teachers replied:

MARK: Everybody. I benefit, the people I work alongside but particularly the pupils

REBECCA: Me ... totally selfishly ... the pupils I teach absolutely definitely ... the members of the department that I foist my ideas on and generate some discussion with ... increasingly other teachers in other school who are engaged in similar projects ... it can be an ever building thing.

NICOLA: Pupils ... visiting ITT students ... other teachers. It just keeps you alive as teacher ... it keeps you permanently on your toes.

But for others, and it has to be acknowledged still the majority of staff in Comberton, research has yet to impact on them either as an opportunity for investigating classroom-enhanced practice or for the personal satisfaction of being a learner. And this remains a puzzle. SUPER has been established in the school for eight years at the time of writing. An effective infrastructure is in place with enthusiastic and respected staff involved. The role of critical friend is in place and has been well received. The enthusiasm of those staff who have become actively concerned with research suggests that within Comberton successful role models exist. So juxtaposing these two situations of the success of SUPER in Comberton with the reluctance of teachers to enter into research raises the question: why? In thinking this through, it may well be that the issue for many teachers is indeed time. Teachers are indeed extraordinarily busy in their professional lives and certainly the earlier views from the headteacher and from Mary identified time as a key concern. The withdrawal of the BPRS scheme and its concomitant funding of release time for research may play a part in this.

Teachers' professional priorities often reflect the day-to-day immediacies of the classroom and research may well be seen by some as a bridge too far. The classroom focus and emphasis on pragmatism in schools may also lead some teachers to remain unconvinced that research is of any real or practical use to them and in one sense, the progression of some staff to MEds and PhDs might have exacerbated this situation – the construction of research as 'academic' and belonging to the university is implicit in the recognition by Comberton of these staff following formalised routes as 'successful' researchers. The fact that as critical friend I am also a university lecturer may reinforce this and perhaps contribute to the view of research and the academic belonging together – and, however far the intention is the opposite, excluding at least some teachers.

Ownership of research in Comberton is still not seen consistently as belonging to the school. But there are also questions about the positioning of research in schools more generally. The government simultaneously espouses school-based research and withdraws funding to support it; success within schools is measured in terms of examination results and league tables and research does not obviously contribute in the short term to improvement in these. Comberton's attempt to situate research in exactly these areas by constructing it as classroom focused and thus to involve teachers in practice-focused research may contribute, paradoxically, to some teachers rejecting research.

We see in some of the examples in this chapter teachers as researchers who have found the major stimulation of the research to be long term and indirect: contributing to their personal and professional feelings of deep involvement in the field of education more generally. A short-term and results-focused version of research may not appeal to this group at all. Research is threatening too. It threatens change at a time when the external pressures on schools do not encourage many teachers to welcome either change itself or the demands on time and energy change brings. Research may too bring to light new problems and issues which may make the school or individual teachers feel vulnerable.

It remains to be seen then whether the sense of gentle but relentless insistence on the importance of research in Comberton will bring about vision of an embedded research culture which will continue to grow over time. Mary concluded:

> I am confident if we can keep the culture going, you know, a different cohort of people next year interested in doing something ... steadily, steadily.

Chapter 5

Netherhall School

A SUPER case study

Keith S. Taber

Context

This chapter discusses Netherhall School and Sixth Form College, an 11–18 comprehensive school in the City of Cambridge, with specialist sports college status, located on two adjacent sites separated by a busy road. Netherhall joined the SUPER project after the other partners, and withdrew two years later. This chapter tells the story of a school keen to enter into partnership, committed to research, having a school researcher and a pre-existing programme of work related to the community themes. It is a cautionary tale of how even the most promising partnership may fail.

This case study is written by the critical friend, who spent time in the school on a weekly basis during the two years. Much of the evidence base for this chapter derives from interviews with individuals in key roles when the school joined the partnership: Graham Silverthorne (headteacher), Phil Evans (teacher research coordinator) and Pam Black (student voice coordinator).

The image of research in the school

When Netherhall joined the pre-existing SUPER partnership at the formation of the Networked Learning Communities (Jackson 2002), the senior management team felt that in one sense they were 'starting from scratch' (Phil Evans), as the other schools had a tradition of working within the partnership, whereas for Netherhall 'everything is new, pretty much'. However, Phil considered that the school was already actively researching its practice and that 'a lot of significant work' was being undertaken, mainly through Best Practice Research Scholarships. Two members of staff had completed some work on inclusion of ethnic minority students, and another had done work related to the use of ICT. There was already work in the school looking at student voice. This project involved sixth formers acting as mentors to Year 8 students identified as disaffected or underachieving. Another member of staff, Geoff Wilson, was the 'school researcher', as Pam Black explained:

The vision of the headteacher was to make Netherhall a centre of excellence in research and there was already a research person in position ... whose research continues and he's looked at birthdate and age in relation to attainment and that's carried on. He's also looking at learning and styles of learning.

Graham Silverthorne described his vision in terms of research supporting the sharing of best practice in the school:

And if I can grow in five, ten, fifteen researchers who in turn can cascade at least some of those skills on into classrooms and to other colleagues then that's a really nice model ... in perhaps a year's time or so we may have four or five research projects which will perhaps fertilise an INSET day where my teachers talk to my teachers about things they've found out.

The school was committed enough to this principle to maintain a 'substantial' research fund ('many thousands of pounds': Phil) to support projects, and a flyer informed staff that 'funding is also available to enable other staff to carry out research'.

The impact of research

Graham believed that the existing research undertaken in the school had already had benefits, estimating that work undertaken relating to independence in learning would impact upon 'about 20–40 per cent of kids' who were 'lucky and get the right teachers'. His aspiration was that by joining the SUPER community and involving more staff in the research, such developments could become part of 'a common set of expectations' that would give 'entitlement coverage' for students. Sixth formers who had worked on Pam's project had already 'gained from being trained as researchers' by university academics.

The school's motivation for coming into partnership

Part of the school's motivation for joining SUPER clearly derived from the existing image of the school as being research active. Graham saw joining the community as part of 'the process of setting up support structures' for research. This included the SUPER steering group, and a 'subset' (comprising Phil, Geoff and Pam) that had been set up by Phil: 'a smaller, instant response team ... who are focusing down on current work going on and targeting new people to get them on board'. The key aim was to expand the research activity 'beyond ... [the] two or three people who did it' (Phil). The school staff were informed that through SUPER, 'all staff will be offered opportunities to participate in conferences and knowledge exchange with colleagues in our partner schools'.

For Graham, being part of the NLC was part of a strategy for implementing the changes he saw as desirable in the school. He had found that ideas developed in his previous post could not be 'exported' directly, so he had to go 'back to basics and regenerate the interest in a different way ... through a Teaching and Learning policy and the Assessment for Learning policy, but there is still a missing piece which I think might evolve as part of the research'.

Joining SUPER was 'an expedient', 'a tool' that fitted with Graham's 'agenda'. As Phil explained: 'We were aware of the SUPER project, were keen that research had a higher profile within the school and that the opportunity was broadened, so it seemed the ideal opportunity'.

Perceptions of partnership in the school

Graham considered the relationship with the university as potentially 'one of those mutually beneficial arrangements where we can learn and clearly we can access resources, but I think we can access expertise'. Phil thought that 'the faculty are key really and they ... really knit the group together and ... they drive the group really and ... act as a conduit as well'. Pam had already drawn upon expertise within the faculty for her earlier research and saw value in such links, but she questioned whether the university should take responsibility to lead the community:

> Who's the senior partner, and the fact that some schools say that they actually wanted somebody to tell them what to do and the university saying, 'No. we're equal partners here'. But there's a dilemma there.

Graham was less convinced about the partnership with the other schools, sensing a lack of direction, as 'if we're not careful we'll be too liberal in terms of allowing things to evolve without a real focus and then it won't have meaning and the schools won't work together because they're too busy actually'. The heads were having difficulty finding suitable times to meet, whereas Phil was regularly meeting TRC colleagues at SUPER meetings. He felt 'more and more part of a group', which was providing 'lots of support', and leading to 'real examples of collaboration and progression' in the partnership. Similarly, Pam talked about a number of specific links she had been making with other partner schools, and described how that had 'helped sustain certainly the research I did because it's enabled me to learn from and with others'. She continued:

> It's the opportunity to step outside the school and reflect and look down at what you've been doing and actually discuss things with other people which helps you to think carefully and think on a higher level about what you've been doing.

Phil had 'the feeling that the *national* partnership has that rather sort of grandiose aim'. Graham reported being 'massively underwhelmed', suggesting that he found the national leadership 'glib, patronising, unfocused really from the school agenda and unrealistic'. Instead of helping forge specific links between individual schools where there was specific value in sharing practice, the national leadership were 'coming out with lots of glossy magazines and well-staged conferences which move you not an inch further forward towards any benefit at all to children'. Pam felt that being part of a national network had not had any impact on the school, just 'a lot of emails with lots of paper and the reality is, on the receiving end in the school, is that it goes in the file'.

Research priorities and activity in the school

The three themes of the research in the NLC, independence in learning, student voice and leadership for learning, seemed to fit well with the school management's aspirations and concerns.

Independence in learning

Phil described 'a strong tradition of work on teaching and learning within the school', and Graham referred to 'a teachers' group called the TALENT group, which looks at all the teaching and learning issues'. He identified the independence in learning theme as 'critical', 'at the very heart of what I want to do' and 'the key to developing learning'. Ongoing initiatives on assessment for learning, enrichment and learning styles, were 'really developing metacognition for learners'. Graham thought that there was relevant work being undertaken, but 'it's happening piecemeal around the school, it's not coherent and that's one of my big aims for this project'.

Student voice

Phil considered work on student voice to be 'in some ways more advanced even than the Teaching and Learning', citing Pam's project to run 'Learning to Learn workshops using sixth form students as the guides and mentors for a group of forty disaffected Year 8 students'. Pam thought this had had very positive outcomes for the sixth form students who acted as mentors: 'the working together as a team, the heightened self-awareness, the understanding of their own learning'. Despite this, Graham viewed student voice as 'not something we do very well here', and wanted the school to 'go quite a lot further', introducing a 'Children's Curriculum Committee'. He saw the SUPER community as a source of support in setting up a means of 'finding out what children think and then doing something about it'.

Leadership for learning

Graham considered that the leadership for learning theme was 'very close to my heart', although he seemed to largely interpret this in terms of seeing the school leaders as continuing to learn themselves, because 'if your leaders aren't learning then you've lost it'. Creating 'an ethos of leadership by all people in the school' was a more distant goal:

> The leader's outside the ball and is preparing the ground and deciding in which direction the ball goes. Now if you've got a leadership team they're all outside the ball. Now they can all dive back in to sort out problems but they're actually all moving the ball together in one direction. I think then you have a very powerful school. I suppose the ultimate there is to have the whole staff outside pushing the ball too.

The delivery

The school's SUPER steering group met once. As well as Graham, Phil, Pam and myself (as critical friend), there was a representative of the governors. Two other members of the group (the school researcher and the chair of the TALENT group) were not able to attend. There was no student representation. There was some discussion on approaches to learning styles, but the main item was a detailed report on Pam's project with the sixth form mentoring of Year 8 students (Black 2003). It was reported that despite the SMT's best efforts to encourage interest from staff, there had been very little interest in applying for the following year's BPRS awards.

In the event the only BPRS application was made by Pam. The application was successful, but she resigned from the school with effect from the end of the academic year, leaving at the same time as Graham. Before this, Pam and a colleague did attend a SUPER Teaching and Learning Research Day to report on their existing work (Wells 2002; Black 2003). Pam attended the whole day, taking part in the discussions, but her colleague was able to be present only for long enough to give his own presentation.

Phil was considering plans to develop student voice 'using students as assessors of teachers', and hoped to form a group of teachers prepared to be involved in a pilot study. As Head of Sixth Form, he was also reorganising the sixth form council to give the students more autonomy in running their own representative body. Some of the upper sixth formers who had been involved in the mentoring project the previous year had worked on an initiative organised by the TALENT group working with lower school pupils, and drawing in some lower sixth students to help as well.

The chair of the TALENT group was Helen Blythe, the Head of Lower School, and she was made joint acting head for the Autumn term, taking over the head's role within the SUPER community as part of her brief. Phil reported that 'we are restarting research'. Angela Brown was appointed SVC for the new academic year, taking over the BPRS project, and spent much of the term familiarising herself with the role, including at a SUPER conference on 'Sharing about Student Voice'.

However, for a variety of reasons, she stood down from the role at the start of the Spring term. Meanwhile Phil left the school at the end of the term, and Helen took over the TRC role.

Theresa Brown took over the SVC role and the BPRS scholarship, and actively started planning her research. She decided to enrol a group of sixth formers to help with research into Year 7 students' perceptions of the transition from primary school to secondary school. The idea was to use this information to inform staff about easing new pupils into the school. Theresa held regular planning meetings with me (effectively the first time the school had made use of my critical friend role), and worked with Geoff to plan the analysis of data collected. She hoped to extend her research by working with one of the feeder primary schools.

Geoff, who had already undertaken published work based in the school (e.g. Wilson 2003), expressed an interest in working collaboratively on exploring some aspects of learning styles. After some false starts, SUPER-associated research seemed to be taking off in the school. However, it was also clear that Theresa was not being facilitated to attend meetings, and did not seem to be getting information about the partnership that should have been arriving in school. The new headteacher did not intend to attend the end-of-year residential conference, and the school booked places only for Theresa and a member of the SMT who had had no previous involvement with SUPER's work. This member of staff did not respond to an offer of a briefing on the project, and did not go to the conference. Theresa, an NQT, attended the conference as the only representative of the school – apart from a message withdrawing the school from the SUPER community.

Changing perspectives in the partnership school

A key feature of the school's period in the partnership was the turnover of key staff (Jackson and West 1999). Graham had been aware that this was a potential issue, 'because year on year with a school this size you can lose four or five new enthusiasts every year who go off to be promoted elsewhere'. What he had not anticipated was that within little more than a year of joining SUPER he would be moving to another headship, the SVC would leave school teaching, and the TRC would move to the advisory service. The loss of Graham, with his strong commitment to research in the school, 'a vision ... enabling those who are interested in doing the research' (Pam), was a major blow to the development of SUPER-related work at the school.

The second year of SUPER membership opened without a permanent head. The new headteacher arrived in January, and over the following months had the opportunity to review activities within the school, and links with other organisations. He decided to leave the community, explaining to me that it was time to focus on issues *within* the school – to find practical ways of using action research to directly benefit the school – and to minimise external commitments, and in particular the time commitment expected of him. He indicated that he believed in the principle of networking, but was unconvinced by the NLC model.

Particular features of the Netherhall case

Case studies are by definition studies of the particular, with their own special characteristics that make them unique. Netherhall is of particular interest in being 'late to the party' and yet still 'early to bed': joining an existing partnership when the community was set up, and then withdrawing two years later. In terms of sustaining partnership, this case is a study of failure rather than success. That does not necessarily imply that there was no benefit for the school or learners within it, or that the partnership may not have benefited from the school's involvement. Nevertheless this is a failure to sustain a meaningful relationship within a networked learning community.

It is clear from this case study that a significant factor has to be the loss of key members of staff who were committed to the school being part of the SUPER community. There would seem to be a number of other features of the school's time in partnership which colluded to make continued NLC membership seem against the school's interests.

Understanding of partnership relationships

Partnership implies shared benefits, shared decision-making, shared responsibilities: above all a commitment to the notion of 'sharing'. Graham and Phil were quite right to focus on what the school could gain from being part of the SUPER partnership, but during the two years of partnership the school was able to offer little back by means of research to share, and time out of school to meet the partners sometimes seemed begrudged. Each school was expected to make a major commitment in terms of staff time for the head, TRC and SVC to be kept available to meet their peers on a regular basis (Jones 2002: 3). Yet Pam was not kept off-timetable during the SUPER meeting slot, attending meetings meant 'hitting some of your classes on a regular basis every month [and] every time an individual with a heavy teaching timetable goes out on a Friday, they're having to prepare three hours of lessons on a Thursday'.

It has been suggested that one of the challenges in developing school–university partnerships is 'how to build equity in the partnership group' (Richert *et al.* 2001). However, Graham seemed to expect the university partner to lead, and Phil characterised time spent debating key community issues and evaluating progress as the community 'busy beating itself up'.

An inability to involve staff

One significant factor in the school's failure to develop its SUPER work was the inability to enrol other staff in the initiative. Despite leaflets and presentations at staff meetings, and the possibility of funding support, it proved difficult to get staff involved. One factor here might have been a high turnover of junior staff. In addition, there was a feeling that everyone was already dealing with a continuous string of externally imposed changes that had to be engaged with, or with initiatives which were already running in the school, leaving little time or energy to volunteer for more. Pam gave an example:

> When the BPRS was presented ... there was interest from one [colleague who] came forward and was interested and she also works on a link project with a school in Africa and she's already doing a project on computer-mediated learning and I think it's assessment as well in Maths ... but she really felt that she'd had enough. She's also doing D-of-E [Duke of Edinburgh's Award].

Pam also suggested that some colleagues saw involvement in the research as 'going out for "jollies" ... not the core job', and felt that no time was made available in the school to take on such work, which 'just becomes an addition to everybody's job'. This lack of time for the role was also experienced by Angela and Theresa.

Fractured initiatives within the school

Another feature of the school's time in partnership was the apparent fragmentation of initiatives in the school – initiatives that would seem to be ideal for linking into a coherent whole. This seemed to be recognised by Graham and Phil, who apparently hoped that involvement in SUPER might bring coherence. The splitting of the school into an upper and lower school, with separate if adjacent sites, and with nominated heads of upper and lower school and the sixth form college, probably contributed here. Phil's ideas on a teaching and learning policy, on learning styles, on introducing more responsibility into the sixth form council, and seeking student feedback on teaching, all seemed to originate in sixth form contexts. Pam was also the Deputy Head of Sixth Form, and it was clear that her focus in her research was on the sixth formers working as mentors, much more than on the younger learners.

The TALENT group, seen as a lower school initiative, was not effectively brought into the SUPER project. Pam commented how 'those who were already doing research don't necessarily feel that they need to be part of SUPER to do what they're already doing'. It was perhaps an incidental, but unfortunate, coincidence that the leadership of the student voice work in the school remained in one academic area with first a biologist, then a chemist, and then a physicist.

The other obvious relevant discontinuity involved the pre-existing action-research group chaired by Geoff that was bypassed rather than developed as the basis of the school's work in SUPER.

Perceptions of imposed structural constraints

At first sight, the demise of an existing active action-research group in a school looking to develop its action research is difficult to rationalise. One interpretation could have been that the SMT did not have confidence in the teacher researcher as a potential teacher research coordinator, but this does not fit with the way Geoff was characterised:

GRAHAM: [Geoff is] the only one here who would know how to set up a research model.

PHIL: [Geoff has] acted as mentor for several [staff setting out on research] over the last few years.

PAM: He's very, very good at what he does, and people who are in the upper school [*sic*] know that he does research as well, and know that he is very exacting in whatever he does.

The explicit reason given was the NLC stipulation that the TRC role had to go to a senior manager, as 'you need someone who is in charge of it, someone whose discrete responsibility is that' (Phil). Yet, this would seem to have been an opportunity to devolve leadership (Hopkins and Jackson n.d.), and other partner schools saw this 'rule' as flexible (Worrall 2002: 3).

This decision resonates with the way the 'leadership for learning' theme was interpreted within the school. It has been argued that 'everyone has the potential and right to work as a leader. Leading is skilled and complicated work that can be learned by every member of the school community' (Harris and Lambert 2003). Supposedly, 'NLCs tap into the leadership potential of all teachers [giving] a commitment to providing a wide range of leadership opportunities' (NCSL n.d.: 6). Perhaps it was this type of rhetoric that Graham found 'glib ... and unrealistic', and that Phil considered a 'rather ... grandiose aim'.

It has been claimed that members of NLCs need 'a focus on dispersed leadership and empowerment' (Hopkins 2000: 6) and that 'academically successful professional learning communities' require 'the collegial and facilitative participation of the principal who shares leadership' (Hord 1997: 4; see also Lieberman and Grolnick 1996). Despite Graham's reference to his whole staff pushing the ball, this did not seem to be how leadership of SUPER work was distributed in the school. Pam certainly had picked up the message that 'leadership for learning' was the concern of the headteacher:

> That's how it's been seen ... I think you'll find that the 'leadership for learning' people are all headteachers ... everybody's a leader for learning, but in terms of the club, in SUPER, it has been seen as where the head goes.

Phil also believed that 'Leadership and learning is a sort of overarching aim which was the preserve really of the headteachers'.

Concluding comments

Although Netherhall was committed to partnership, and to learning from partnership, the school seemed to want a different sort of partnership to the NLC that SUPER had formed. The action-research group, the school researcher, the existing pockets of active work that fitted extremely well with the SUPER research themes, all would seem to have made Netherhall an ideal partner in the NLC. But the SUPER research never became part of the school dialogue (Jackson and Payne n.d.): it was always very much a minority interest, perhaps partly due to 'structural barriers' (EPPI-Centre 2002), such as the discrete identities of the lower school, upper school and sixth form. Perhaps the fit was too good ('Just a really nice opportunity to jump on a bandwagon that was already going the way I wanted to go': Graham), to encourage creative thinking about how to make the partnership work.

This chapter is dedicated to the memory of Geoff Wilson.

Chapter 6

Queen Elizabeth's Girls' School

From teachers as researchers to students as researchers

Colleen McLaughlin

Context

Queen Elizabeth's Girls' School (QEGS) in Barnet, Hertfordshire is a fully comprehensive 11–18 girls' school with 1,145 students. The school's Ofsted report (Ofsted 2003b) describes it as having the following characteristics. The proportion of pupils identified as having special educational needs (9.4 per cent) is below the national average. Pupils come from a wide range of ethnic backgrounds and there are some signs of deprivation. The school is oversubscribed and was also a Beacon school. It is situated forty miles away from the Faculty of Education and is geographically the furthest school from the others in the partnership.

The school's association with SUPER grew from a longstanding partnership with the Faculty of Education, begun in 1996 and led in the school by Non Worrall (James and Worrall 2000) and this will be fully explored in the following section. Non Worrall was the deputy head in the school; between 1996 and 2003 there were three headteachers at QEGS. This is important because Non Worrall was the link and also the original driver of SUPER in QEGS. She was teacher research coordinator for QEGS and a co-leader of the Networked Learning Community for two years before she left QEGS, so she had a role beyond the school. She presented papers at the British Educational Research Association conferences as part of SUPER symposia. This chapter is my own view of developments as the critical friend to QEGS and is informed by interviews with staff and students, questionnaires administered to a representative sample of the whole staff group and students, and public writings about QEGS and SUPER.

A tradition of research

The school has a tradition of classroom-based research and experience in supporting staff in this research. Between 1996 and 1998, all staff were trained in research techniques. The school supports teachers in taking up 'Best Practice Research Scholarships' and is a member of the 'Network Learning Community' linked to Cambridge University School of Education. Over recent years, staff development days have covered many issues relating to using a range of teaching and learning styles; the positive impact of that professional development is clearly visible in many lessons. ...

Pupils, as well as teachers, engage in research work. Groups of the more able students in some years have been trained as researchers and these students work with others in their year on specific projects. A group of year nine pupils, for example, is currently researching 'what makes a good lesson'. Through such projects and others, the school has set a climate of investigation and encouraged pupils to pose and answer their own questions.

(Ofsted 2003: paras 22 and 29)

This tradition of research (summarised in Box 6.1) for both staff and students goes back to 1989 when Non Worrall, then a senior teacher and INSET coordinator, enrolled on a sixty-hour course at the then Institute of Education, taught by Mary James. 'In Mary's opinion, the enthusiasm with which she embraced the idea that changes in policy and practice should be evaluated on the basis of evidence was critical for their future collaboration' (James and Worrall 2000: 95). This shared understanding led to a more formal collaboration with the school.

The then headteacher created a five-year school development plan focused on curriculum and staff development. Her aim was to facilitate the transition from a grammar to a comprehensive school and in particular to develop collaboration among staff. The important focus for the development was cross-curricular working. During the five years from 1991 until 1996 the staff worked in cross-curricular groups in a range of ways, supported by Mary and the School of Education at Cambridge. Non Worrall and Mary James researched these developments. In the conclusion to her Master's thesis, which studied this work, Non Worrall concluded:

It is important to seek evidence of progress to enable us to ensure that learning is taking place; to establish a culture of reflection amongst students as well as teachers that could lead to the achievement of a school ethos which places the highest valued on what Desforges (1992) calls 'mindfulness'.

(Worrall 1994: 61, cited in James and Worrall 2000: 99)

Box 6.1 The tradition of research at QEGS

1989–1990	Individual research by inset coordinator in school
1991–1996	Cross-curricular groups of staff work on planned programme delivered and planned in consultation with a member of the then School of Education
1996–1998	Raising Achievement through Action Research Project
1999	QEGS joins SUPER

This led to the Raising Achievement through Action Research Project, which ran from 1996 until 1998. A new headteacher had been recently appointed and wanted to focus more specifically on staff development. The aim was to establish 'a critical mass of colleagues who shared and would really strive to achieve the vision of a school of collaborative reflective practitioners' (James and Worrall 2000: 99). During this next phase the whole staff of seventy received a six-day programme of training and support from various colleagues at the School of Education, led by Mary James, to enable them to undertake practitioner research on their own teaching and learning. Mary James and Non Worrall identified the following as the key elements for a successful programme:

- All teaching staff were involved.
- The Project was a cooperative venture with Higher Education in terms of both planning and support.
- Accreditation was made available.
- Peer support was built in through the establishment of critical friendships, group supervisions and discussions.
- Dissemination to all colleagues in the school was built into both the six-day programme and the regular programme of staff meetings.
- The Project was underpinned by a theory of learning and teaching as well as a theory of action research.
- It was on based on an assumption, supported by evidence, that research and reflection will lead to improvements in teaching and learning which will raise standards of achievement.
- Substantial investment in terms of time and money were made in order to create the conditions for success.

(James and Worrall 2000: 101)

In the period from April 1996 to July 1998, 62 teachers participated in the Action Research Project. Most worked individually but 23 worked in pairs or threes.

(James and Worrall 2000: 101)

In 1999 the second dimension of the work at QEGS began. This was the introduction of students as researchers. Michael Fielding had organised a conference at the Faculty of Education on Students as Researchers, which Non Worrall had attended. QEGS had been invited in 1999 to join the SUPER project but Non Worrall had heard of the work of Michael Fielding.

This brought the school into contact with others with immediate results, in that work with student-researchers being carried out at a Bedfordshire 'beacon school' (Sharnbrook Upper School) and involving Michael Fielding from the University, provided an additional stimulus to involve students directly in school-based research.

(James and Worrall 2000: 103)

This was in many ways a natural development since the students had already been involved in evaluating aspects of the previous developments. This will be discussed further in a later section.

Joining SUPER

This tradition of research clearly informed and shaped the work of the SUPER partnership at QEGS and the key connections between Mary James and Non Worrall were central. Non Worrall became the teacher research coordinator at QEGS. The work with both teacher and students continued. In 2001 a new headteacher also came to QEGS. Mary James no longer worked with the school and I took over as critical friend to QEGS, undertaking half-termly visits to the school, training and supporting the teacher and student research as well as researching the processes in the school and sharing my findings with the headteacher, the teacher research coordinator and student voice coordinator.

The previous work linked very strongly to the work undertaken initially in SUPER. The common focus on thinking skills that was the starting point for SUPER was developed and researched. Then under the aegis of the Best Practice Research Scholarships work continued. Box 6.2 is a summary of the completed teacher research projects.

A further seven projects were completed under BPRS in 2002–2003 involving ten teachers. The partnership with the University of Cambridge continued in the same way. The university provided research training and supervision for the BPRS holders as had been undertaken in the previous projects.

Non Worrall continued in her collection of data on the processes. She undertook a BPRS project herself on the development of a research culture and presented two papers at BERA (Worrall 2002, 2003). In these papers she was reporting research undertaken in a sample of the SUPER schools, including QEGS, and she addressed three central questions: 'Why do practitioners undertake school-based research?' 'How do teachers feel about doing research?' 'Why do teachers choose to further develop or neglect their skills in undertaking classroom-based research?' (Worrall 2005). These questions are central to the work at QEGS as well as to the work within SUPER. To the first question she received the replies shown in Table 6.1.

To the second question of how teachers feel about doing research, Non Worrall concluded thus:

> Pursuing in interviews the question of why teachers carried out classroom research revealed a shared perception amongst research-active teachers of the fundamental desire to deepen one's own understanding of the many inter-related strands that characterise the complex processes of teaching and learning. These teachers viewed themselves as learners, as needing to generate more self and subject knowledge that would enable them to function ever more effectively as teachers. They express a restless concern to pin down

Box 6.2 Teacher research projects undertaken in 2000–2002 (all BPRS holders)

- Can music help to develop thinking skills in history?
- How would a thinking skills approach to teaching improve the Year 7 media unit in English?
- By using thinking skills across the curriculum will the thinking skills of students with special educational needs improve? (two teachers)
- What impact can using thinking strategies in teaching English have on the motivation and progress of girls in a Year 7 class?
- Can using an enquiry approach in the teaching of an A level Ethics class enable students to foster and develop meta-cognitive thinking?
- Mobile phone and mobile minds
- Using thinking skills as a means of preparing students effectively for examinations in AS level Media Studies.
- How can the use of ICT improve the writing skills of low-attaining students in modern foreign languages? (two teachers)
- What factors and attitudes encourage or impede teachers carrying out classroom/school-based research?
- What are the most successful ways of enabling Year 10 students to control their own learning the PSHE/ tutorial programme?
- How can we integrate thinking in to the PHSE programme for Year 7 students? (two teachers)

Table 6.1 Why did teachers decide to carry out classroom-based research?

Reason	No. of responses
To generate greater understanding of specific issues in teaching and/or learning	23
To solve immediate problems	10
Effective self-directed continuing professional development (CPD)	9
To regain professional control over and confidence in what happens in own classroom	9
Part of higher degree/programme giving access to promotion	8
To satisfy intellectual curiosity about issues of teaching and learning	6
To capitalise on collaboration with colleagues	5
To provide evidence and feedback on aspects of school improvement plan	5
As part of reflective practice	4
To promote development of teaching as evidence-based profession	4
To provide data for external researchers	3

answers, to search for solutions to questions that will not go away. A significant proportion drew attention to their personal disposition as the key factor
in their research-active profile.

(Worrall 2005: 141)

Regarding the third question on why teachers choose to further develop or neglect
their skills in undertaking research, she highlights the key factors as professional refreshment and engagement with classroom problems, and engaging with
students about practice, Furthermore,

> As the conversations continued, most teachers drew attention to the necessity
> of working within a school culture that is, at the very least, sympathetic to
> researching teachers:

> > 'It's a lot easier to carry out research activity if there is some sort of research
> > culture and I wonder if one could have research activity, meaningful
> > research activity without some notion of a research … well, within the
> > context of a research culture'. (Teacher research coordinator, School B)

> > 'Is a mixture really of the work that has been done within the school and
> > the links with Cambridge and also the links with other academic institutions
> > and it has become kind of natural really to become part of a reflection on
> > the teaching and so rather than being an "add on" it becomes something
> > that's part of the teaching'. (Head of year, School D)

(Worrall 2005: 143)

Non Worrall's research also pointed up the vulnerability of the work, for many
teachers had stopped doing research. She identified the need for some form of
external pressure, the time and responsibility of day-to-day professional life, the
personal dispositions of individual and a feeling that research was something done
to teachers 'by people outside', as well as 'a deep unease about the motives of their
political masters' (Worrall 2005: 143). These factors were also borne out in QEGS
and the history of the work demonstrates this.

The impact of the work

Some themes had been built on and developed over all this time. One example is
the current work on transition from primary to secondary school. This topic had in
fact been part of the impetus for the original engagement with research. In 1989,
Non Worrall had been of the opinion that the lack of continuity was a key factor in
teaching and learning. She had become concerned with the compartmentalisation
of the secondary curriculum. She had started here and this theme has been
systematically pursued over the years and particularly by the current Head of Year
7. The Ofsted report noted this as a strength of the school's work. There had also
been sustained exploration of key themes such as thinking skills, as we saw in Box
6.2. In the 2002 QEGS report to the partnership, the work is summarised thus:

In developing a research culture we had adopted an approach, which encourages individual teachers to examine particular issues in their own classroom practice and then attempts to harness the findings into our School Improvement Plan by linking the outcomes to the improvement of teaching and learning across the curriculum. By using the SUPER focus on Thinking Skills we have attempted to provide an overarching thematic approach that should make communication and collaboration easier.

Individual teachers chose and designed their own involvement in research but were provided with as much support, both practical and theoretical, as possible. Time was made available for teachers to conduct research and discuss their progress with colleagues, their HE [higher education] mentor and the TRC. This 'individual' model ensured real involvement and commitment on the part of the researchers but embedding the outcomes in the practice of teachers outside the research group remained extremely difficult. Research was still seen by most teachers as a minority activity, although there has recently been an increasing interest in accessing what has been found out through the research projects by other teachers.

In summarising the impact of the teachers' research work, James and Worrall (2000) state:

> No attempt had been made to implement the stages of the programme described above as experiments with randomised controls. For this reason, claims for the impact of these developments over the impact of other interventions, such as the introduction of academic review and target setting, cannot be made with absolute confidence. However, in that so much of the school's resources had been put into this developmental programme, it would be reasonable to assume that improvements must at least be partly attributable to it. It is worth noting therefore that from 1992 to 1999, the achievement of students on the most frequently quoted indictors of success (five or more A*–C grades at GCSE) rose from around 40 to 68 per cent. As might be expected, because it is easier to make strides from a low base, improvements had been rapid in the first five years and more gradual thereafter, with occasional 'blips'. The predicted level of achievement in 1999, based on intake, was 38 per cent five A–C grades, suggesting that by this time the value added of the school was approaching 100 per cent.
>
> (James and Worrall 2000: 110)

This trend in the school's results has continued. The figures for five A–C grades at GCSE in the period 2000–2003 are as follows:

2000	67 per cent
2001	75 per cent
2002	66 per cent
2003	71 per cent

In 2003 a series of events brought about some changes. Best Practice Research Scholarships ended, Non Worrall left the school, and there was a shift in emphasis to students as researchers rather than teacher research. The teacher research activity proved to be the most vulnerable but the students as researchers activity developed apace. This is not to suggest that teacher research has ended but rather that it is less visible and not as central to school developments as it was. It is not surprising given its close connections to an individual and it will need time to be reshaped and to rebuild.

It had been a principle of the partnership that the teacher research coordinator should be a member of the senior management team. When Non Worrall left, there were two new senior appointments and the school was also applying to become a specialist Arts school. This meant that there was not a senior member of staff designated to be the TRC. The headteacher felt strongly that a volunteer should fill this position and at that point there was no one in the SMT with a commitment and/or willingness to take up the post. There was considerable enthusiasm for the work of student voice coordinator. Two members of staff, Adele Christofi and Abigail Manning, volunteered for the work of teacher research coordinator and student voice coordinator. They shared the work between them, but after one year Abigail Manning stopped work on the project to focus on other professional issues. Adele Christofi was very keen to develop the work on the students as researchers and she focused on this aspect of the work over the next two years. She was young and enthusiastic but also had a full teaching load, which meant that she had to prioritise the work undertaken, given her capacity. As a result the focus shifted to the work with the students. Evidence of the reduced impetus can be seen in this extract from an interview with a teacher in 2004. She was not involved in research and when asked about her awareness of research activity said this:

> I knew about it from a couple of years ago, probably when I knew that people were involved in research and they organised INSET for us, or I think it might been a management meeting where various people had undertaken some research, kind of gave us their, whatever you call it, their blurb about what it was that they were doing, and how they were going to do it. And since then, to be honest, I haven't heard much else. There was talk about putting together a folder so that people in the staff knew what kind of thing had been done and so on. But I don't know any more than that.
>
>   I don't know if it really has a place at the moment. I think it probably should have, although I don't understand a great deal about it. But, I think there was a big drive to try and implement it and make a place for it, which then, with certain staff leaving and stuff, perhaps, it kind of stopped. So I don't think it actually does have a place at the moment.

Students as researchers

As has already been said, the origins of this work were in the evaluation of the two major projects prior to the SUPER enterprise. The students had been involved in giving feedback on the developments being undertaken by the staff. The training of students and the explicit move to students as researchers took place with the investigation into personal, social and health education (PSHE). This was as a direct result of contacts with Sharnbrook Upper School, a partner in SUPER. Originally this had been seen as 'a central plank in the provision for Gifted and Talented Students, enabling students with particular academic and interpersonal skills to extend their learning opportunities' (QEGS partnership report 2002). The students were chosen initially on the basis of their SATs scores, although this has since changed.

The process that the students experienced in researching the PSHE provision at Key Stage 3 is described in a handout from the school, which was produced by the students (see Box 6.3).

Box 6.3 The process of undertaking the research and the training received

Step 1 Four students were selected from each Year 10 form to carry out the research (30 students in total).

Step 2 We took part in a training day with Dr Dave Ebbutt. The skills we were taught included communication skills, idea-developing skills and skills for interviews and questionnaires.

Step 3 We decided on a list of topics we were interested in researching.

Step 4 We were put into groups according to the subject we wanted to research and were allocated to a teacher.

Step 5 We met up with our group once a week to discuss how we were going to conduct the research.

Step 6 Each group carried out their research in different ways, using questionnaire and interviews.

Step 7 We had to target our questionnaires and interviews at Years 7, 8 and 9 because they were the ones who would benefit from the research the most. Also the students from Years 10 and 11 were not available as they were either on work experience or on study leave.

Step 8 We collected our data with the help of Dr Dave Ebbutt and presented it in relevant graphs.

Step 9 We shared our findings with all the staff at our school, the governing body, who were interested in the food research findings, and the school council, who were looking into our recommendations to decide which ones to follow up. We disseminated our research findings in a presentation at De Montfort University.

Table 6.2 Student projects at QEGS

Year	Year group involved	Topic
1999	Year 10	Students' views of Key Stage 3 PSHE
2000–2001	Year 12	What do students think Citizenship consists of? How do Year 8 students define learning?
2001–2002	Year 9 into 10	How healthy is the food available in the school? Are students happy with the school environment? Do students find the system of rewarding achievement satisfactory? What extra-curricular activities are available to students? Would additional team-building activities help to resolve problems?
2002–2003	Years 7 and 8	What do students think of the ways that they are inducted into their new secondary school? (Year 7) How does the school enable students to develop as individuals? (Year 8)
2003–2005	Years 7, 8 and 9	The use of ICT across the curriculum. The development of the student voice in school.

By 2001 the school was also part of the 'Involving Students as (Co)-researchers' research programme that was part of the Teaching and Learning Research Programme, funded by the Economic and Social Research Council. This project was run by Dr Michael Fielding, and based at Sussex University. Over the period 1999–2005 the QEGS students had undertaken the research projects listed in Table 6.2.

At every stage of this development, research has been undertaken by both teachers and university-based colleagues, as well as the major research project on the work. Aileen Naylor, who has since left the school, undertook a BPRS study on the question, 'What effect there was on students' learning once they were trained as students as researchers?' She interviewed and gave questionnaires to the students involved. These were her conclusions.

Which research processes did your pupils find helpful?
Through reflecting and evaluating their experience as researchers the students recognised that certain features of research were particularly beneficial to classroom learning. These were: learning as a team, acquiring and applying research skills to subject learning, enhancing self confidence and learning how to manage time effectively. Key factors to improved classroom learning were: improved skills in analysis and report writing, better management of time and meeting deadlines and the ability to use their research skills in other subjects.

What were the learning points you gained from undertaking the research and what were your findings?

My expectations of the research were that I would find that students had different views of their experience. They would have a different perception of the role of their school in relationship to their lives and that they would suggest further ways of improving the school/pupil relationship. I expected these students to be stronger and more confident individually.

Whilst the student responses fulfilled my expectations, they also exposed the importance of student solidarity. The students questioned the differentiation brought about by being part of a chosen group and were clear in their view that this should be an opportunity open to everyone. The responses to the questionnaire revealed a largely positive overall judgement to being a participant as a student as researcher. The students involved were surprised and pleased by their ability to cope with the demands of research.

The majority of students saw the process of being selected and trained to carry out research as a positive experience and emphasised their delight at being chosen to carry out such a demanding task. Many students drew attention to the issues surrounding the selection of researchers. Most students welcomed the opportunity to contribute to the improvement of the learning environment of the school.

Students recognised the problems centred on getting back information via questionnaires to provide them with sufficient data and problems finding time to organise meetings to discuss their research. Despite difficulties the researchers were very positive about the value of their experience and felt that this opportunity should be extended to more if not all students.

(Naylor 2004)

In 2002, as critical friend to the school, I had undertaken the role of training and supporting the students in their research and had also researched their perceptions. The issue of the selection of students had emerged in this work too. Adele Christofi took on these issues and developed links between the School Council and this work. She initiated a process whereby a discussion about this place took place in the Student Council, which then led to a debate in form groups and the election of students to undertake the research. She also introduced the notion of research mentors. Students who had experienced the process mentored those beginning the year after. This worked well, as Adele reflected:

Having been through the process of students as researchers I have discovered that it is much more than a regimented training session with extra work for the students that would have to be completed in their lunch time and free time. It is about nurturing students of all abilities and helping them to develop in a social, cultural and spiritual sense, in addition to encouraging them to take responsibility for their own learning and developing them as independent learners. The research feedback is important in terms of reaching a goal and completing a project, but for me the pastoral development of the students that evolves from such an experience is far more superior.

Adele also noted that the involvement of younger students had worked well and that the mentoring showed considerable sophistication in taking on a facilitative role. The commitment had endured and she saw it as a highly motivating process. She also felt that the process 'raised many issues in terms of the effect of research upon the student's personal development, whole school understanding of the role of students as researchers, student voice and developing the students as independent learners.'

The students valued the process of working independently in teams but it was the most challenging. The parts of the training that they found most valuable were the group work and interactive participation; the technical support in research training; the accessibility and availability of advice from school staff; highlighting issues and resolving them; and preparation time. One of the first students as researchers, who was in the pre-SUPER phase, described her experience and sums up the feedback from many students:

> As well as learning different research skills. I have also learnt a great deal about myself and my individual learning. I have learned how to work independently, have gained more confidence in my own abilities and how to stay motivated when there is not pressure from teachers to meet deadlines.
>
> (Nikki Wheeler, Year 13)

Apart from the impact on those involved in the research work, the work has directly impacted on various aspects of school policy. It has resulted in the toilets being decorated and changed (something of considerable importance to the girls and concerns about bullying); transfer from primary to secondary school has continued to develop informed by the students' research with new and current students; and it has informed curriculum developments. There is an awareness of need to strengthen the dissemination to key staff members including heads of department.

This work continues to be a priority and is being developed in the local area along with other local schools. QEGS decided to leave the SUPER partnership in 2005 and to pursue this as a priority in the local area. The school wished to continue the link with the Faculty of Education in the training and support of the students as researchers work.

Concluding remarks

This case study is testament to the deep commitment of the school over a long period of time to professional development and school-based research. It is also the story of a longstanding collaboration between the Faculty of Education and the school, with some partners changing as well as some staying constant. The nature of the partnerships was very different. The first was tightly bound to professional and school development, with higher education providing facilitation and accreditation. The second was a more open partnership with a wider agenda and less clearly framed outcomes. However, the personal connections have also been shown to be central to the work. Whether this is a story of the fragility and vulnerability of teacher school-based research or whether it is the story of natural progression and development, only time will tell.

Chapter 7

St Ivo School

Stories of research

Kristine Black-Hawkins, with Diana Wilson and Dan Wilson

Context

This chapter examines the nature of the research that has taken place at St Ivo School during its membership of SUPER. It does so by exploring a number of perspectives from within the school and considering how such views and understandings have changed over time. The chapter sets out to illustrate what has been particular about this school's research stories, while recognising that there have been similar experiences, concerns and achievements in all the schools. It is based on evidence collected primarily between 2002 and 2005, including interviews with staff and students, observations of lessons and meetings, and documentary information including reports and records of research activities.

Following this introduction, the chapter is arranged in four sections. It begins by considering the headteacher's understanding of the purposes of members of a school engaging in research, including collaboratively with a university. Subsequent sections relate the two principal stories of the partnership work at St Ivo, which are rooted in the headteacher's vision for school-based research. These are the development of research projects undertaken by individual teachers and the role of student voice as a means by which to improve teaching and learning. The chapter ends by reflecting on what might be learnt from St Ivo School and, in particular, how its successes and difficulties might shape its future intentions, including its membership of the SUPER partnership.

St Ivo School is a large coeducational comprehensive for students aged 11–18, with approximately 1,800 on roll. It is the only secondary school serving its local town and surrounding area. Some families have connections with this popular school that go back over generations. It was awarded Beacon status in 2001, Sportmark in 1996 and has several community awards. When it was last inspected by Ofsted (in 2003), the inspectors described it as 'a good school with a significant number of strengths'.

Purposes of educational research: a headteacher's perspective

St Ivo is one of the original members of the SUPER partnership. Mike Mahoney was headteacher at the time and continued in post until August 2005, thus covering the entire period of the project until that date. There has been a longstanding research relationship between some members of the school and the Faculty of Education. For example, prior to SUPER, St Ivo was one of three English schools which formed a partnership with the faculty, as part of an international action research project, known as Action Research in Teacher Education (ARTE 2005). Mike considers that he too has benefited, as a headteacher, from his links with the university: 'It's had a significant impact ... Things like this [SUPER] ... That's why I wouldn't give it up.'

Mike has supported and encouraged collaborative research with the university throughout his time as headteacher. However, he has clearly articulated views about the purposes and functions of such partnerships and these understandings emanate in turn from his deeply held beliefs about the purposes and functions of a school. He is strongly committed to supporting the full participation of all students and of valuing the different contributions that each of them can make. Involving the school in any form of university research must be of 'direct benefit' to students, and not simply serve the publishing needs of academics:

> I'm not here just to be a research department. I'm not in that business, these kids are too important. I want to be certain that they get direct benefit in a learning sense ... and that values them and makes them feel part of it all.

While acknowledging that university researchers have to publish their findings, he does not consider their pressures to be his concerns. He describes as exemplary the research activities at St Ivo of one particular academic from the Faculty of Education:

> I never felt that her answer was 'Let me do this bit of research ... because I'm going to write a book.' ... She does have to do that but I never got the feeling that's why she wanted to engage with the school. ... Somebody has got to bring the findings into the real world for us, and that's what [she] was good at doing.

Mike's understanding of the purposes of practitioner research is that it too should be grounded in the reality of school life and be directly beneficial to students. However, and of equal importance, he sees such activities as helping to transform the cultures of a school.

> [It's] about liberating people ... Giving people opportunities to go in search of stuff which otherwise wouldn't be there for them. There's a great sense of

liberalism and a great sense of democracy about it as well. So you're pursuing significantly high-order aims.

To help to fulfil these aims, Mike identified two related areas for further improvement at the school. First, he wanted to provide opportunities and incentives for individual teachers to pursue research that mattered to them and was exciting. Second, he wanted teachers to consult students so that they could support subject staff when developing the curriculum in terms of its content and materials.

The initial three years of St Ivo's membership of SUPER (1999–2002) were predominantly devoted to developing the school's work in relation to teachers' research. As in the other partnership schools, a teacher research coordinator (TRC) was appointed and took on the role of supporting and promoting school-based research as well as being involved in partnership activities. In addition, the university researcher, Dave Ebbutt, visited St Ivo to provide research training and guidance to staff as required. Together, these developments helped to make practitioner research a familiar, albeit a minority, practice at the school. During this time, Mike's second priority, regarding the consultation of students, made far less progress, although some teacher researchers were beginning to draw more directly on students' views as a means of gathering their research evidence.

In 2002, however, a major shift took place when it was decided across the whole SUPER partnership that each school should appoint a student voice coordinator (see Chapter 1 for details). This proposal provided a valuable catalyst for Mike. His determination to promote this initiative, and the value he ascribed to it, was demonstrated when he appointed an assistant headteacher as the school's first SVC. The post was given the specific responsibility of working with students on curriculum development across the entire school. In an interview later that year, Mike stated:

> By the end of summer 2005, which is when [SVC] is going to finish his first three years ... I think we'll get there. ... We will have bedded in departmental teams of staff and students working together on curriculum reform.

This seems to be particular important to Mike and is based on his understanding that students are extremely knowledgeable about what does and does not help them learn and that teachers should draw on this rich source of information to support their decisions about curriculum design. It also accords with his beliefs regarding the need to acknowledge and value the contribution that students make to a school: that 'sense of democracy' noted earlier. From the outset, Mike has recognised the ambitious nature of these intentions, describing them as requiring a significant cultural shift in the attitudes of both teachers and students.

These developments in student voice and the research work more generally have been part of Mike's intended legacy to St Ivo School, before his resignation in 2005.

Having the senior teacher post given over to pupil voice, having a dedicated teacher practitioner like [TRC] ... and having opportunities for funding research work in the school ... is a solid piece of work. Once it's in place ... the next head coming in, is unlikely to be able to unpack that because it will be part of the culture.

It is Mike's aspirations which provide the context for the following two stories regarding individual teachers' research and the development of student voice work at the school.

Stories of individual teachers' research

Since 2002 there has been considerable progress towards fulfilling Mike Mahoney's aim of providing opportunities for teachers to engage in research. In St Ivo's most recent Ofsted report, 'research' was identified by the inspectors as one of three 'examples of outstanding practice' from across the whole school: 'Excellent opportunities for teachers' research are helping to improve the quality of teaching and learning' (Ofsted 2003c). Box 7.1 provides a small selection of some of the research undertaken by members of the school between 2002 and 2005. Many of these have been as a result of successful Best Practice Research Scholarship awards. In the last year of this national scheme (2003–2004), nine teachers applied for a scholarship, seven were successful and the other two were funded by the school.

The role of the TRC has been crucial in promoting and supporting this work at St Ivo. Since 2002 there have been two TRCs at the school: David Jones, a science teacher (2002–2004), and Diana Wilson, Head of the Religious Education (RE) Department (2004–2005). During this time they have undertaken their own research, mentored colleagues engaged in research and participated fully in SUPER meetings and other partnership activities. They have also had responsibility for coordinating research more generally across the school: arranging termly steering group meetings, presenting at staff meetings and producing materials to promote research activities. The headteacher has supported and encouraged their work and

---

Box 7.1 Some examples of research at St Ivo

- Years 6 to 7: induction programme
- Literacy and practical assessment in science
- Stimulating creativity in Art GCSE
- Formative assessment in music at Key Stage 3
- Interactive ICT in science at Key Stage 4
- Student retention in the sixth form
- Left-handedness and learning
- Thinking skills and independent learning in Year 7

provided them with protected non-teaching time. Approximately every half-term the TRC has coordinated a day's visit to the school for Kristine Black-Hawkins, as the university critical friend. During this time she has offered additional mentoring for practitioner researchers, discussed with the TRC the progress of their work and interviewed staff and students to support this case study.

The brief outline of structures, roles and research activities (described above) suggests that, for those teachers who wished to engage in research, St Ivo has provided real opportunities and strong support to do so. Both TRCs have fulfilled their responsibilities conscientiously and capably and have worked well with staff from across the school. What has proved less straightforward for them has been how to make best use of the research after it is completed. Individual researchers have drawn on their findings to adapt teaching and learning in their own classrooms, but their research has generally had a limited impact on lessons that take place elsewhere in the school.

Stories of research: developing the role of TRC

Early on in his post as TRC (March 2002), David Jones wrote a report for the headteacher. In it, he identified some of the strengths as well as weaknesses of teacher research in the school:

> The strength ... seems to be the involvement of staff in an area in which they have an interest and can ... develop their understanding. ... This leads to increased professional development and motivation. The weakness is that there is little effective dissemination of the key findings, or celebration of the development of good practices across the school.

Just over a year later David contributed a paper to the British Educational Research Association conference (Jones 2003). Again, he grapples with how to make the most of the research taking place in the school, so that those teachers who do not engage *in* research can at least engage *with* the research of their colleagues and thereby benefit from the efforts of others. However, his tone is more optimistic as he describes individual research projects which he considers to have become 'part of the school's strategies'. He outlines some of the changes that have taken place in the four terms since his earlier report which have supported these developments. In particular, he highlights the increased number of BPRS awards for teachers that year, thus broadening the research across subject departments. He emphasises the impact of the structures put into place when the SUPER partnership became a Networked Learning Community, in September 2002. At St Ivo, he argues, this has helped to raise his profile as TRC as well as supported the establishment of a research steering group. Finally, there has been a greater commitment to research generally in the school, as evidenced in its inclusion formally in the school's development plan. Nevertheless, he ends on a cautious note, reiterating his concerns from the previous year:

> The impact of research ... has extended beyond the individuals who are con-
> ducting the research but is still limited to [their] immediate colleagues. ...
> There have been developments made in departments as a result of work
> completed, but having a wider impact across the school is the challenge for the
> future.
>
> (Jones 2003: 6)

In his final year at St Ivo and as TRC, David Jones set out to embed research
further into the work of teachers in the school. He had experienced considerable
success in terms of acquiring funding through the BPRS scheme. Together the
seven successful applicants in 2003–2004 brought approximately £17,000 into
the school. This paid for mentoring support from the Faculty of Education, some
supply cover for the researchers and the opportunity to purchase research-related
materials and equipment. It also accorded a status to the research work itself. In
addition, the format of the scheme was manageable, with structured and fairly
undemanding outcomes in terms of writing. David was concerned that when the
scheme ended (and he left the school), opportunities for individual teachers to
undertake research might be dissipated. It was decided among the research steering
group to find a way to replace BPRS and hence the St Ivo School Bursary Scheme
was established. Monies were allocated by the governors to fund this scheme and
all teachers were invited to apply, with members of the research steering group
deciding on the suitability of proposals. Diana Wilson, as the newly appointed
TRC, was to oversee the scheme generally.

Stories of research: continuing the role of TRC

Diana Wilson became the TRC at St Ivo in September 2004. However, the story
of her engagement in research at the school is of a longer duration. Her experiences illustrate the value of providing individual teachers with the opportunity to
engage in research which is directly related to their classroom concerns. In this
way, she is a clear example of the kind of research that the headteacher referred to
earlier, which he intended to be 'liberating' for teachers.

In January 2003 Diana was one of three teachers in the school, that year, to
be awarded a BPRS. Her project was entitled, 'Creative use of images in RE'.
Students were given disposable cameras to take photographs of images that had
spiritual meaning for them and these were to be used as teaching and learning
resources in Diana's lessons. Her research focused on the effects of doing so on
students' understanding of the concept of spirituality. Kristine was her research
mentor and, in their early meetings, Diana expressed some uneasiness about
whether her ideas constituted 'proper' research and also whether, because of the
demands of teaching, it would be possible to undertake the research 'properly'.
By the end of the year her concerns had been alleviated:

> It's been great ... it's given me the chance to do something I'm really interested
> in and to try something out. ... I said [to students] 'You've got to do this

because I need it for my research' ... and that was a really important message that the teacher was also the learner and interested in things to do with learning and to do with the ideas.

By summer 2004, she had sufficient confidence in her research skills and experience to apply for, and be appointed to, the post of TRC. In the mean time she had been awarded further funding from the DfES to extend her BPRS research into other curriculum areas in the school and to the religious education advisory services in the LEA. She had presented her findings at a SUPER conference and worked with teachers from a school in Northern Ireland. Towards the end of her year as TRC she wrote a contribution for this chapter, examining the development of her recent thinking about practitioner research (see Box 7.2).

There is here a strong sense of the value and excitement of undertaking research: of finding out for oneself and being given the opportunity to do so. These sentiments are similar to those held by other practitioner researchers at St Ivo (although not all). However, in this context and following on from the school's considerable success with the BPRS scheme, it has been both surprising and disappointing, to members of the research steering group, that the offer of school-based bursaries has been largely ignored by teachers. (Diana described herself as 'perplexed'.) During 2004–2005, she made great efforts to promote research in the school, giving presentations to the whole staff and canvassing individuals, but with little response. Two teachers applied for bursaries: one was accepted, the other withdrew.

Since early 2005, as it became explicit that teachers really did not want to undertake research in this way, the steering group has had to consider alternative ways of encouraging them to do so. At the time of writing, the main emphasis has moved from individual teachers to attempting to build research into departmental development plans. The intention is for each department to identify two or three key topics they need to investigate as part of their ongoing development. In a discussion between the headteacher, Diana and the critical friend, Mike Mahoney suggested that departments should be asked to consider the following question: 'What would you be doing anyway that you could do even better with some extra time and resources?' It is not yet possible to assess how successful this approach will be.

Stories of students' voices

In answer to an interview question, 'In all that is happening in the research ... is it the idea of involving students that particularly engages your interest?', Mike Mahoney replied: 'More than anything.'

Since 2002, there have been two main stories about student voice at St Ivo, which have interwoven with the tales of teacher research. The first of these started in September 2002, when a new position in the SMT was established and Tony Collins was appointed assistant head and SVC for the school. This story ended in Easter 2004, when Tony moved to another job. There was then an interval of

Box 7.2 Extract from 'What is the impact of research and enquiry in a school?'

Normal teaching does not allow much time for reflection or experimentation. In religious education, for example, a class teacher with a full timetable may see literally hundreds of different students across any one week. The danger of teaching without built-in research 'breathing spaces' is that the teacher is always conscious that there could be better ways, but that there is no time to explore these. Over a period of time, this gap between what the teacher recognises as their present performance and their potential becomes a source of frustration. . . . [This] leads teachers to leave, take part-time work, move schools or simply work below their own expectations. I first became interested in research through BPRS initiative. It allowed me time and space to try teaching the same material in a different way. It also allowed me to work with a professional [university critical friend] outside the school who asked questions which an insider wouldn't. I appreciated the opportunity to talk to someone about my work who did not have an agenda beyond teaching and learning.

   One danger of small-scale research in schools is that findings, valid and interesting though they might be, remain locked inside the heads of individual teachers and are therefore insufficiently disseminated. There are two main reasons for this. First, schools operate within a culture reluctant to share good ideas and that teachers are instinctively protective of holding on to what works for them. Schools are still competitive, career-driven, environments. Research can be shared effectively on the intranet and through meetings, but another reason why research findings may not be sought out is that like all learners, teachers can only move on in their thinking when they are ready to do so. Learning comes through experience and being told 'research shows another way of teaching and learning is more effective', simply does not have the impact of finding out for yourself. This is why it is important for teachers at all levels and at all stages of their careers to be involved in research. . . . There is a need for new blasts of fresh air, for collaboration and discussion and thought, if teaching is not to become stale and dry.

some months before the second story began. In September 2004, Tony's replacement, Dan Wilson, joined the school, where he continues to work. The prelude to both these stories has already been related in the first section of this chapter and is illustrated by the above exchange between the critical friend and headteacher. The unifying theme which runs throughout is Mike Mahoney's steadfast belief that students have an important contribution to make to the development of teaching and learning in the school. 'In the end there are thousands of kids on the receiving end of this curriculum, what do they think about it?' Therefore, opportunities for teachers to listen to their views should be provided, and especially through students' attendance at departmental meetings.

Stories of research: developing student voice

When Tony Collins became SVC, Mike Mahoney had definite views about what he wanted him to achieve, and why. He was also clear about the nature of the difficulties he might face. For the work to be successful, there would have to be a change in the attitudes and behaviours of both staff and students, and a shift in the nature of their relationships. That is, staff would need to feel comfortable about being advised (criticised) by students, and students would need to learn how to contribute to meetings in a constructive and confident manner. Mike outlined three related concerns that he considered had to be addressed by the SVC. First, students should not be patronised:

> As long as ... we don't end up patronising ... if [students] are there as a gesture ... then it's a waste of time. ... They need to be able to say things which make a difference.

Second, a broad range of students' voices should be heard:

> Articulate middle-class girls ... who would typically find themselves in such groups are very, very obedient, and sometimes you need less articulate boys ... [who] say the very awkward things that you don't feel very comfortable with but ... you should be finding out.

Third, neither students' nor teachers' voices should be privileged:

> I don't believe that it should be taken to an extreme, whereby the only stuff that matters is what the students say. ... They happen to be, at the moment, a minority voice, they need to become part of the voice ... as long as everyone involved is seeking what's in the best interests of the school.

From the start, Tony was aware that the role of SVC was to be a challenging one, if he were to fulfil the headteacher's expectations about bringing about complex whole school changes. Tony approached the work, understandably, with some caution. In his first year (2002–2003), he set out to get to know the school, its students and staff. His intention was to gain the confidence of a few colleagues and to ensure that any research undertaken with students had a serious purpose. He promoted the notion of student voice with teacher and students, for example, in staff meetings and assemblies. He experimented with student voice in his own lessons, such as asking students in his Years 10 and 11 English classes to evaluate the usefulness of feedback he gave them in response to written tasks. He asked for teacher volunteers from across all departments to work collaboratively with him to undertake other student voice activities. This led, for instance, to a small group of staff investigating two areas with Year 9 students. The first was entitled 'What helps you learn?', and the second, 'What do you think should be offered for you to study in Years 10 and 11?'

The findings from both activities were shared with staff more widely. As part of his broader role in SUPER, along with some of his SVC colleagues from other partnership schools, Tony successfully applied for a joint BPRS award. Its focus was 'Pupil participation in teaching and learning development'. The research was to start at the beginning of the following school year (September 2003).

Like Mike Mahoney, Tony was committed to focusing on students' experiences in the classroom, rather than on the social aspects of school life. However, he was concerned that students were not necessarily comfortable with this approach:

> It seems that there are certain sort of limited areas which are the top of their priority. .... The pupils don't tend to go to the curriculum for the first thing they want to say about, but I don't think that's because it's not important to them.

A major achievement at the end of Tony's first year was the inclusion of student voice work within the school development plan (SDP) for the following year, placed in the section on 'whole school issues' and under the heading of 'community'. Student voice had not been prominent across the school in this way before. Tony set two broad objectives: the first was 'to promote the development of formalised pupil interaction between year groups and the direct transmission of student voice'; the second was 'to make the development of pupil voice a matter of active practice for all teachers'.

It seemed that the foundations for effective student voice work had been laid and Tony's second year began optimistically. However, when the autumn 2003 term started, there was a hiatus of sorts. Many staff became increasingly concerned about the school's forthcoming Ofsted inspection, scheduled for later in the term, and student voice was not necessarily a priority for them. Tony encountered some reluctance from staff to support his work, and this affected his own BPRS research project, which was then postponed. The Ofsted inspection came and went, with the inspectors setting action plans for improvements across the school. Members of the SMT were keen to rejuvenate student voice and a decision was made to utilise the Ofsted action plan as a vehicle for this. That is, each department was asked to consider how they could use a student voice approach to address an area identified by Ofsted as requiring improvement.

To embed these procedures further into the workings of the school, the spring term (January 2004) began with a whole staff development day. Its focus was teacher research, with a particular emphasis on student voice. Staff were reminded about the commitment to use this approach as a way of resolving departmental concerns raised by Ofsted. However, the day itself was a mixture of success and disappointments. At the end teachers were asked to identify anonymously their 'hopes' and 'concerns' with regards to student voice. Box 7.3 provides a selection of their comments. It suggests that, whatever progress had been made, the attitudes of some staff and (their perceptions of) the attitudes of students were proving resistant to change. Meanwhile, an opportunity for a new job arose for Tony, and a few weeks after this development day he resigned. He left St Ivo at the end of the spring 2004 term.

Box 7.3 Selection of teachers' 'hopes' and 'concerns' regarding student voice

Hopes
- 'Teaching and learning will become more effective'
- 'Staff will begin to appreciate what it feels like to be a pupil at St Ivo'
- 'They solve the problem of lesson disruption by the few students who spoil lessons'
- 'We are able to find a way to involve as many pupils as possible'

Concerns
- 'Unrealistic expectations from pupils which can't be met'
- 'Students are frequently concerned with changes to school rules or privileges rather than teaching and learning'
- 'That the benefits of such a large investment of time, effort and money will not outweigh the costs'
- 'Could go too far – encourage misplaced arrogance and blur the teacher–pupil boundaries'

Stories of research: the sequel to student voice at St Ivo

About six months passed before, in September 2004, Dan Wilson took up his post as St Ivo's next SVC and assistant head. Like his predecessor, Dan considered that to do the job well he had to get to know the school, its teachers and students and they had to become acquainted with him. He also needed to re-establish the role of student voice work in the school which had, during this second hiatus, lost further momentum. In addition, this was the first term for Diana Wilson as TRC, so the two main research coordinating positions were being undertaken by teachers new to their roles. During their first year they worked collaboratively and Dan is clear about the relationship between student voice and school-based research:

Implicit in the process of student voice work is developing the skills of staff to undertake research, and the desire and interest of staff to do so. … Student voice is an extension of this … to enhance the learning experiences of students and generate knowledge that directly impacts on how students are taught.

Dan took over the work on the Ofsted-based departmental action plans but also had other ideas about expanding student voice activities. Towards the end of his first year, he wrote a contribution for this chapter, describing his role as SVC and the development of his thinking about it. Box 7.4 provides an extract from this, focusing on the type of activities in which he has engaged.

In addition to the example below noted, Dan has been involved in coordinating student voice research activities in the following areas: students' perspectives on

---

Box 7.4 Extract from 'Student voice work at St Ivo'

The desire to dive straight into working with students on pre-planned ideas that I had formulated over the summer break was great. I had an almost overwhelming desire to make a dynamic start and to be seen to 'make an impact'. In the end I decided that the best approach was to spend time meeting staff and students. I wrote an action plan addressing the issues that I became aware of in those first few weeks, and identified how I might deal with them.

All departments had to undertake a formal evaluation of their Ofsted Action Plans and were encouraged to use students to evaluate any aspects of the plan that related to teaching and learning. To allow this to happen I outlined to staff and students, in various forums, what the aims and processes should be. The level of interest that this developed with students was phenomenal: many stopped me around the school to discuss the work. As students got involved they wanted to tell me about their input and thoughts on the process. This was my first real taste of the power of Student Voice within a school.

An example of student voice research: Different departments have used a whole range of approaches to support Year 11 students' revision for GCSE exams. We decided to evaluate which were the most useful to students and why. Therefore, all Year 12 students were given a questionnaire to complete about their experiences the previous year. This evidence was supported by interviews with a large sample of students. The findings were presented to staff at a whole school development day so that individual departments could plan how they would prepare the current Year 11 students for their exams.

learning modern foreign languages; the purpose of work experience for Year 11 students; approaches to teaching and learning for students identified as being 'gifted and talented'.

Despite his enthusiasm for the work, Dan is aware that teachers' attitudes to it are complex: 'From staff who do not "buy into" the consultation of students, staff who implicitly feel threatened by the process and find it perfidious, to the work becoming tokenistic and of no real value'. In a report to the SMT on the progress of the Ofsted-related work, he noted that the quality of the student voice work had been variable and that although some departments were committed to the work, others were 'merely taking part because they have to'. In a second extract from Dan's writing, he outlines his general impressions as his first year at St Ivo came to an end (Box 7.5). Alongside his commitment to the work, a sense of wariness emerges. He emphasises the importance of support from the headteacher: this was a concern for Dan since Mike Mahoney was leaving the school and a new head-teacher had been appointed for September 2005. Dan reiterates the connections between research and student voice as well as developing a 'culture' in which both take place.

Box 7.5 Successes and difficulties in student voice work at St Ivo

For student voice to be successful, it is imperative that the headteacher is fully behind the SVC and understands that it is not always possible to have an immediate impact when starting new to the role and new to the school. The initial impetus for this type of work will come from a committed head-teacher and then be developed and sustained by the SVC. There needs to be a culture of staff as researchers established in the school. The best student voice work is when students are used to provide opinions or guidance on work that is on the school's agenda and is taking place anyway. In this way it is possible to ensure that the student voice is focussed on valid topics and will influence practice. It is important to avoid it becoming 'bolt on' and a peripheral activity. Trying to make it central to practice in the school is challenging, but essential.

Reflecting on the stories of research from St Ivo School

Between 2002 and 2005 it seems that there have been not only notable achieve-ments in the research activities at the school but also, perhaps, some disappointments in the rate of associated developments that have taken place. This is partly because of the turnover of key people (TRC, SVC and now the headteacher) and the time that new appointments need to establish themselves in a different school and/or post. It is also partly because of the fluctuating professional priorities of teachers, such as preparing for Ofsted inspections, when research seems less urgent. However, the structural and cultural changes that Mike Mahoney set out to implement required fundamental and complex shifts in the attitudes and beliefs of staff and students. His aim for the 'end of summer 2005' (noted earlier in this chapter) was to have 'departmental teams of staff and students working together on curriculum reform'. Progress here has been uneven, with several successes but also some resistance and apathy from staff. It may well be that more time is required and the 2002–2005 period should be seen only as the beginning of this process.

The future seems a little uncertain for research at St Ivo at time of writing. The school year started in September 2005 with no TRC in place to coordinate research activities. The school's membership of SUPER is in abeyance, as it awaits the new headteacher's decision about its commitment to the partnership. Dan Wilson remains as SVC but his role in the SMT may need to be adjusted to accommodate the new leadership of the school. Nevertheless, there are positive signs for the future as well. The new headteacher is moving from another SUPER school, where he was also headteacher. There he was a strong advocate for teacher research and an active member of the partnership. It seems likely that he will wish to continue St Ivo's relationship with the Faculty of Education.

Although it has been disappointing that teachers at the school have not applied for the internal research bursaries, the BPRS research activities of the recent past means that there is a pool of research knowledge and experience among the staff, on which the new headteacher may draw. Finally, teacher research and the supporting role of student voice are more evident in the school than ever before, and are now accepted as part of the structures of the school, such as the school development plan. Therefore, the potential for research at St Ivo School may be described as being tentatively optimistic.

Chapter 8

Sharnbrook Upper School
Stories of research

Kristine Black-Hawkins, with Jennie Richards,
Alison Gill, Peter Garbett and John Clemence

Context

This chapter comprises a series of accounts about practitioner research at Sharnbrook Upper School, which focus on the SUPER partnership between the years
2002 and 2005. However, the school's history of involvement with research and
universities stretches back further in time. Therefore, the chapter begins by
considering some earlier stories of research, including Sharnbrook's membership
of SUPER from the project's inception in 1999. The second section is concerned
with structures and roles which currently promote and support research at the
school. In the third section more recent stories of SUPER are told. The chapter
concludes by considering what might be learnt, from Sharnbrook, about developing a 'researching school'.

Sharnbrook is a 13–18 mixed comprehensive school, serving a predominantly
rural catchment area. It has specialist status for media arts, is a designated training
school and also a Beacon school. It has been the subject of two highly successful
Ofsted inspections. The school is popular with local families: established in 1975,
it has grown considerably to its present size of about 1,700 students. Partly because
of its size and partly because of its community education provision, the school has
formed two key leadership roles. The principal, Peter Barnard, has overall management of the school, while the head of school, John Clemence, has day-to-day
responsibility for the students and staff. It is John who is more directly involved in
supporting research activities in the school.

This chapter draws on evidence gathered through interviews with staff and
students, observations of lessons and meetings and documentary information
including reports and other records of research activities. It is likely that those of us
who have been most willing to contribute to this chapter are also among the more
enthusiastic about its subject matter. However, because Sharnbrook has a longer
institutional history of engaging in research than many other schools in SUPER,
some of its staff are extremely experienced as practitioner researchers and able to
be highly reflective about their work.

There are, of course, many tales that can be told of Sharnbrook and choosing
those which illustrate best the fundamental concerns of the book has not been
straightforward. First, Sharnbrook, like any school, is a dynamic organisation and

descriptions of (and by) the teachers who work and research there do not remain static. Second, all such stories are partial, in that they are shaped by the values, knowledge and experiences of those who relate them. This chapter does not intend to smooth out differences over time and inconsistencies in perspectives, but rather to provide a means by which they might be more clearly understood.

Stories from the past: shaping current and future research

The foundations for Sharnbrook's involvement in SUPER were laid some years earlier by the previous principal, David Jackson. During his time in this position (1988–2000) he encouraged teachers to engage in research and he also established links with university education departments. The relationship with the Faculty of Education developed when a group of teachers undertook an MA in Education. Then, in 1993, the school joined a research project called Improving the Quality of Education for All (IQEA) involving a number of schools working in collaboration with the faculty (Hopkins *et al.* 1994). A programme of students as researchers was established around this time, to which the faculty also provided support. In 1999, Sharnbrook, with the support of David Jackson, was one of the original schools to join SUPER. The ways in which these projects were managed, the purposes for which they were primarily intended and the nature of different members' involvement, have helped to shape how practitioner research is understood in the school even now. Despite changes in staff membership, including the principal of the school, these legacies have permeated, and continue to shape, the current work at Sharnbrook.

The IQEA project

Sharnbrook participated in IQEA for eight years and during that time a range of organisational research models were trialled and developed. In the final model (1999–2000) eighteen teachers were directly involved, forming six cross-curricular 'trios', each responsible for researching a single whole-school issue. However, *every* teacher was required to join one 'trio' as an 'associate member'. While involving all staff was intended partly to ensure that none felt marginalised from the core work of this high-status project, the element of compulsion was resented by some. This was exacerbated by the SMT's decision to include IQEA-based work in teachers' targets, as part of the 'performance management' scheme newly introduced by the government. This proposal was viewed with suspicion by some teachers and its links with IQEA were perhaps misunderstood. However, as Jennie Richards (2003: 9) notes: 'Teachers were aware that future pay and career prospects depended on satisfactory completion of the work'.

When, in 2003, Jennie interviewed staff about their recollections of the IQEA project, she found that a range of attitudes remained, both positive and negative in nature.

I felt hounded into it. Although I do see the value of research, it was a fait accompli, I had no choice.

Your own concerns were not valid, if your concern was how to survive at the chalkface.

There are benefits from research in school. Some cross-curricular links are needed to stop us being too inward looking.

It would have been better if the research had been at departmental level, then we could have moved forward as team.

It seems that, as a whole-school research project, IQEA generated both enthusiasm and also resentment among staff. Researching in cross-curricular groups was a creative opportunity for some, whereas for others working with members from their own departments might have been more appropriate and possibly less threatening. Finally, and perhaps most importantly, engaging in practitioner research appears to have made most sense to many teachers when its purpose was explicitly about improving the teaching and learning directly taking place in their own classrooms. (For further details of Sharnbrook's story of IQEA, see Richards 2003.)

The Students as Researchers (SAR) project

SAR started in about 1995, partly developing from, and alongside, IQEA (Raymond 2001). Central aims of both projects were to promote school-based research to an increasingly broader membership and to use that research to enhance whole school improvement. There was strong support for SAR among the SMT and, in particular, from one member who took overall responsibility for the work. Under her direction, the conceptualisation of SAR developed in the school. Initially, staff were expected to use students as sources for their research evidence as part of IQEA. However, over time this shifted so that students were encouraged to be independent researchers.

When the main advocate for SAR left the school, the momentum for the project diminished. Some staff attempted to continue the work but, with the end of IQEA and the arrival of a new principal, who was less sympathetic to the programme, it became marginalised. Also, some staff were sceptical about the value of the work, claiming that the research undertaken was insufficiently focused and had little impact on the school. Others argued that those involved were not representative of the student body as a whole. These concerns are reflected in the following comments by two teachers, recorded by Jennie Richards in 2003.

Too many groups doing too many things . . . very dependent on staff input.

Students as Researchers were a 'Brownie pack'. They seemed radical, but they were selected students who would say what people wanted them to say. They were part of the system, not a solution.

It was in this context that, in September 2002, Alison Gill was appointed as the school's student voice coordinator. Shortly after she took up the post, she described a conversation with some students:

> I said, 'What do you think Student Voice is?' They said, 'It's just Student Council' ... I said, 'But it's so much more ... it should be you being able to feedback to us about your learning experiences or teaching, anything that affects you within the school because it's a community and this is your right to do that'.

The shift in perspective noted here, from *some* students undertaking independent *research* to *all students* exercising their *democratic right to be heard*, is important and seems to have come about for a number of reasons. First, the SAR programme appears to have been too dependent on the support of a few key staff, who when they left the school took the impetus for the work with them. Second, despite the best intentions of SAR, participation was insufficiently democratic and was viewed by some as privileging a few students only (the 'Brownie pack'). Third, by encouraging independence in the choice of research foci, there was always the risk that students' findings would have little effect on major developments taking place in the school. The sequel to Alison's story is told later in the chapter.

The Cognitive Acceleration in Science Education (CASE) project

Peter Garbett introduced the CASE project to Sharnbrook in 1994 and continues to lead it. He learnt of the research through courses run by members of King's College London (see, for example, Adey and Shayer 1994; Adey *et al.* 2001). After sharing his enthusiasm for the work with colleagues in the science department, they collectively decided to join the project. The school approached Unilever plc (a local company, with major research laboratories) for substantial financial support, who agreed to fund a two-year training programme with King's College as well as teacher cover for training, in-class coaching and other CASE-related activities.

King's later became interested in expanding the work into additional subject areas and phases of education. At Sharnbrook, other departments experimented with developing cognitive acceleration and the science department introduced the work into local middle schools. Peter describes this time as: 'Exciting ... [as] we rapidly became one of [King's] sources of research data and increasingly felt part of the broader project.' He argues that the effect of the CASE project on the science department was considerable, in terms of: 'The development of teacher skills and the establishment of a research culture within the department. ... [It] opened up all sorts of new avenues for fertile discussion about classroom practice'. He describes the CASE work currently taking place at the school as being 'much quieter' but with lessons being taught routinely across a wide range of curriculum areas, including science, mathematics, English, the arts, technology, and physical education.

The story of CASE illustrates some of the benefits when a school and a university research together. First, the work itself had an explicit conceptual basis which Peter and his departmental colleagues understood and valued and which they considered to be highly relevant to the development of their own classroom teaching. Second, the role played by members of King's was vital: not only did they provide useful support and training but also they kept Sharnbrook staff informed about the project findings. In these ways they were able to sustain a sense of belonging to and responsibility for the project overall. Third, the substantial funding obtained from local sponsors was crucial to lighten the burden that practitioner research necessarily brings. Finally, although Peter's enthusiasm for the work is evident, the project's success required the collaborative support of his colleagues and the science department provided an important organisational structure for this.

Establishing the SUPER project 1999–2002

Sharnbrook has been an enthusiastic and committed member of SUPER since its inception in 1999 and, since then, the school has introduced, examined and modified a range of research activities, foci and support structures. Furthermore, all three of the projects described above (IQEA, CASE and SAR) have overlapped at different times with SUPER and have, to some extent, contributed to and been influenced by, the work of the partnership. From 1999 two important roles were established as part of the overall project, both of which were influential to the work of Sharnbrook (see Chapter 1 for details). First, a researcher from the University of Cambridge was appointed. This position was first held by Dave Ebbutt, who worked with all the schools, providing research support while also exploring what the schools wanted and needed from the partnership. In effect, his role was similar to that currently taken by the 'critical friend', except, because he supported *all* the schools, his time was necessarily spread rather thinly among them. The second role, established in all the SUPER schools, was that of the teacher research coordinator, who was expected to be released from teaching for one day a week for partnership work. In Sharnbrook, this position was originally taken by Peter Garbett (CASE project leader) and his role was central in terms of promoting and supporting research across the school as well as collaborating with colleagues from the other schools. Then, in 2002, Jennie Richards took over the role, while Peter continued to manage CASE.

The period 1999–2002 was a challenging time for Sharnbrook in terms of practitioner research and its relationship with the university. In many ways, the school was considered a key member of SUPER: Dave Ebbutt (2002) identified it as having the 'most embedded research culture' of all the schools and thus able to offer something of a model to others within the partnership. However, this period also brought internal changes for Sharnbrook. The principal, David Jackson, who had been an extremely strong advocate of practitioner research, left the school just a year after SUPER was introduced and the incoming principal inevitably chose to establish fresh ways of working and changing priorities for the school. Sharnbrook's membership of SUPER became crucial in helping to maintain the momentum of its research activities.

Recent stories of SUPER: promoting and supporting research 2002–2005

This section describes four key roles/structures at Sharnbrook intended to promote and support research at the school. These are the TRC, the SVC, the research steering group, and the university critical friend. In 2002, SUPER applied for funding to become a Networked Learning Community (NCSL 2002), and writing the accompanying bid provided all members with the opportunity to re-think the partnership's structural arrangements. In response to this, it was agreed that the role of TRCs would continue but their work would be supported and extended through the establishment of SVCs. In addition, each school would set up a research steering group and be allocated a designated research critical friend from the university. Jennie Richards, the school's current TRC, considers these structural changes to have been important to Sharnbrook because they have helped to 'ensure that research is no longer so dependent on the enthusiasm of a few key players, who may leave at any time'. Also, John Clemence, as head of school, has encouraged staff to make creative use of existing school structures so that research is more firmly embedded in its everyday working practices.

The structures/roles noted above are used flexibly to support and promote *all* research activities at Sharnbrook and, as such, are not considered to be exclusive to SUPER, even by those most directly involved in its work. Not only does the school belong to other partnerships but also other opportunities to engage in research are promoted within the school, and staff and students do not necessarily make distinctions between different projects or their associated sources of funding. As in all the SUPER schools, the way that different structures work and are used is shaped by the circumstances of each particular school, including the resources available and the value assigned to research. The contribution made by key individuals also varies: different people bring their own experiences, knowledge and interests to the work. How this is currently resolved at Sharnbrook is described below.

Teacher research coordinator

In a discussion with Kristine Black-Hawkins in April 2005, Jennie Richards considered the nature of her work as TRC. She identified her main contributions as being to support, coordinate and promote the research activities of her colleagues, both within and beyond Sharnbrook School, as well as to engage in her own research. To fulfil these demands, Jennie is guaranteed the equivalent of one day a week non-teaching time. The importance of this cannot be underestimated, not only in practical terms (which is crucial) but also in terms of the signal it gives across the school about how highly her work, and research more generally, is valued, particularly by members of the SMT. The support of John Clemence, the head of school, is especially appreciated: 'My time is properly protected ... if ever I've wanted to go to a conference or I've been asked to do things. ... [There] has never been any question of me not going'.

Student voice coordinator

When Alison Gill was appointed as SVC, the post was not only new to her but also relatively untested across all SUPER schools. However, unlike other SVCs, who are usually teachers, Alison is the school's resource centre manager and librarian. Since 2002, it has become clear that this position has proved to be advantageous. Part of Alison's work is to induct new students into the use of the resource centre, which includes developing their research skills. Therefore, unlike many of Sharnbrook's teachers, she has direct contact with *all* students in the school and the focus of that contact is research. Also, because much of her day is not timetabled, she is able to be flexible in working with students as well as attending outside meetings and visits. She receives support and information from a range of people but Jennie Richards, as TRC, and John Clemence, as head of school, are particularly valued. Alison is now much more certain about her role as SVC. She identifies the main contributions she makes to Sharnbrook and SUPER as coordinating all student voice activities, including liaising with and feeding back to staff. She also represents the school at meetings within the SUPER partnership and beyond. Furthermore, like Jennie Richards, she regularly engages in her own school-based research.

Research steering group

This group has fulfilled an extremely useful role in maintaining the momentum of research at Sharnbrook. John Clemence describes it as 'essential', in terms of structuring, coordinating and supporting research. 'In a complicated school ... with loads of strands to our work ... it's a way of trying to pull it all together ... It's probably ... the only time when we set aside dedicated time.' That it is valued is apparent both in the time that it is allocated and in its membership (including three of the SMT). The group meets half-termly, during the school day, and teachers are released from timetabled commitments to be there. Its membership comprises TRC, head of school, SVC, head of the training school, CASE coordinator and university critical friend. The research administrator is also present to support the meetings. There has been full attendance at nearly every meeting since

2002. Students and other staff are also invited to join some meetings to report on their research activities.

Critical friend from the university

The principal purpose of a university research critical friend, within the SUPER project, is to research the nature of the developing partnership between the school and the university. In doing so, the critical friend would hope also to be in a position to support the school's research activities. For example, in Kristine's first year as Sharnbrook's critical friend, she made fourteen visits to the school, some for half a day, others only for an hour or so. In addition, she met Sharnbrook staff when they attended SUPER meetings at the university, in particular, the TRC, SVC and head of school. All these opportunities have contributed to meeting her research requirements as well as providing research support for the school, although some have met the university's research needs much more directly (such as interviewing staff and students), while others have more clearly fulfilled the needs of the school (for example, mentoring individual teachers' research).

Towards the end of that first year, she asked Jennie Richards how she perceived the purpose and value of a critical friend, from her perspective as TRC. Jennie was certain that the relationship was mutually beneficial. A summary of key points is given in Box 8.1.

Jennie was particularly clear about the final three points. She argued that involvement with the school gave the critical friend valuable opportunities to see

---

Box 8.1 Mutual benefits from a research critical friendship

Benefits to school: activities undertaken by critical friend
- Asking questions of individuals but also at meetings
- Supporting key individuals: e.g. TRC, SVC, teacher researchers, head of school
- Providing practical information about research: e.g. faculty courses
- Helping the development of research beyond individual projects
- Being a physical presence in the school and meeting people informally
- Supporting the research integrity of the school
- Providing a link with other schools in the partnership

Benefits to critical friend: research opportunities provided by the school
- Access to a school in which to gather evidence for research purposes
- Detailed insight into a range of school activities
- Involved in experiences grounded in messy reality and 'busyness' of school life

staff and students in ways which would not necessarily be provided to outside researchers. This privileged access was available as a direct result of her supportive role in the school.

Recent stories of SUPER: the place of research 2002–2005

This section provides accounts of research at Sharnbrook between 2002 and 2005. Each indicates how the structures and roles (described in the previous section) work in practice. However, they have also been selected because they illustrate the place of research at the school; that is, why some teachers decide to undertake research and what they choose to do. The effect of research is also considered, in terms of its impact on individual researchers as well as more broadly across the school. Together the stories show how very different approaches and uses of research can successfully coexist in one school. The first is an account of research undertaken by an individual teacher who had a very specific classroom concern that she wanted to address. The second continues the story of Alison Gill in her role of SVC in which she endeavours to ensure that the voices of students from across the whole school are properly heard. The third provides a selected summary of recent research projects at Sharnbrook to illustrate the range of activities there.

An individual's story of research

Although this story is about one teacher, it is illustrative of the experiences of many others at Sharnbrook who have sought to engage in practitioner research either as individuals or, somewhat less frequently, in pairs. Such research has often been funded through schemes such as the DfES's Best Practice Research Scholarships or, more recently, that offered by the Learning and Skills Development Agency (LSDA). In all cases, the research starts from the specific professional interests or concerns of the teachers and has a sharp focus on understanding better, and thus improving, the experiences of students.

Joan Stainer's professional concern focused on the relatively poor performance of boys in geography GCSE course work compared to their examination results. She wanted to understand why this happened so that she could help students to improve in future. In 2004, she successfully applied for a BPRS. She began by looking at quantitative data already available in the school to check the accuracy of her hypothesis about boys' results. In particular she considered the breakdown of marks for different elements of the GCSE from previous years. She then studied the past course work of students, to establish areas of strengths and weaknesses in relationship to the demands of the examination board. She also interviewed a group of boys in Year 12, who had completed their geography GCSE the previous year, to establish their views on undertaking course work and the nature of diffi-culties they had encountered.

Joan's findings and recommendations were written up as a BPRS report and were also shared with departmental colleagues. She presented at a SUPER conference to teachers from across the partnership schools. Joan's research was supported in a number of ways. She worked closely with another geography teacher who had also been awarded a BPRS and Jennie Richards gave them both in-school advice and guidance. Joan and her colleague also attended a research training programme at the Faculty of Education, provided for all SUPER teachers who were recipients of a BPRS. Kristine Black-Hawkins also contributed to these sessions and so was able to work with Joan at the faculty as well as at Sharnbrook.

For Joan the primary purpose of the research was to improve the Geography GCSE examinations results of future students and her findings were directly relevant to her classroom practices and those of her departmental colleagues. However, the process of engaging in research also seems to have been of particular value to Joan in terms of her sense of professional refreshment:

> This research enabled me to come out of the box we all live in, the classroom. I could seek, see and reach out for new horizons. You're never too old. After thirty-six years in the classroom did I know it all? Research made me sit up and re-evaluate my ideas and take on new challenges.

Stories of student voice

When Alison Gill was appointed as SVC, she looked at existing structures at Sharnbrook and decided that there appeared to be no effective mechanisms that allowed students' voices to be heard. She considered, and rejected, reviving past schemes such as student year councils or SAR. Instead, she capitalised on significant changes happening elsewhere in the school. In 2003, Sharnbrook introduced vertical tutoring and an associated house system. These arrangements were intended to allow staff to tutor, both academically and pastorally, a small number of students from across each year group. Ideally, this was to provide every student with a real 'voice'; that is, regular opportunities, on a one to one basis, to discuss with their tutor, their views about school life, academic or otherwise.

Supported by the TRC, SMT and the school's critical friend, Alison decided to form a vertical focus group comprising students of mixed ages and gender. Its purpose was to gather ideas from students across the school about what they considered student voice to mean and how it might be properly heard. Their findings indicated that students wanted to be represented by a body that reflected the school's new vertical tutorial/house structures; its membership should be determined by a democratic election and it should be known as a Parliament. These views accorded with Alison's:

> It seemed to me imperative that the Parliament be as inclusive as possible, that we should use the opportunity to ensure that Student Voice consisted of as many voices as possible. In the past we had fallen into the trap of listening to the voices we wanted to hear. The only people benefiting were those students

and staff involved in the research: there was no feedback feature in our student voice to the larger student body.

Because each tutor group is mixed by gender, ability and age they represent a cross-section of the student body. Alison has successfully promoted the vertical structure of Sharnbrook as an efficient means for staff and students to gather students' views and experiences for a range of research projects at the school. The Parliament has also been asked by other students, staff and the SMT to look at a range of issues affecting school life, as well as being consulted by external agencies on various subjects affecting youth, both locally and nationally.

Alison continues to evaluate the workings and constitution of the Parliament to ensure that it can fulfil the role for which it was intended. Nevertheless, this initiative has clearly increased opportunities for students' voices at Sharnbrook to be heard. The work is shaped by clear principles relating to the democratic rights and responsibilities of all students. In this context, student voice work in its current form is very different from that of the earlier SAR project. On the one hand, it is notably more widespread, acknowledging the value of listening to all students, rather than a selected few only. On the other hand, it is more contained, in that its purpose is to be instrumental to the research of others (staff and students) in the school. Although the work is still developing it would seem that this breath of representation alongside a more clearly defined set of functions will help to reduce some of the difficulties experiences in the past.

Selection of research topics

Box 8.2 provides a small selection of recent and current research undertaken by members of Sharnbrook since 2002. It illustrates the range of different activities, topics and approaches that coexist within the school. It is notable that much of the research, like Joan Stainer's, focuses on immediate and practical classroom concerns. However, others do have a wider school relevance, such as Alison Gill's. Research is conducted by individuals (e.g. thinking skills in geography and physical education), in pairs (e.g. performance data in effective academic tutoring) and larger groups (e.g. assessment for learning).

Examining why research takes place

Understandably, the majority of teachers at Sharnbrook are principally concerned with the teaching and learning which takes place in their own classrooms. Practitioner research is just one possible way of developing their teaching so as to improve students' learning. It is a *means* to an end, and not an *end* in itself. It is not about the generation of new knowledge but about producing practical outcomes which make a difference to the experiences of students in the school. As one teacher explained, research must be 'useful ... it either validates ... the types of teaching that [teachers are] doing or initiates a change in the way that they're

> *Box 8.2* Examples of research at Sharnbrook
>
> • The application of cognitive acceleration teaching and learning methods
> • Use of ICT in teaching science
> • Science practical work: teachers' expectations compared to students' actual gains
> • Effective learning styles in history
> • Developing thinking skills in geography and physical education
> • Exploring the pedagogy of geography fieldwork
> • Developing ICT databases and network infrastructures for whole school use
> • Assessment for Learning: translating formative assessment into practical teaching and learning methods
> • The impact of vertical tutoring on the support processes
> • The use of performance data in effective academic tutoring

teaching and the students are learning'. Thus, research is a professional development tool which can be used to address or solve professional interests and concerns. In this way the use of a teacher's time and other school resources can be justified.

That the primary purpose of research at Sharnbrook is to improve teaching and learning through professional development is strongly emphasised in the staff brochure, 'Research Opportunities at Sharnbrook'. However, a number of associated reasons for engaging in research are also suggested. In particular, research is offered as a means of enhancing individual teachers' prospects of promotion and career development. This is considered especially pertinent to those who have chosen to participate in accredited courses, such as Masters degrees.

The reasons why teachers might chose to engage in research are similar to those which underpin why research activities are promoted in the school by the SMT, notwithstanding the latter's broader understanding of the potential value of research to the school as a whole. For them, the development, or improvement, of individuals' practices in classrooms can be translated into possibilities for school developments, or improvements, taking place at an organisational level. Likewise, this justifies the employment of the school's time and other resources. For example, John Clemence describes why Sharnbrook chooses to fund its membership of SUPER:

> I hope our work with the faculty and the other schools will help us to sustain the culture that we value so highly ... of challenging our thinking about what we do and making certain that we're looking for ways to improve our practice.

Furthermore, individual teachers are funded by the school to study for higher degrees because there is an expectation that not only will they undertake research which will benefit the school, but also that they will stay in post for, at least, the duration of their studies. Like many British schools, the retention of staff is a key concern to the SMT of Sharnbrook.

Developing a researching school: purposes and balance

The overarching purpose of practitioner research at Sharnbrook is to contribute to school improvement, both at the level of the classroom and across the whole school. Evidence from this case study suggests that developing a researching school supports such improvements in a number of important ways. These include:

- Encouraging individual teachers to question their classroom practices in constructive ways.
- Supporting individual teachers to reach well-founded conclusions, based on evidence, about their classroom practices.
- Offering individual teachers increased intellectual satisfaction in their work.
- Providing stimulating and rewarding opportunities for teachers to think collaboratively about their teaching.
- Supporting new, or validating existing, SMT and departmental decision-making through the use of sound research findings.
- Offering opportunities to benefit from the stimulus of engaging in national and regional research enterprises.
- Encouraging the learning of valuable research-based ideas through contact with external organisations.

Furthermore, membership of a schools–university partnership, like SUPER, can contribute to each of the above and, particularly, in terms of providing support for research, working collaboratively and benefiting from external perspectives.

At Sharnbrook, the balance between the *act* of engaging in research (how *being* a researcher is a form of professional development) and the pursuit and establishment of robust *findings* (evidence-based practice) fluctuates depending on the intentions and needs of the researcher(s) and the school. This is partly, but not always, related to whether the research is primarily concerned with the improvement of *individual teachers* or across the *wider school*. If the latter, however, it is probably even more critical that the research is of a robust nature.

It seems clear that the range of research opportunities offered by Sharnbrook is a real strength of the school. While there is no longer any sense of compulsion that all staff will engage in such activities, huge efforts are made to help anyone who wishes to do so. The structures and roles which support research have been developed to be flexible and responsive to staff's needs. Furthermore, members of Sharnbrook's research steering group (and John Clemence, in particular) have been creative about acquiring resources and making them available so that research can take place. They have also been inventive about using existing resources, such as employing the school's librarian as SVC. Finally, this allocation of time and other resources to research is a strong signal to staff and students that such activities are valued by the SMT and are valuable to the school as an organisation.

Members of the research steering group argue that the engagement of staff in research contributes to the school in other ways, which are more intangible but are nevertheless still important. Research is considered to have a positive effect on staff recruitment and retention by engendering an excitement and sense of professional autonomy by those involved. After seventeen years as a teacher in the school, Jennie Richards describes her work as TRC as giving her 'a new lease of life ... It has done my self-esteem and enthusiasm for my job, the world of good.' From a very different perspective, a philosophy teacher who is completing a doctorate degree, explained that his research is 'the reason I am still in teaching'. Part of this enthusiasm relates to how research can alleviate the isolation of schools and teachers. For Sharnbrook, the SUPER project has been a conspicuous example of encouraging outsiders into the school, and insiders out. A range of staff and students have visited other schools in SUPER and have also participated in wider partnership activities, including those at the University of Cambridge.

Learning from Sharnbrook

Although the stories related in this chapter are specific to the context of Sharnbrook, they offer some useful insights into the nature of practitioner research and how it might be developed across a school as well as in partnership with a university. The following is a summary of key points.

- A school's history shapes its present activities and future aspirations for research.
- Clarity about the primary purpose of research (the balance between professional development and the pursuit of robust evidence) may support the quality and usefulness of both these activities.
- The quality of research undertaken by teachers is always important but it becomes increasingly critical when findings are used to determine policies and practices that apply to wider school issues rather than individual classrooms only.
- For many teachers, research is a means by which to improve their teaching and their students' learning. Making a difference in this way is considered a justification for the use of their time and efforts and other resources.
- Whole school research can be exciting but also restrictive. Providing and promoting a wide range of research opportunities for staff is more likely to produce useful research than compelling all teachers to be involved in one project.
- Researching in groups can work well, but trust and a genuine interest in a common research purpose are important; departments are a good basis for research teams in secondary schools.

- Establishing flexible structures and roles to support research is essential. However, these remain vulnerable to staff changes and the need for strong, committed, thoughtful and creative leadership is vital.
- When students are encouraged to contribute to school-based research, careful consideration of issues relating to participation, representation and power need to be made.
- There is value in exploiting links with other institutions and organisations. Universities can provide helpful sources of research training as well as a broader understanding of related research issues. All members of a school–university research partnership should be mindful of costs as well as benefits.

Chapter 9

Soham Village College

From research question to policy development

Colleen McLaughlin, with Howard Gilbert and Chris Tooley

'Belonging to the school, not to individual teachers'

Before Howard Gilbert became headteacher of Soham Village College in 1999, he had been headteacher of Chesterton Community College, another SUPER partnership school, and had also been one of the initial group of headteachers to discuss the idea of a schools–university partnership. Howard had learned a great deal from these experiences:

> We did lots of research but it became like a little comet in the firmament for a while and then fizzled. The individual teacher may have changed practice but did many others?

In his second headship, Howard wanted to explore and develop the notion of research as a school rather than an individual teacher practice. The three concepts of research as a sustained activity central to school policy-making; focused on teaching and learning; and central to change and reflection in the classroom and staffroom pervade what happened at Soham Village College. The conceptions of research and its purposes will be shown though the views of the teachers, faculty heads, other senior managers and the public statements. There are many different layers to this story and the first part emphasises the vision of the initiators and planners – the senior managers in the school.

The school

The school is described in its 2003 Ofsted report thus:

> Soham Village College, a foundation technology college, provides education for pupils in Years seven to 11, who transfer from a range of near and distant primary schools. About 50 per cent of the pupils travel to the college by bus each day. The college is bigger than most other comprehensives with 1,314 pupils aged 11–16, and has steadily increased in size over recent years. About 80 per cent of pupils transfer at the age of sixteen to sixth form colleges or to

schools with sixth forms. Virtually all the remainder go into employment. The number of boys and girls in the college is similar in each year group. Most of the pupils are white and very few are from ethnic minority backgrounds. Very few of the pupils do not have English as their mother tongue. A small number of pupils are the children of travellers. The proportion of pupils identified as having special educational needs, 18 per cent, is broadly in line with the national average. About 2 per cent of pupils have Statements, a similar proportion to that found in most schools. Overall standards are above average. The area around the school is socially and economically mixed but advantaged overall. About 10 per cent of the staff leave the college each year and at the time of the inspection the school had about 7 per cent of the staff on temporary or short-term contracts.

Soham Village College is a very good school. It provides a caring learning environment where pupils are well taught and they strive for success. Pupils do very well in examinations, achieving very good GCSE results – 70 per cent of the pupils achieved five or more A*–C grades and 98 per cent attained five or more A*–G passes in 2002. The pupils' achievements are very good. The leadership provided by the principal, supported by the governors and his senior staff, is of the highest quality. College management, with its strong focus on making teaching and learning as effective as possible for individual pupils, is very successful.

(Ofsted 2003d: Part A, p. 6)

A researching school: knowledge creation and evidence

The concept of the 'knowledge-creating school' (Hargreaves 1999) was very visible. The website (www.sohamcollege.org.uk/knowledgecreation) has a section on research and development and Hargreave's article is referred to here, as it is in the headteacher's presentation on this work. A knowledge-creating school is one which

> *Audits* its professional working knowledge
> *Manages the process* of creating new professional knowledge
> *Validates* the professional knowledge created
> *Disseminates* the created professional knowledge.
> (Hargreaves 1999: 125)

This was also visible in the strategy employed to develop the research in the school. The concept of creating new knowledge rather than sharing best practice was emphasised by Howard Gilbert, who often quoted Hargreaves (1999): 'The dissemination of *existing* good practice is an inadequate basis for making a success of schools: we need to generate better knowledge and practices'. The process of developing the research was planned and managed very carefully. Much was learned and modified along the way but the strategy was clear from the beginning and will be detailed later. It was also informed by senior managers' clear view of practitioner research, its purposes, processes and limitations.

The purposes and processes of school-based research

The aim at the beginning was to establish a process of research that would bring about change in the teaching and learning practices in the school and the necessity for the research to have clear results in the classroom through the faculty system was firmly stated by Howard Gilbert: 'To move away from an approach where people did research individually and learned a lot from it, to an approach that could get embedded in faculty and school structures and which was supported by pupil evidence'. The sustainability of research knowledge within the school was a key aim and the problem of individuals leaving and taking the knowledge with them was seen as one that needed addressing. The faculty structure came to be seen as the fulcrum for this process.

The generation of a reflective research culture in which teachers focused on and talked primarily about teaching and learning was also an aim. However, the notion of evidence was central. Key concepts used and talked about by many of the researchers were validation, extension and replication. Howard Gilbert commented: 'My frustration with the past research has been that findings happened but then they're not replicated or validated. I'm a statistician by trade and that's what you do with research'. What was wanted was a process where knowledge was built upon through a process of extension from the work of one teacher to a group of teachers in the same subject area, through to the faculty and finally to inform a teaching and learning policy.

The analogy for replicability used to characterise this was the mutation of cells. Chris Tooley, the assistant principal and teacher research coordinator, explained:

> When a human cell divides by mitosis, it first makes a copy of each of its forty-six chromosomes. The chromosomes separate so that a full set are on each side of the cell. The cell then divides to form two identical cells – it replicates. However, the process is not always so neat. There can be errors in the copying process and the separating mechanism can result in non-identical outcomes. There is also the possibility that a mutation will occur – a change in the chemical composition of a single gene along the length of a chromosome. In these cases the impact is most often negative but it can also lead to an advantageous outcome, which will then be passed on to every cell descended from the mutated one.

This is a useful metaphor in that it shows the role and importance of extension and learning from negative outcomes. Both the teacher research coordinator and the headteacher acknowledge the limitations of this metaphor and the influence of their scientific backgrounds on how they conceptualised the process. Zina Payne, one of the science researchers, also acknowledged that the scientific idea of replication of conditions and testing cannot be applied to education: 'You can't have fair tests, you can't compare like with like'. The other idea of adaptability to real classrooms or action research was equally important. The aim was to extend the practice and the research in order to see how it developed under the influence of different teachers, students, classrooms and subject areas.

The validation of the knowledge was seen as coming from three sources. It was a triangle of teacher experience and reflection; data on pupil outcomes; and data on the pupils' experience and attitudes. This was seen as giving it credibility, as Chris Tooley explained:

> Right from the beginning every one of our research projects has had to have, as much as possible, three different forms of data which could be used to triangulate. Where possible we've asked for some empirical statistical data. It's got a clear aim, and that is to change practice within the faculties, and that's what we want to do. We want to test out what people say works about learning, to find out how it works within the context of certain subject areas, and to make the outcomes able to be put into practice. Some people are really taken by the data. If the data says it they'll do it. Other people are much more taken by other colleagues and what they've said and what their experience has been, whereas some say, 'Well look, the kids are the ones in the classroom; they're the ones we're here for. If they're saying it's good for them, that's enough for me. By building all three into every project, we kind of make it as compelling an argument as possible to win the hearts and minds of the teachers involved.'

The processes of evidence collection had to build credibility but as far as possible they had also to be manageable. The criteria for trustworthiness and the model used are clearly influenced heavily by a scientific paradigm and the biographies of the key players are important here. There has been a growing respect for the more qualitative and experiential work over the years.

The leaders were fierce in their protection of the efforts and focus of what they were doing. A key criterion was that the research activity was 'helping us to move forward and not causing us to do extra things that we wouldn't normally have done' (Chris Tooley). It had to be a process that 'had impact on practice' (Howard Gilbert).

What engaged the teacher researchers was the focus on classroom processes of teaching and learning and in particular the engagement with the views of pupils. Paul Heffer, a religious education teacher, said of his involvement:

> I could identify with the fact that we had to look further at how children learn. You go on teaching day to day, doing things that you think work – pretty sure work – but it really appealed to me to look at new ways to explore.

Laying out the stepping stones – the strategy and the process

Howard Gilbert talked of the excitement of the challenge and that having formed a clear idea of where they wanted to be, they began to plan the journey, but they did not know exactly what it would look like. A long time was spent planning the strategy, trying to incorporate the elements described above and the learnings from past experience. Box 9.1 summarises the different phases of the development.

Box 9.1 The research process at Soham

Phase 1 Preparation of research and strategy
Term 1 Reading, thinking and planning
- Headteacher and teacher research coordinator (who is also assistant principal) discuss and plan strategy
- Management salary points are allocated for four teachers to research pupil recall
- The teachers meet and spend the summer holidays reading selected writing and research on learning, neuroscience and pupil recall

Phase 2 The research in three classrooms
Term 2 Starting out
- All meet with the teacher research coordinator and pool ideas and reflections on reading
- All establish research questions
- Start work in their own classrooms and collect three kinds of evidence:
  - statistics on pupil performance
  - researcher's impressions of the work and the issues, e.g. diary
  - pupil data, e.g. questionnaires
- At the end of the term the evidence and the experience are examined and recommendations drawn up for two other colleagues in the faculty

Term 3 Extending and replicating
- Two other colleagues from the teacher researcher's faculty follow the recommendations made, receive training and support and adapt it to their own classroom practice
- Collect and review new evidence of the same type as collected before

Term 4 Reviewing and recommending
- Together the three faculty teacher researchers review the evidence and make recommendations to the whole faculty

continued

Box 9.1 Continued

Phase 3 Extending across the year group
Terms 5, 6 and 7
- Discussion with the whole faculty and training in using the researched practice
- The faculty implements the enhanced recommendations across the whole of a particular year group
- This is also researched as before
- Faculty adopts the researched practice, refines it and it becomes part of the faculty's teaching and learning policy
- Becomes part of the faculty review process

Phase 4 Informing a whole-school teaching and learning framework
The outcomes of the research are used to build criteria for excellent lessons in each subject area. This framework also acts as the stimulus for deciding on foci for further investigations.

The first phase involved planning the strategy and initially the research was conceived of as a one-term project. (Soon came the realisation that this was unrealistic.) Four teachers applied to be teacher researchers for a year and they were to be given a salary increase or a management point for this work. This was intended to give the work status and also to send a message that research was an important activity. Howard Gilbert talked of how these salary rewards are often given for administrative or resource management tasks and that he wanted to reinforce the focus on teaching and learning. The teachers were not given extra time to conduct the research. They never mentioned the financial reward as the key motivator, but it clearly sent a message. They said it was important at the beginning and became a support, but one teacher summed it up thus: 'I am not doing it because I am getting paid for it. I am doing it because of my interest and its impact'.

Reading, thinking and planning

The Teaching and Learning Group was formed and they were given the summer holidays to read various key texts on learning, neuroscience and particularly pupil recall. The work of Mike Hughes (1999) was seen as a good starting point. The prospect did not necessarily excite them all but Rachel Hollingworth, a mathematics teacher, talked of how soon she became engaged and struck by the power of working on the improvement of pupil recall. Paul Heffer described this as having his appetite whetted and said that it convinced him 'that this was worth trying'.

The four researchers, all from different core faculties (English, science, mathematics and humanities), came together to plan their research at the beginning of the next term. Chris Tooley, the TRC, led the team, supported by me as the university critical friend. The first task was to narrow down to a research area and questions that could be focused on in a term and which would fulfil the criteria described above. The group focused on the notion of pupil recall based on this rationale, given in the following extract from the report to the governors.

The review cycle

The following reports are based on research evidence of worldwide research into the rate at which information is forgotten in the absence of review. [Figure 9.1] shows a dramatic decline in memory in the first twenty-four hours after a learning experience.

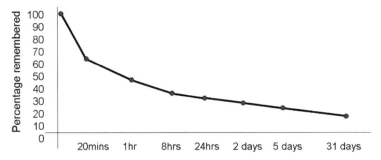

Figure 9.1 The Ebbinghaus curve of forgetting

[Figure 9.2] shows how this decline in memory can be overcome by strategic-ally timed reviews of work. These reviews occurred ten minutes from the end of a lesson, the next day, one week, one month and then six months later.

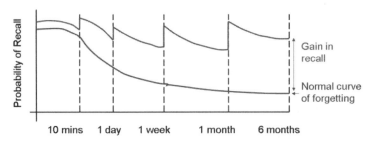

Figure 9.2 Gain in recall following strategically timed reviews

Whilst these particular timings of reviews may be impossible due to time-tabling constraints it is always possible to conduct the initial review in a pupil led plenary session at the end of a lesson and to review again in the subsequent lesson and using the weekly homework slot.

(Report to Governors on the work of the Teaching and Learning Group, Autumn 2004)

This done, the group spent a term initiating a practice in their classrooms. For example, science teacher Zina Payne explored the use of mind maps as a learning tool. Paul Heffer tested the use of a ten-minute review at the end of lessons on pupil recall in religious education. Rachel Hollingworth explored using a three-stage review process consisting of a review five minutes after the learning period, one twenty-four hours after the learning period and one a week after the learning period; she found that this helped pupils to improve their ability to recall information learnt in lessons.

The work was recorded by the teachers, existing pupil empirical data examined and new student data collected. The evaluation criteria included the following:

- In science, Zina collected teacher perspectives on the value of the model, test results as a function of the Yellis (Year 11 Information System) data compared to the previous cohort and pupil comments regarding motivation and learning.
- In mathematics, Rachel collected written comments from pupils (focused on enjoyment and learning) and teachers (focused on the amount of work on the part of the teacher, differences observed with the group and any improvements noticed during lessons). Assessment data, from classes taking part in the review process as well as their comparison groups, in the form of module test results combined with Midyis (Middle Years Information System) data.

Examples of this and other research undertaken in the school are summarised in Box 9.2. The researchers had time to share what they were doing with other colleagues during faculty meetings. This stage of the process was fairly unproblematic since the core group were clearly interested and working alone in their classrooms. They had one-to-one meetings with Chris Tooley, the teacher research coordinator, which were very important to them, and termly group meetings with myself as the university critical friend. One teacher talked of how interesting the Teaching and Learning Group discussions had been and that it was a rare opportunity for contact across faculties.

Box 9.2 Synopses of a sample of the research undertaken

(A full list and the full reports are available on the Research and Development Website - www.sohamcollege.org.uk/knowledgecreation)

Rachel Hollingworth (Mathematics)
Investigations were undertaken with Year 9 classes to determine whether introducing a three-stage structure of reviewing key learning points would make a difference to pupil recall. Initial results suggested that this was the

continued

Box 9.2 Continued

case; replication by other teachers confirmed the findings and was persuasive enough to lead to the development of a review policy for all Key Stage 3 classes.

Vanessa Summers (English)
Investigations were carried out into when pupils prefer to carry out review techniques and the specific techniques that were preferred. Pupils indicated that beginnings and ends of lessons were most desirable and that mind mapping and oral techniques were most highly favoured as techniques.

Zina Payne (Science)
Year 10 pupils were introduced to the skill of mind mapping. Significant gains in recall and pupil motivation were found where this skill was introduced. The process was then repeated with the whole of Year 7 with highly positive outcomes. Additionally a great deal was learnt concerning the optimal process for managing this type of initiative to bringing about successful change in practice.

Caroline Howard (Physical Education)
Visualisation is an excellent additional way to encourage pupils to take charge of their learning without losing out in terms of lesson time. It allows pupils to practise at home, without the need for equipment / facilities and has the potential for setting simple homeworks. The process needs to be well structured at the start so the process becomes automatic. Visualisation doesn't seem to suit all aspects of PE, particularly in game play situations. However, it can be used to enhance skill development which in turn can be used in game play.

Vanessa Summers (English) and Rachel Hollingworth (Mathematics)
These investigations suggest that visual, auditory and kinaesthetic learning styles (VAK) questionnaires are not a useful diagnostic tool for determining strategies for whole class teaching. Rather that, as a general rule, pupils' learning is enhanced when information is presented in as multisensory a manner as possible. Pupils seem to respond very positively to a range of techniques but that kinaesthetic options are particularly favoured. VAK questionnaires may, however, be of use in identifying and devising strategies for helping individual pupils with highly skewed profiles.

From lone researcher to working with colleagues: extending and replicating

After a term the teachers each enlisted two volunteers from the faculty to join them in the research and development work. This involved the researcher working with two other colleagues who adopted and adapted the teaching and learning strategy and used it for a term in their classroom. Data was collected on the new extension. This was an interesting but also a challenging phase for the researchers. The activity was significantly different as it now required working with colleagues and not just being a lone, enthusiastic researcher. The researchers found this the most difficult part of the process and one that had not really been anticipated in the planning stage. One researcher had to enlist support from the senior managers when one of the colleagues involved in replicating the work did not follow through on the data collection. This had been professionally complex. Another researcher had found being in a training or expert role challenging and initially uncomfortable. The move to a change or development role was a significantly different one from that of researching one's classroom practice and placed the teachers in a new relationship to their colleagues, who were sometimes senior in age, experience and position. However, there was a commitment to involve all members of the faculty and especially the head of faculty, which came through very strongly in interviews. One head of faculty described how he and other colleagues had also found this stage difficult:

> At first it was hard and maybe it was because we didn't know what she knew and all the research and the reading that she had done. So therefore she'd got ideas in her head, she knew exactly what she wanted to find out.

He had found the faculty discussions invaluable and that the process took time. The second year had established a more shared understanding and purpose.

The whole staff group were informed through regular reports in the staff bulletin and through staff meetings. The group described feeling supported and high profile in the staff group, but not all responses were positive and for enthusiastic researchers this too was not easy when they went beyond the initial group.

Reviewing and recommending

The final term of the first year was when the teacher researcher along with the other colleagues drew up recommendations for the faculty. This led to the next stepping-stone – inducting *all* faculty colleagues into the new practice, writing recommendations and preparing to work across a whole year group.

Going faculty wide and informing policy

Three major faculties extended their practices across a whole year group of pupils and with all the staff involved in that teaching. Finance was given to the faculty to use on this enterprise as they would. This was a big extension and provided the opportunity to examine the evidence on a much larger scale. It was also developmentally a much bigger task. The further out the researchers went into the staff group, the greater the range of attitudes and motivations they were going to encounter and they encountered scepticism and critique. Younger staff found their lack of seniority an issue initially but not later on as understandings of the work spread. The support of heads of faculty was key.

Although the model described was the final and preferred strategy, other models were also being tried. There was an initiative on assessment for learning and the approach here was to ask one member of staff to become an expert on the current research and thinking. His goal was then to draw up guidelines, using pupil evidence, and effect change in two faculties. The third strand was an audit of skills and talents in the school under the broad remit of the development of education for the gifted and talented. Howard Gilbert described them as 'three pilots' but the main strand, which was supported by the partnership, was the research and development on teaching and learning.

The strategy largely held up and the final goals of improving pupil recall, influencing policy across faculties and producing a policy statement to influence teaching and learning have all being achieved. Howard Gilbert recently acknowledged that the work had spread but was not fully embedded in the sense that there was still staff who were not fully aware of the extent of the work. Staff presentations at staff meetings had raised awareness of this and had made the senior managers aware that communication and dissemination were constant processes. There was an ongoing need to be flexible and opportunistic.

The last phase of the development has been in place for a year at the time of writing. This is a collaborative project with City of Ely Community College under the aegis of the Leading Edge Initiative. The research is now being extended to another school. This collaboration involves taking what was learned at Soham and developing the research in the Community College in Ely. There has also been great opportunism in financing the development. The partnership schools used funding from the National College of School Leadership (Networked Learning Communities), DfES's Best Practice Research Scholarships and grants from the Gatsby Charitable Foundation to finance the considerable amount of money being spent on this work. In Howard Gilbert's view the finance was important because it enabled the school to secure the work. Finance was used to enhance salaries, enable release for group meetings, improve ICT support and pay for the university's support in the Leading Edge Initiative.

Research on teaching and learning

The research studies were summarised in Box 9.2. One of the research reports is shown in Box 9.3. It gives a good sense of the actual research undertaken. Some of the research has challenged assumptions and expectations. The research on learning styles in particular challenged the notion that there were groups of learners who used a set learning style and who were evenly distributed. The final report arrives at the conclusion that the use of a multisensory approach was what could be recommended. The final framework for teaching and learning has been produced and forms a part of the framework for review of teaching and learning.

The research instruments used were questionnaires designed by staff and reproduced ones such as that on learning styles; interviews with individual and focus groups of students; research diaries; statistical analysis of data on pupil tests and performances.

Box 9.3 Research report: Rachel Hollingworth (Mathematics) and Vanessa Summers (English)

Aims
To analyse the learning preferences shown throughout a whole cohort: Year 8
To test the effectiveness of VAK starter (English) and plenary (Mathematics) sessions
To ask whether knowledge of the distribution of learning styles within classes forms useful diagnostic information for teachers

Brief description
Every Year 8 class in English and Mathematics was given a questionnaire to determine their learning style. A profile of each class was then produced.

In Mathematics three modules were chosen from the Year 8 scheme of work and a learning style was allocated to each one.

* Fractions, decimals, percentages and ratio – Visual
* Graphs – Auditory
* Circles – Kinaesthetic

Six key concepts were identified from each module and a plenary activity devised for each. The visual activities were devised by members of the Mathematics faculty and the auditory and kinaesthetic activities were devised with the Cambridgeshire LEA advisory teacher. Once the activities had been devised, resources were made and presented to the rest of the faculty. The activities were then briefly evaluated, any required changes made before reproduction for each faculty member.

Each member of the faculty then used the plenaries while teaching the module to their Year 8 classes. The pupils were informed of the project and asked to think carefully while doing each activity about how useful and enjoyable it was.

continued

Box 9.3 Continued

In English the decision was taken to concentrate on starter sessions to see if pupils preferred any one particular style and if any one significantly enhanced their learning. The faculty collectively devised a series of six lessons with appropriate resources to cover a two-week teaching period on each of the learning styles – visual, auditory and kinaesthetic. Each Year 8 class was taught exactly the same starter in exactly the same way, but not always at exactly the same time of day due to timetabling restrictions. The pupils were informed of the project and asked to think carefully while doing each activity about how useful and enjoyable it was. All of Year 8 was included.

Evaluation criteria

• Pupils and staff were given a questionnaire at the end of each set of activities asking how useful and enjoyable the activities were, this became known as the Pupil/Teacher Satisfaction rating. All responses were numerical so that the data could easily be entered into a spreadsheet for analysis.

• Teachers were asked for opinions throughout the project and their suggestions taken on board.

Outcomes

Question 1 Does the profile of the Year 8 cohort match published research which suggests that the population is split into thirds of visual, auditory and kinaesthetic preference?
The pie chart shows that the proportions found match very closely the published data.

Total VAK comparison

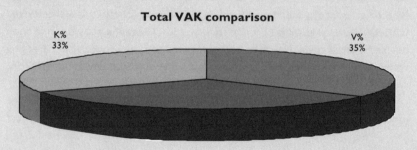

continued

Box 9.3 Continued

Question 2 Is there a recognisable pattern drawn from comparison of the sets?
Conventional wisdom is that high ability pupils often tend to be visually biased whereas low ability pupils lean towards a kinaesthetic approach. However, the percentages for the sets in English and Mathematics contradict this, being incredibly similar. It is also significant that there was no distinction between Mathematics and English sets which had significantly varying compositions. The implications of these finding are that assumptions should not be made about the learning preferences shown by pupils in particular sets.

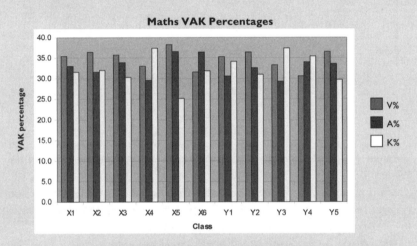

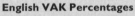

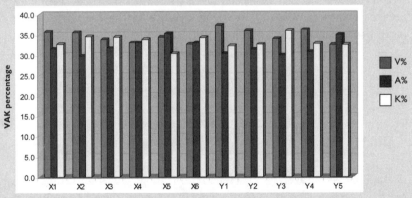

continued

Box 9.3 Continued

Question 3 What sort of spread is there within a group? Are there extremes present in all classes – should this lead to multisensory teaching?

The graph shown is that of one set of pupils only but is representative of the whole cohort. A really big spread of results can be seen across every class including some notable extremes. This suggests that multisensory lessons are vital if all pupils are to be able to maximise their personal learning potentials.

Variation of VAK preferences per pupil

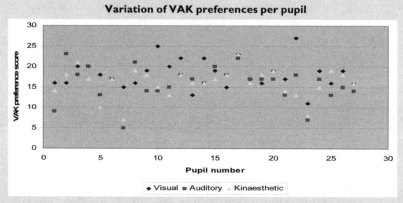

Question 4 Do pupils' and teachers' satisfaction ratings reflect or confound the VAK profiles?

There is no set rule here but, more often than not, the teachers' satisfaction ratings are mirrored by the pupils. This may indicate that teachers' enthusiasm for particular methods influences pupil perception – or vice versa!

Here is one set of results (8 × 2 Maths) as an example:

Graph A shows the VAK scores for the class and it is clear that there is very little difference between the learning styles, with the class being slightly more visual than auditory or kinaesthetic.

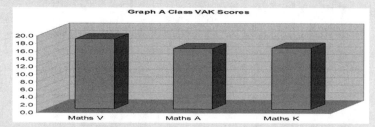

Graph B shows the average pupil satisfaction ratings and Graph C the average teacher satisfaction rating. The teacher rating reflects the VAK profile of the class more than the pupil ratings.

continued

Box 9.3 Continued

However, a notable trend throughout the data is evident here: pupil ratings are very positive towards the kinaesthetic activities. There are several possible reasons for this finding (which was found throughout the data) but a major factor may be that the kinaesthetic activities involved the pupils getting up and moving around the room, in stark contrast to their usual classroom experience.

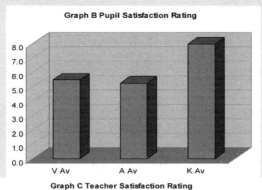

Graph B Pupil Satisfaction Rating

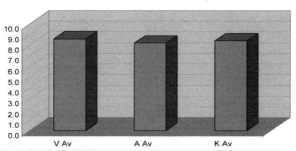

Graph C Teacher Satisfaction Rating

Graphs D, E and F show the relationship between the pupil response and their VAK score. We would expect to see a positive correlation for all of these graphs, that is, the more visual a pupil (x-axis), the higher the rating they would give to visual activities (y-axis). However, the data shows very little correlation at all. This suggests that it is not simply a case of the modality of an activity determining levels of pupil learning, but rather that the specific nature of the activity and the context and manner in which it is presented are more significant factors. This is exemplified again by the kinaesthetic results where pupils shown by the VAK questionnaire as very low in kinaesthetic preference showed very high levels of satisfaction in terms of the learning benefits from these methods.

continued

Box 9.3 Continued

Graph D Visual score
against pupil satisfaction
rating

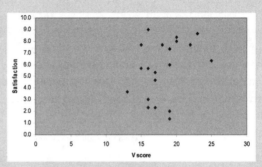

Graph E Auditory score
against pupil satisfaction
rating

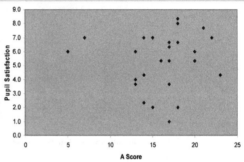

Graph D Kineasthetic
score against pupil
satisfaction rating

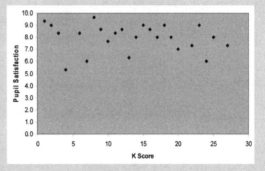

Summary of outcomes

These investigations suggest that VAK questionnaires are not a useful diagnostic tool for determining strategies for whole-class teaching. Rather that, as a general rule, pupils' learning is enhanced when information is presented in as multisensory a manner as possible. Pupils seem to respond very positively to a range of techniques but that kinaesthetic options are particularly favoured.

VAK questionnaires may, however, be of use in identifying and devising strategies for helping individual pupils with highly skewed profiles.

The focus on student voice: fear of scrutiny

One of the themes that the partnership was pursuing was the development of student voice in teaching and learning. The students were being consulted and questioned as part of the research on teaching and learning. However, there was an attempt to develop this work by involving students more formally in the faculty review process. It seemed like a natural development. It was not. It raised fears of inspection and reporting on staff in unfair ways and the whole notion was pulled back. The students had always been involved but this was a reminder of how delicate this work is, especially in a national climate of scrutiny and accountability. Ofsted's consultation of pupils as part of the process can lead to associations of inspection and be a barrier to the work. This also occurred at a time when the college and staff were under considerable pressure due to the murders of two girls on the site and it may have been symptomatic of the pressure they felt at that time. Since 2004, this is an area that has begun to be developed again.

The experience of and the effects on the participants

Shifting to a focus on learners and learning

The first teacher researchers talked of the immediate impact on them of under-taking the reading. One said: 'It made me think, it made me realise that in front of me are a range of learners'. Another said: 'I was very interested in the theory and to see it working changed my mind-set and my practice'.

The most powerful drivers were the responses of the pupils to the work being undertaken, the process of data collection and the data itself, as two teacher researchers commented:

> Thinking how the students will respond has changed. Getting feedback from the pupils was very important and new. Thinking about it from their view-point was new and powerful.

> It has made me focus much more on the diversity of learners in my class-room.

The questioning and reflective stance adopted towards their teaching and in particular to the pupils became something valued and seen as ongoing. However, the readiness to change and be open to evidence was also part of the process that became a tenet of these teachers' professionalism. One explained:

> If you are not researching, you are going to get stuck in your ways. If you are not prepared to look into how to change the classroom it will get worse. Research is part of it but you have got to be prepared to change.

The experience was not without its difficulties. There was often an increase in frustration and the difficult awareness of complexity. During the process of necessary disturbance the support of the other researchers was very important and the regularity of it was also key. The experience of the TRC, who has a Masters in educational research, was highly valued. The wider support from the SMT was noted. 'Every time I did something for the bulletin I got a response from the head and the teacher research coordinator' (teacher researcher). Other teachers reported a growing confidence in the research group and that as the researchers' confidence grew so they became more convincing. One head of faculty talked about a researcher in his department:

> She's got sort of better at what she's doing and her research and that is then filtered down to the rest of us. Whereas last year she wasn't as on the ball.

Time was of course an issue. One teacher researcher commented that anything extra would always be seen as burdensome but that since the gains were so apparent, the burden seemed lighter and worth carrying. The concept of manageability recurred as an important theme in the conversations with teacher researchers and leaders of research.

Another theme was that the shift to working in the faculty could be the most difficult aspect and was the aspect for which the group were the least prepared. One researcher felt that the group would have benefited from a session where this was discussed and they were formally supported in this area. Other aspects that were found to be supportive were working as a group and across faculties.

The force of the research

The researchers have already been reported as describing the effect on their view of the classroom and their own learning and practice. Other teachers too who experienced the faculty focus reported how the research began to change conversations, thinking and practice. One head of faculty reported that new conversations were occurring between colleagues:

> We often sit and talk about things and talk about the activities, and things that we are doing, you know. As it's useful people are always enthusiastic.

Other teachers interviewed also reported this shift in the content of teacher talk. There was also a shift in the type of reflection. This researcher suggests a change in how activity in the classroom may be judged:

> People are thinking about [learning], which they wouldn't necessarily have done before. It would have just been 'oh that's a nice activity, that will work well' and not necessarily think well it will work with 90 per cent of the class but not with the other 10 per cent.

Practice in the classroom and policy in the faculties has been changed but other teachers not directly involved have also noted that the students now talk actively about revision and recall, including sophisticated discussions of how they go about it. The visibility of the work has affected the way teachers discuss ideas and are open to debate and new practices. There is a more widespread reflection on practice.

The Ofsted report noted that there were visible signs of the work:

> The University of Cambridge education department is supporting a number of research projects, initiated by Soham Village College, on teaching and learning skills. These are having a very good impact on practice in the college. Several of the successful teaching and learning characteristics identified in the research were seen in observed lessons. The use of mind maps in science, regular reviews in modern foreign languages, reviews at the starts and ends of lessons in design and technology and visualisation in physical education are some of the successful techniques employed. In a very successful Year 7 physical education lesson, for example, pupils looked at pictures of Olympic gymnasts, then closed their eyes and visualised their own positions before carrying out the gymnastic activity required. This reflective approach resulted in very good progress and achievement for each pupil.
>
> (Ofsted 2003d: 14)

The partnership and the connections

The partnership with the university

University colleagues were involved in various ways. As critical friend, I visited regularly, led meetings with the researchers, undertook research training and support, undertook interviews and fed back the emergent issues to the headteacher and TRC. In addition, Susan Barnett, a visiting research fellow from Cornell University, is currently undertaking a research study, which is in the area of the school's concerns (Barnett and Ceci 2002). The staff are helping to design the research in a school setting. Chris Tooley and Jackie Bullock, a previous member of the Teaching and Learning Group, are also working on the T-Media project with Sarah Hennessey from the Faculty of Education. The work with the university is valued for many reasons. It is seen as giving validation and status to the work of the teachers, as adding an external, informed, critical perspective from which all benefit. Howard Gilbert explained:

> You [the university] bring a rigour to what we do, which we wouldn't have otherwise. You bring an external challenge, which again we wouldn't have otherwise. It's given a structure to the framework as well. It's excellent to be working with people in education research and picking up allsorts.

However, this involvement with research must not take the school off track in its work. The TRC, Chris Tooley, argued that the work and the university involvement 'must help us move forward and not cause us to do extra things that we wouldn't normally have done'. The university fulfils a role as a bridge to the wider world of research knowledge and is also the servant of the needs of the teachers. Chris added:

> One thing that certainly isn't going to happen is actually me being able to chase research because, you know, I don't have time to eat in the school, let alone chase research. But being sent a sort of summary of research findings is useful.

An aim of the work in the partnership was to make the research of colleagues in the university accessible to the schools and this was seen as the least successful part of the work, although there were some presentations from university colleagues at the whole partnership research conferences. Reviews of research such as Coffield *et al.*'s (2004) review of the research on learning styles was found to be useful. Accessibility was a wider issue. Teacher colleagues were critical of the language of research articles and there was a need to be a bridge to the world of the teachers and their style of communication. Howard Gilbert said:

> There needs to be communication that goes across in a way that's very readable. There's some research articles where you need your dictionary beside you and it doesn't seem to speak the same language.

The connections and partnership with the other schools

The work has been shared with other school partners and with schools outside the network; however, again the theme is that the contact must support the work being done in the school itself. The work with other schools is highly valued and the new collaboration, which extends the contacts in the local context, is seen as very important. This is the most difficult aspect of the work for the teachers, however, and is also a feature of the geography of Soham, which is rural. The recent development of the website has been very important here and teachers in Ely talked of how important this was, but it was not a substitute for face-to-face contact.

Conclusion

The processes which Hargreaves (1999) identified as central to a knowledge-creating school, that is auditing the professional knowledge, managing the creation of new professional knowledge, validating the professional knowledge created and disseminating the created professional knowledge have been systematically engaged with in Soham Village College. The validation is particularly important here since so much has been built on those first steps. The key theme is the alignment of all that occurs in the school to the central purposes. As this case study is being written, the headteacher and the teacher research coordinator are leaving to go to new positions. This will be the test of whether the work is now central to how they do things in Soham or not.

Chapter 10

Bridging and bonding
Perspectives on the role of the university in SUPER

Vivienne Baumfield and Colleen McLaughlin

The potential benefits of collaborations between schools and universities have long been recognised and can be summarised as follows:

- A chance to work across institutional boundaries in a loose organisational structure
- Participation in a community that respects teachers' knowledge as well as knowledge from university research and policy-makers
- Opportunities for teachers to both absorb and generate knowledge about teaching and learning
- Flexibility and informality
- An environment that supports experimentation and taking risks.

(Adapted from Lieberman 1999)

While there is a growing body of work on networks and other forms of collaborative research and inquiry (McLaughlin *et al.* 2004), there is still much to learn about how they function in specific contexts and the role of universities in such partnerships is an under-examined aspect. The final overview of the School Based Research Consortia (an initiative funded by the Teacher Training Agency to explore the potential of partnerships involving schools, LEAs and universities to promote evidence informed practice) confirms the value of relationships between university staff and the teachers in the schools but concludes that, while there was evidence of the breaking down of traditional hierarchies

> The task of learning across boundaries formed the working environment, a research goal, a means to the end of improving teaching and learning – and a perpetual puzzle.

(Cordingley *et al.* 2002: 2)

The perspectives of the university staff associated with the Schools–University Partnership in Educational Research project make a contribution to the unravelling of this puzzle and help us to understand better the role of the university in a collaborative research partnership.

The view from within the university: visions, strategies and challenges

The notion of partnership with schools, in particular of collaborative action research work, was not a new one in the Faculty of Education or its predecessors (the Institute, Department, then School of Education, and Homerton College). Many examples of such work exist, such as Marion Dadds (1995), Susan Hart's work on teacher inquiry (see Dadds and Hart 2001), Jean Rudduck's work on learning (see Harris and Ruddock 1993), the IQEA project (Hopkins 2002), the work of the Collaborative Action Research Network (CARN), the general approach to continuing professional development (Bradley *et al.* 1994) and the current initial teacher education (ITE) partnership. However, as was pointed out in Chapter 1, the notion of the SUPER partnership was different in its intentions and its focus on working on research at school level rather than individual practitioner level. It aimed to explore the possibility of a partnership with schools built around supporting, developing and collaborating on research: its prime purpose being to research the conditions necessary for effective research to take place within individual schools, across individual schools and between schools and the university. This was an exploratory and open agenda. This section explores what was learned and what challenges this presented for the university as a partner in this enterprise.

After a year of initial discussions, the university responded in a familiar way: it applied for research project funding to the Wallenberg Centre and a researcher was appointed to research the development for three years. This funding also supported the financing of a teacher research coordinator for one day a week in each of the schools. The university hosted meetings and administered some of the communication between the partners. There was immediately a tension in that the school partners seemed to look to the university for leadership, albeit of a democratic and negotiated sort. This was particularly a tension for the person in the research role and something was resolved at the end of the three years by separating out two aspects of the role, that is having a researcher but, in addition, a lecturer in the university to act as a coordinator and clearly identified as such. The issues of leadership and power within the partnership remained, but one aspect had been resolved. This development also seemed to put the university in a more traditional service and research role. The introduction of new personnel was a natural point at which to reflect with the schools upon the progress in terms of the university's role.

The key issues that emerged at this point were ones that continue to be key ones within the faculty:

- the nature of the partnership, collaboration and leadership within it
- the different needs, conceptions and pressures on the different partners
- resourcing and financing the partnership
- working towards a more structural view of research partnerships within the faculty.

The nature of the partnership, collaboration and leadership within it

When a review was made of the activities that the university had undertaken, after seven years of SUPER, it looked as if the university was in a service role. The university undertook the following activities:

- actively seeking funding on behalf of the partnership, e.g. the Wallenberg funding and then later the Networked Learning Communities funding
- providing start up and maintenance support, plus research training in the school context through meetings, mentoring and providing support materials for teachers in the schools
- promoting and helping in the writing, critique and dissemination of the school-based research between the schools and to the wider educational community
- developing professional development opportunities for teachers undertaking inquiry, through accreditation and presentation opportunities
- supporting the teacher research coordinators in their role as site-based coaches and facilitators of inquiry in the school setting
- supporting students and student voice coordinators in their inquiry activities
- liaising with headteachers and facilitating meetings
- providing space and facilitation for meetings when required
- providing support services such as the maintenance of a website and communication services between groups.

The role of critical friend was introduced and was a key strategy. The aim was to tighten the connection between the university and the school. The critical friend could fulfil a number of very important functions. First, they could work alongside the schools in researching the uses and understandings of research in the schools and in the partnership. This research could be fed back regularly to the schools so that it fulfilled a developmental role. Second, the critical friend was able also to support individuals and groups undertaking research in a continuous way. This enabled the work to have continuity and depth and was a very important step in the development. It was also an opportunity for the faculty team to invite new colleagues to join and this provided an opportunity to develop links with schools through the initial teacher education partnership. This imposed greater demands on the university colleagues: because the team were to operate in this way, they needed to meet regularly, update each other and be kept in the picture. This proved to be difficult and immediately raised issues related to communication, resources and time allocation to the work.

The set of personal connections between colleagues and their schools was not only a strength of the work, but also a potential pull against the group as a network, in that allegiances and connections between subgroups could become more important than the allegiance to the whole group. This has implications for the team-building and communication work within a university team as some colleagues had more time to meet with the whole group of TRCs and headteachers and this inevitably created different understandings and connections.

Leadership within the partnership is an ongoing issue. The schools clearly expected some form of leadership from the university. They expected research expertise to be shared and for the university to take on many of the administrative and communication functions, since these were seen as too demanding for teachers or headteachers. The financing arrangements reflect this in that money was set aside to pay for this. However, within the partnership the schools had a high degree of autonomy within their research agendas and this has been a push and a pull within the work.

Whether collaboration means all working together on the substantive research agenda or whether it means collaboration on the process of research is a topic of continuing debate within the partnership. There were examples of research projects located within the partnership where the leadership taken by the university was much tighter i.e. where the university framed the research topic, shaped the research questions and the school partners undertook the research, including the design, in their own way. In general, many faculty members have not used the partnership to negotiate and develop research projects. Early in the life of SUPER there was an attempt to find a common research topic within the partnership and Thinking Skills was chosen. Then there was a move to three overarching themes within which the schools could integrate their own agendas. Currently there is an attempt is to collate these different research projects and assess what has been learned about the themes. The assumption of a very high level of autonomy for each school has been a critically important factor in shaping the nature of the partnership and perhaps the future resides in learning from the research and providing leadership on that basis.

The different needs, conceptions and pressures on the different partners

There was a need to teach each other about our institutions and the ways in which they worked. The school partners did not understand the connections between publication, research and finance in universities and nor did they understand the financial constraints under which university colleagues were often working. A critical moment in the partnership was when Donald McIntyre talked to the TRCs about how the university worked in terms of finance and staff allocation. All partners needed to understand the pressures and ways of working of the different organisations involved in order for trust and mutual tolerance to develop. The other major topic of constant debate was that of research. There were big differences between the purposes, timescales and forms of research work undertaken within the partnership. The boundaries between sharing practice, continuing professional development and research were often indistinguishable for many colleagues. The different demands made of the research within the partnership organisations were also clear.

Resourcing and financing the partnership

Finance was a constant pressure for all partners. The time consumed by applying for funding and servicing the funding providers is always an issue in this work. The high resource model used, the mismatch between university colleagues' teaching schedules, especially those working in high input teaching programmes, and the communication needs of the partnership were ongoing tensions. There was a constant search for mechanisms to support the work of teachers and university researchers, which were economical of time and effort, and there is a constant tension between the need to set up structures that might be helpful and the danger of being consumed by the processes of administering these structures. The stage of development currently being implemented (i.e. the partnership MEd aimed at supporting the development of inquiry leaders within the schools) is the latest attempt to do that. The ways of financing the partnership fit the financial planning of schools and the university in a more conventional and recognisable way, it is less short term and appears at this stage to be suited to purpose, although there are challenges for the university in terms of the forms of assessment and the notion of what counts as teaching contact hours.

Working towards a more structural view of research partnerships within the faculty

Within this work there is an implicit assumption that the University would explore the development of a more structural research partnership with schools, as exists in initial teacher education. This was and is still being explored. An open, invitational meeting was held in the early stages (2002) with interested, university colleagues to discuss this and the issues raised. The aims of the meeting were to explain the SUPER pilot project: to explore and formulate a vision of school–university research partnerships; to identify key issues for the university partners and to take the first steps towards policy formulation.

The key concerns and questions raised by colleagues in this very preliminary discussion were related to the funding of the research and the differing needs and purposes of research. In relation to funding, the key challenges were how to marry the funding mechanisms of universities with the funding mechanisms of schools and also relate to the criteria for the research assessment exercise (RAE). One question raised was whether RAEs in the future would require greater collaboration between schools and universities and if so, how would this work? Other questions related to the nature and conduct of research:

- Who would decide what topics were researched and how would the long-term development of research marry with the more immediate needs of schools?
- How would the faculty plan their research?
- What would be the implications for the appointment of staff?
- How could differences in the perceptions between schools and the faculty about the nature and purposes of research be addressed or reconciled?

- What would be the implications for the writing up and publication of research when schools are co-researchers?
- How should research agendas be decided?

Currently in universities colleagues decide their own research agendas and have high degrees of autonomy. The partnership poses the question of whether it is possible to work towards a middle position where staff continue to be involved in a research project about which they feel passionately, while others are directed towards work in partnership with schools on particular topics?

The view from the schools

SUPER holds an annual residential conference attended by headteachers, teacher research coordinators, student voice coordinators and, from the university, the critical friends, the director of SUPER and the research associate. The first stage in exploring the impact of SUPER on the university was to interview the school staff at the conference with a view to understanding the schools' perceptions of the role of the university in SUPER and any benefits and tensions resulting from their partnership. The benefits of SUPER were easily identified by the respondents and they included being associated with a prestigious university, access to research expertise through the relationship with the critical friend, the opportunity to collaborate across institutions all of which motivated staff and helped to develop a 'research friendly' ethos in the schools.

Tensions referred to in the interviews tended to reflect issues associated with the management of the partnership in terms of adjusting to different cultures as evident in the difficulty of matching the pace and timing of activities and different expectations across the schools as to what should be a priority for SUPER. Links between individual schools and the university were strong but this was sometimes as much a consequence of a history of overlapping contacts through ITE, CPD and individual research projects as more directly through SUPER, but as far as the respondents were concerned this was not important as they did not make such distinctions. However, problems in communicating effectively were raised and the extent to which individual schools had an overview of what was happening across the partnership was questioned. The tendency to channel activity through the university was criticised by some teachers who felt that this restricted the scope to learn from the expertise of school leaders or distribute leadership and there was a suggestion that this issue was becoming more acute due to the expectations of the Networked Learning Group. However, this was a minority view and all the respondents were enthusiastic about being a member of SUPER and valued the contribution of the university; it is mentioned here only as an indicator of the complexity of leadership in the partnership.

Unanimity as to the benefits of the link with the university through SUPER overlay differences in the scope and extent of the partnership for the different schools. For some the benefits were conceived of principally in terms of professional development for staff, for others the link was part of a strategy for school improvement through teacher research, in one instance expressed explicitly in terms of the concept of knowledge creation and for others it was the opportunity of collaborating in university led research projects based in their school. There were also differences in the extent to which the partnership with the university was exclusive as opposed to one aspect of a more diverse set of contacts with external agencies, including other universities. The diversity of activity and conceptions of the purpose of SUPER in terms of being principally an agent of change through promoting professional learning, school improvement or research was not presented as a problem by the school staff who saw all aspects of their involvement in SUPER as potential benefits; however, such distinctions did pre-occupy the university staff.

The view from the outside in: a moment in time

The perspectives of the university staff discussed in this section were gathered through a series of semi-structured interviews which attempted to capture their views at a particular moment in time. The period in question was one of transition as one source of funding, as a Networked Learning Community, was coming to an end and negotiations had begun to establish a partnership MEd as the means of supporting SUPER activity in the future. The perspectives informing this case study are shaped not only by the point in time in which they were elicited but also by the degree of immersion in SUPER of the informant. The SUPER schools, in common with other schools in the region, have a number of natural points of contact with the university: as partners in ITE, employers of graduates from the ITE programmes, through CPD and consultancy, and as sites for funded research projects. These multiple points of contact enrich the relationship between the schools and the university and so can be fruitful for SUPER but they also contribute to its complexity and make it difficult for the achievements of SUPER to be visible within the university.

Figure 10.1 illustrates who was interviewed and their relative proximity to SUPER: the core group (Colleen McLaughlin, Kristine Black-Hawkins and Donald McIntyre) consists of those within the Faculty of Education directly involved in the day-to-day managing of the partnership and who are also critical friends to some of the schools; the next layer (Keith S. Taber and Sue Brindley) consists of members of the faculty who act as critical friends within SUPER and who also have links with some of the schools through an overlapping partnership based on ITE; the next layer (David Frost and Kenneth Ruthven) consists of faculty staff whose work involves collaborative research with schools, sometimes schools in SUPER, but who are not members of SUPER; the final layer represents Dave Ebbutt, a retired member of staff who was involved in the early stages of SUPER. Establishing the identity of SUPER within all the overlapping activities and school–university links across the faculty is problematic and so the different positions of the respondents enabled multiple perspectives on SUPER to be canvassed.

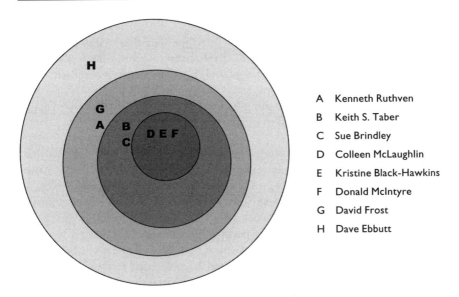

A   Kenneth Ruthven

B   Keith S. Taber

C   Sue Brindley

D   Colleen McLaughlin

E   Kristine Black-Hawkins

F   Donald McIntyre

G   David Frost

H   Dave Ebbutt

Figure 10.1 Faculty of Education members of staff involved with SUPER

As we have seen, the decision to establish SUPER was at the instigation of a group of headteachers who saw benefits in establishing a collaborative research partnership with the university in order to explore the concept of the knowledge creating school (Hargreaves 1999). The university responded positively to this request as they were interested in learning more about what the implications of such a partnership might be, particularly in the prevailing climate of criticism of education research as lacking in relevance for practitioners (Hillage *et al.* 1998). The informal, loosely coupled origins of SUPER gave the partners the scope to be innovative and flexible in the pursuit of mutual benefits and the partnership as an organisational structure has many of the features of effective networks (Lowndes and Skelcher 1998; Lieberman 1999; Putnam 2000; Hannon 2005). However, the partnership also faced the problems that this way of working can present and the tension between the relationships and activities of SUPER and institutional cultures is also part of the story. This case study focuses on the impact of SUPER on the university and in doing so begins to probe the wider question that is emerging across the public sector:

> What remains unanswered – and to some extent unasked – are the conventional questions of the pluralist debate: who has power, who gains and who loses as the policy makers' obsession with networks and partnerships grows?
>
> (Lowndes and Skelcher 1998: 331)

Inside the academy

Within the university there is a commitment to the idea that working collabor-atively with schools is a core activity of the Faculty of Education and that the relationships with schools should be reciprocal. Kenneth Ruthven commented:

> I was very conscious that the thing had to be planned, so that everybody got something out of it ... it had to be a coalition of interest.

All of the respondents were positive in their appraisal of practitioners' know-ledge and experience, which they respected and wanted to acknowledge as not only a valid independent means of understanding teaching and learning but also one that can and should inform their own work. SUPER was founded with the intention of asking the question of what would be the implications for schools and the university of working in a research partnership and there was consensus across all the respondents that they had, and still could, learn a great deal from the partnership. Positive evaluations of what had been learned tended to focus on having a better understanding of what was happening in the schools, as one person phrased it, 'the texture of what is happening in schools'.

One of the achievements of SUPER was providing a channel for open and honest debate between school and university staff about the benefits and frustrations of working in partnership in which both parties gained a better understanding of the opportunities and constraints presented by their respective institutional cultures. For some people this enhanced mutual understanding was of benefit in that it meant that working with schools within a more traditional university led research project framework was facilitated as they could be more realistic in their expectations of what they could reasonably ask teachers to do and in turn, teachers were more informed and so better informants (Kenneth Ruthven). However, respondents were also agreed that they still knew little beyond their individual experience about the implications for the faculty and that evidence of impact and structural change beyond those involved in SUPER was sparse.

Tolerance of ambiguity

The potential to promote wider collaboration and a more integrated way of work-ing across a range of activities involving links with schools is widely recognised as is the potential of SUPER as a means of learning more about how this can be achieved. However, in a partnership not all of the potential benefits are definable at the beginning and participants need to be prepared to work within a fluid, multidimensional entity and not be alarmed by 'the irregular heartbeat of a partnership organization' (Lowndes and Skelcher 1998: 330). Among those university staff most closely involved, there is a high level of tolerance of the ambiguity of SUPER, which is seen as a source of potency rather than a deficiency. As Kristine Black-Hawkins explained:

It's not a project with a pre-defined end product – it's like a jelly, amorphous and shifting. You don't know how it ends.

For some staff it is the excitement of the unpredictability of working across different cultures that is interesting and they are willing to revise their views on what is expected of them and how this might influence their own research activity. Kristine Black-Hawkins said:

I think if I want stuff from them I have to be a bit more flexible so that then I realise that I'm taking up my research time and the schools have got different backgrounds and different histories and the people have different ideas about how SUPER operates and I feel responsive to that, and also the serendipitous nature of research fascinates me.

Motivation can also come from a commitment to the need for structural change in order to promote equity and the recognition that this requires the open and honest exchange of experiences and a willingness to learn. All the partners have a contribution to make to the improvement of teaching and learning which is the common purpose that underpins their work. From this perspective, partnership requires integrity and its success depends on the quality of the relationships. Colleen McLaughlin commented:

It has to be driven by people's beliefs and you can't short circuit that I don't think, well you can, but would you want to?

Intellectual curiosity also plays a part in so far as an interest in seeing what will happen and a degree of detachment from a particular outcome can sustain involvement in the midst of uncertainty. From this perspective the partnership is a process of academic inquiry and not a project and so will be fruitful whatever the end results may be. The flexibility SUPER affords can be beneficial to some staff as it offers the possibility of achieving the integration of a research dimension to their existing roles, this is particularly true of some ITE tutors for whom SUPER affords the opportunity to combine links with schools as teacher trainers with the role of critical friend and so achieve economy of effort. SUPER for these staff also represents the 'reclaiming of the thinking agenda for teachers and teacher trainers' (Sue Brindley) by addressing the question of what it means for teaching to be an evidence-informed profession.

Within the university there are different degrees of comfort with uncertainty and ambiguity as an aspect of working in partnership. The different strategies for dealing with this can be interpreted in terms of seeking to work in a way that promotes bridging across the different points of contact and activity or working towards bonding participants together. In the views expressed by the staff most closely involved in SUPER we can see a range from the most flexible, bridging, orientation that embraces the serendipity of research to the pursuit of integration that in its tendency to promote bonding between the partners may lead towards accommodation and so limit radical change on the part of the university.

The literature on social networks (e.g. Putnam 2000) categorises bridging as a form of activity in which the ties are weak and the aim is to be inclusive through accommodating broader identities and the wider diffusion of ideas; such networks support innovation. Bonding, on the other hand, seeks stronger ties and a closer identity which leads to more exclusivity and while providing solidarity requires specific reciprocity. SUPER has a specific focus on research and the way in which this is conceptualised by the different participants is a key factor in the identity of the partnership within the university. We have seen that the schools are able to work with broad definitions of research in which distinguishing between professional learning, school improvement and research is not necessary. The same cannot be said for academic staff who are more preoccupied with the question of whether the work of SUPER can or should be described as research.

Making distinctions

Two of the university staff working with schools in research projects, but who were not themselves part of the SUPER team, referred to a tension between developing research questions that were academically coherent while at the same time professionally useful for the teachers. There was a sense that in fact for schools the interest would always be in finding solutions to particular problems rather than developing an awareness of what Kenneth Ruthven describes as the wider research enterprise:

> But I think the difficulty is that often schools and teachers, simply because it's not part of their world, part of their work, it's very difficult to understand the research enterprise as something that's bigger than a single institution, bigger than a single country and in effect you are part of a community which is ongoing in time and is right across the world and that is trying to generate knowledge which is more than just of local interest which is also ... tried and tested in a whole range of ways that is understood.

This perspective focuses on the status of the knowledge produced and sees this as the determinant of whether the process by which it is acquired can be termed research. According to this view, teachers' knowledge is characterised by its concreteness and contextual richness as opposed to the generalisability and context independence of research knowledge, which is by definition public, open to scrutiny and so verifiable. Some writers have argued that there are processes whereby practitioners' knowledge can be developed into a form that can be shared and examined publicly and so acquire the characteristics of academic knowledge (Stenhouse 1975; Hiebert *et al.* 2002) but whether this means that this is research as opposed to the codifying of professional knowledge is as yet not agreed.

One view expressed by university staff was that given the problems of defining the activities of schools as research and the complexity of managing large partnerships, it would be better to think in terms of SUPER as a CPD activity in which case it would not be necessary to justify the work by claiming that it was contributing to the wider research enterprise. According to this perspective, one outcome from a schools–university collaboration would be a better understanding of research and the confidence to be honest about the different roles and contributions that schools and the university can make to education, as Kenneth Ruthven explained:

> If any of this is going to work successfully, it has to be people recognising that there are different projects and different roles you know to contribute and being comfortable about that.

Aspects of this response resonate with another perspective which is less pessimistic regarding the possibility of defining practitioner inquiry as research but argues that it may be making too many demands on teachers to ask that they should be researchers. Donald McIntyre reflected:

> There are long-term intellectual and very practically important issues – should we be asking teachers to be researchers? Is this scandalous? What about restructuring schools and rethinking the role of the teacher so that it is a more collaborative enterprise – there are lots of directions from which to approach it – many aspects.

Underpinning both perspectives is a view that it may also be making unreasonable demands on university staff to work in collaborative research partnerships given the demands it makes on their time and the fact that it is difficult to represent this expenditure of effort in terms of their own research profile, especially in the current climate of the auditing of research outputs through the research assessment exercise, as Donald McIntyre pointed out: 'The pressure of the RAE means that it is not an efficient way of investing energies'. Kenneth Ruthven agreed:

> Quite demanding in time. I mean, what I'm conscious of is it would be hard, even impossible, to run that model just on the staffing that would be available.

For other respondents it was not the feasibility of teachers carrying out research that was problematic but rather whether the type of research was appropriate. One argument put forward was that the intensive, context-specific model of action research resulting in a case study was not only demanding on the individual teachers but also of limited utility in persuading policy-makers or effecting real school improvement. Questioning of the current drive in government policy to support teacher research was evident in the responses of Dave Ebbutt, a member of the university who was an advocate of action research:

I've become sceptical about research as the government sponsored route to professional development. I think that there are all sorts of other groups and ways of enthusing teachers ... the claims about what research can do for you in your school are somewhat overblown.

Getting the balance right between enabling teachers to use research, engaging with research, and doing their own research was also raised and it was suggested by David Frost that teachers would be best served by being encouraged to focus on school improvement, not because they were not capable of conducting research but rather in order not to dissipate their energies and to focus on bringing about real change in schools.

Visibility

The interviews did not focus directly on the issue of what counted as research, this was not one of the questions asked, but the respondents all touched upon this issue at some point in the conversation. The preoccupation with definitions of research came up most often in answer to the first question exploring their views on the main achievements of SUPER or in replies to a question on how SUPER fits in with their work in the faculty. Given that SUPER was set up to investigate what the nature of a school–university research partnership might be and its impact on both schools and the university partner, there need not be any obligation to prove that teachers are engaging in research in order to establish the validity of the project. However, defining the activities of SUPER in a way that is recognisable to the rest of the faculty is important in terms of the credibility of the staff involved and their research profile in the faculty. Respondents did in fact find attributing any tangible achievements to SUPER problematic and this has implications for the viability of the partnership within the university in what is increasingly a culture of accountability. Kenneth Ruthven commented:

I don't have a sense of SUPER itself.

Keith Taber concurred:

I'm a bit out of it, I'm not so involved any more. I do know somebody involved ... I'm not sure how much commitment is there that was.

Of course, to be simply unaware of what one's colleagues are doing is not an unusual state of affairs within a university faculty, as Colleen McLaughlin described:

Two years ago we went to BERA [research conference] and we met at the airport, and there were half my colleagues, and we all looked at each other and said, 'I really don't know what you're doing' and so we actually set up something called Camera as a result of that where we share our own research within the university so that is not just a problem about SUPER, it's actually about how universities work.

What would be of more significance would be if any achievements of SUPER were not recognised within the university because they were not valued as research activities or credit was given to projects not recognised as having any link with the partnership and there is some evidence in the interviews of both of these things happening. While SUPER is exploring a way of working that is relatively new to both schools and the university, bringing about change in schools, although slow, appears to be less difficult than securing structural change within the university. The problems of bringing about change are linked partly to the difficulty of identifying tangible and prestigious, in academic terms, outcomes but also to the nature of the institutional culture which has been notoriously averse to any attempts at leadership. Colleen McLaughlin said:

> Roles and relationships within the university are complex and I've learned that those different agendas and cultures have to be put on the table right at the beginning and worked out right and again I come back to bravery. If you are in the position of holding out your hand and trying to persuade, I think it makes you less brave or clear about what you're doing.

Currently, universities are going through a period of change and few institutions have escaped a programme of major 'restructuring' in order to become more competitive and while this can offer opportunities it can also lead to greater insecurity. During the period of the interviews, the university was in the middle of major restructuring as previously discrete sections were brought within the faculty structure and relocated to a new, shared, building. One respondent commented on the fact that there are two main groupings of staff in the faculty, each with different sets of priorities and values, those whose main identity is as researchers and those closely involved in teacher development and school improvement. Interestingly, given the decision to develop the partnership MEd in SUPER, these different orientations are seen as coming into conflict in the area of accreditation where academics come together in boards of studies to adjudicate on academic standards, as David Frost explained:

> Those differences are magnified of course when you're talking about passing or failing students' work, that becomes a drama, whereas if it is a seminar it's just a difference of view. So I think it is an urgent thing to see how are we valuing the work of the teachers that we come across and what does that say about our own values and priorities.

The decision to use a new MEd programme as the means of funding SUPER was made partly to secure resources that were not tied to a particular project or initiative and so provide more autonomy but also because this was a way of engaging the university more directly in the partnership. What may at first appear to be a conservative choice to pursue partnership through an accredited post-graduate degree framework, and one that might also be seen to privilege the university, may in fact prove to be a radical step. If the presence of the partnership through the MEd becomes more deeply embedded in the core structures of the university and at the same time it opens up the debate about valuing teacher's professional knowledge and its status then it may be that the level of commitment already present will indeed be transformed into more profound structural change. It remains to be seen if the next stage in the life of SUPER enables the mutuality between academics and teachers evident in the responses and the desire to forge a coalition of interest can overcome the problems of aligning activity so that costs and benefits are balanced. For those closely involved in SUPER there is a sense of urgency, as described by Colleen McLaughlin:

> I think what is going on at the moment is about are the universities going to get seriously into practitioner research because if they don't now, it's a crucial time and we'll be overtaken because we are so small and we will be like the dodo.

Afterword

The university is to continue the debate, the new Masters programmes are aiming to develop this link, and the headteachers are exploring with external bodies such as the Specialist Schools trust ways of recognising the research task of the school. The view of the university as a mediator between the world of external research and schools is still seen as a viable option and one that the Faculty of Education would like to pursue. The university has invested and will continue to invest con-siderable resources and effort. It is hoped that SUPER will go towards providing some insights into these questions.

Chapter 11

The SUPER partnership

A case study

Kristine Black-Hawkins and Donald McIntyre

Having considered the diverse cases of each of the SUPER partners, we are left with the task of giving an account of the partnership as a whole. In our efforts to understand what school–university research partnerships could and should be like, we are conscious that this SUPER partnership is just one case. It represents our best efforts as yet to form an effective research partnership but, like the cases we have described of the individual institutions involved in it, it is one particular case, shaped by the concerns and preconceptions of the people involved and by the practical and financial constraints of its historical context. Before going on to consider what we have learned about school–university research partnerships from our experience, we must first try to understand and articulate what has happened in this particular case.

This account will be structured in terms of three historical phases of the partnership. In the first section we shall briefly reflect on the beginnings of the project, from 1997 to 1999. The second section is about the years from 1999 to 2002 when, with the help of a grant from the Wallenberg Centre, the partnership started actively to pursue its goals and to learn both about the rewarding things that it could achieve and about the problems that it faced. The third and longest section is about the third phase, from 2002 to 2005, during which the partnership benefited from lessons learned earlier, and also enjoyed the benefits and suffered the constraints following from the agenda of its new Network Learning Communities funding body.

Phase 1: the beginnings of SUPER 1997–1999

As described in Chapter 1, SUPER grew out of both national and local concerns. Nationally, the change of government in 1997 brought with it not only a new level of government interest in educational research, but also a highly critical debate about the quality and especially the usefulness of academic educational research. For example, a review of educational research commissioned by the DfEE concluded that 'if the purpose of educational research is to inform educational decisions and educational actions, then our overall conclusion is that the actions and decisions of policy-makers and practitioners are insufficiently informed by research' (Hillage *et al.* 1998: 46). David Hargreaves, one of the School of Education's professors, was nationally the most prominent critic of academic educational research. One of his main proposals for resolving the problem was that much more educational research should be done in schools by teachers, with the active support of university staff (Hargreaves 1996, 1999). Donald McIntyre, the other professor, was also active in the national debate (McIntyre 1997, 1998; McIntyre and McIntyre 1999), but was more sceptical about school-based research as a solution to the problems. The two professors were, however, in total agreement about the desirability of an exploratory schools–university research partnership at Cambridge to examine the possibilities and problems of such arrangements.

They were also responding to local concerns as expressed by two secondary school headteachers who independently approached the School of Education, seeking a special relationship concerned with research in addition to relationships they already had with the School of Education for other purposes. And, as explained in Chapter 1, they were building on a tradition developed by the Cambridge Institute of Education, and in particular on the longstanding research relationships with three other secondary schools that had been established by different groups within the Institute. The heads of two more secondary schools had not only provided active leadership in the Faculty of Education's secondary ITE partnership, but also been keen to broaden the basis of that partnership. All seven schools accepted the invitation to join the partnership, which was formed in 1997.

One important thing to note about the SUPER partnership is that it was formed spontaneously, entirely on the basis of the interest and enthusiasm of its members. It was not formed, as other TTA and NLC partnerships have for example been formed, to pursue an externally determined agenda. On the contrary, there was from the start a deliberately open agenda, so that the partnership could be responsive to its members' diverse research concerns and understandings, and so that the viability and fruitfulness of various possible agendas and arrangements could be explored. This lack of a tightly conceived agenda of course brought its own problems.

During the first eighteen months of the partnership, there were several meetings to explore possible ways forward. These meetings were attended by the headteachers, the professors, and other interested (mostly senior) members of the partner institutions. Many ideas were discussed but, interesting and informative as these meetings were, it gradually became apparent that little progress was being made. There seemed at the time to be one main reason for this, although in retrospect a second reason also seems to have been important.

This latter reason was that there was little early consensus about the value of radical new partnership activities that would be time-consuming or that would impose constraints on members. One suggestion, for example, was that members of the School of Education should, when planning new research projects, submit them to a panel drawn from the partnership schools to get advice on the attractiveness and usefulness of the proposed research. This was not at all a popular idea with academic staff, who were finding the demands on them to be active and productive in research quite demanding enough without the imposition of any extra hurdles. But nor was it an attractive idea to school members of the partnership, no doubt because it would have meant extra work for them without any obvious benefits to their schools. The suggestion was quietly dropped.

The more obvious reason for the lack of progress was the simple fact that none of the institutions had resources to spare to devote to partnership activities. As has become even more apparent since that time, an effective research partnership is quite expensive; and the lack of an obvious source of finance for research partnership is a fundamental problem. The schools could have invested in the partnership only by taking money away from other more obviously necessary things, like teaching time, new computers or roof repairs. The School of Education could invest in the partnership only if it was clearly part of its own teaching or research obligations.

Phase 2: learning about research partnerships 1999–2002

The obvious centrality of the problem of resourcing the partnership led, in the spring of 1999, to an attempt to find at least a temporary solution to it. The Wallenberg Centre for Educational Improvement had been established in the School of Education, with the support of a generous grant from the Swedish philanthropist, Peder Wallenberg, to fund research projects concerned with transforming the nature of schools. Donald McIntyre therefore made a bid to the Centre not for funding for the partnership, but for a research project to explore the idea of schools–university research partnership. The bid was successful and underpinned the work of the partnership during this second phase. The nature of the bid made it necessary however that the main costs identified were those of investigating the partnership, not those of allowing it to work. And, although some of the costs of making the partnership operational were nonetheless embedded in the bid, the lack of funding for some of its basic work was to be a problem during the next three years.

The Wallenberg Centre funding was primarily used to fund the full-time post of project researcher (Dave Ebbutt for the first two and a half years), and the posts for one day per week of teacher research coordinators in each of the seven schools. The major questions with which the research was concerned were about whether and how such a partnership could effectively serve the research interests of both partners. Implicit in that was a question about the similarity or complementarity of these research interests. The focus was on whether the research interests (about doing and using useful educational research) of both parties could effectively be met through such partnerships. Was this a possible solution to the problems diagnosed by Hargreaves (1996) and Hillage *et al.* (1998)?

Joint research projects

One initial assumption, at least on the university side, was that the partnership would consider and jointly decide on projects of common interest proposed by any of the partners, which would then be pursued in a unified way by the university and by at least most of the schools. This turned out to be a false assumption about the main way of working of the partnership, but there are lessons to be learned from the projects that were accepted or rejected within this framework of thinking.

One early idea for research, generated by the headteacher of a school with a widely spread and diverse rural–urban catchment area, was about the resources for learning available to pupils in their home communities and about how schools could help pupils to make optimum use of these resources to complement those available to them in schools. The headteacher and one of the professors developed this idea into a research proposal, and shared it with the other schools. However, when two of the more confident headteachers pronounced the idea to be 'too academic', the proposal was abandoned. This story exemplifies well the early commitment to seeking projects based on consensus across the partnership, and also the difficulty of identifying such projects.

Another idea that did not progress far, but for a different reason, was concerned with the impact of class size on teachers' and pupils' teaching and learning strategies and on pupils' attainments. The proposal, initially made by two of the university staff, was accepted as being useful by four of the schools and was fully developed in collaboration with their TRCs. The proposal was submitted to the Economic and Social Research Council, which rated it highly but decided not to fund it. This proposal too was therefore abandoned.

One project that had a more complex fate was undertaken as part of the Consulting Pupils about Teaching and Learning Project directed by Professor Jean Rudduck as part of the national Teaching and Learning Research Programme. This particular project involved a researcher interviewing pupils about what they found helpful and unhelpful for their learning, in particular volunteer teachers' classes. The researchers then fed this information back to the teachers, exploring with them the changes that they might make to their teaching in light of the pupils' suggestions. These changes were then followed up both in the short term and six months later. With the support of their TRCs, two teachers in each of four subject departments in different schools volunteered to participate in this project.

From a partnership perspective, the important thing about this project was the sharply different evaluations of it according to different criteria. Most of the individual teachers involved in it clearly found it interesting and helpful in terms of their own professional development. The project was also successful from an academic research perspective, leading as it did to interesting conclusions and a number of well-received conference papers and written reports (Morgan 2000; Arnot *et al.* 2004; McIntyre *et al.* 2005; Pedder and McIntyre 2006). From the perspective of the TRCs, however, it was an unambiguous failure. The main problem was that the university staff were not able to analyse the data they collected quickly. In part, this was because the research officer employed for the project had to move on to a new post almost immediately after the work with the teachers and pupils had been completed. In part, however, it was because the process of rigorously analysing the data was inherently time-consuming. Two years passed before the academic findings and conclusions were available for discussion in the schools, and by then the momentum of the project in the schools had gone and those not directly involved had totally lost interest.

The partnership project that was generally the most successful, also initiated by a member of the university staff, Professor Kenneth Ruthven, and funded by the Wallenberg Centre, was concerned to identify what teachers judged to be good practice in the use of ICT in their subject teaching, to elucidate with them the grounds on which these practices were claimed to be good, and thence to seek evidence to demonstrate and test the validity of these claims (Ruthven 1999). Subject departments in six of the partnership schools and several members of the School of Education participated in the project, which achieved significant success in relation to both academic and practitioner criteria. Through the articulation of not only good practices but also rationales for these practices, and the sharing of these within and between subject departments, the schools found the project to be highly productive in terms of the professional development of staff. At the same time, useful research-based conclusions were derived and reported in academic papers (e.g. Deaney *et al.* 2003; Ruthven *et al.* 2004, 2005; Hennessy *et al.* 2005a, 2005b).

Even in this project, however, it proved difficult to create conditions under which schools and teachers would give priority not only to reviewing and renewing their own practice successfully, but also to framing and evaluating such practice in terms which would persuasively establish its wider significance and effectively support its broader dissemination. Indeed, while a follow-up study (Deaney and Hennessy, in press) confirmed that almost all of the participating teachers had disseminated their practice informally or formally within their own schools, notably within their own subject departments, often consolidating it into the departmental scheme of work, by contrast there was little dissemination beyond that particular school, even within the partnership itself. In effect, the research process was treated and valued by schools and teachers as a primarily local mechanism for developing the person-embodied and setting-embedded expertise required.

It is noteworthy that in a later contribution, Kenneth Ruthven argues for research partnerships based on more explicit recognition of the need for effective coordination of the differing and complementary global and local concerns of researchers and teachers, so as to achieve more effective 'synergy of scholarly and craft knowledge' (Ruthven 2002). This approach is reflected in a new ESRC project Exploring Teacher Mediation of Subject Learning with ICT. In this a group of teachers and researchers, most of whom have been brought into contact through the original SUPER partnership, are working collaboratively to develop this type of knowledge synergy, and to represent it through multimedia case studies (Hennessy and Deaney 2005b).

A fifth joint project was one on Thinking Skills. This was a project that the TRCs, after extensive discussion, agreed upon as one that reflected concerns of all the schools and which they wanted to pursue as a research theme in each of the schools. Considerable efforts went into sharing ideas about work in this area, including a day conference, at which Vivienne Baumfield reported on the Newcastle partnership's research on thinking skills. It was significant that this project initiated by the schools was consistently conceived as a common theme which each school would pursue independently, asking its own questions and investigating these in its own way, and then reporting back on its work to the partnership. This was reflected in the diversity across the schools, both in the importance attached to this theme and to the nature of the initiatives taken. Despite that, the theme was an important focus of common interest across the partnership over a considerable period. And the model it offered of a common theme pursued by each school in whatever way seemed most helpful and most feasible for that school set a pattern for the next phase of the partnership.

The role of the project researcher

The key figure in this phase of the research was the full-time university-based researcher, Dave Ebbutt. His primary role was to investigate, with the help of the TRCs, what kind of partnership, if any, could most effectively meet the needs of both the schools and the university. To do this, he first had to explore both the aspirations and the needs of the schools. Much of this he had to do informally, especially through conversations with the headteachers and the TRCs, in which he could explore what it was that they wanted and gauge their reaction to suggestions that he made. In addition, he conducted surveys of teacher attitudes in the partnership schools (Ebbutt 2001, 2002), demonstrating wide differences both between and within the schools. One of his conclusions was that 'the differences between the research cultures of the schools that I have been talking about look very much like developmental stages along an evolutionary path', implying that 'should schools wish to develop to the point of embracing an embedded research culture, they will need to evolve through the prior stages'. He and some of the TRCs were also able, on the basis of his research, to reach tentative conclusions about the nature of the tensions between schools and university departments that were endemic in their different cultures (Ebbutt *et al.* 2000). Dave's research role also included the substantial (but ultimately dispiriting) task of writing research proposals to a number of funding bodies so that investigation of the partnership could be continued beyond the initial three-year period.

None of the schools, however, had research cultures that were sufficiently developed for them to feel able to pursue their research agendas independently. Indeed their primary reason for wanting a relationship with the university was that they wanted the university's support for their engagement in research. There was thus a considerable demand from the schools for strategic advice and for training and support for staff. University staff, however, all had substantial teaching loads already and there was no real incentive for them to take on such tasks. The fruit-fulness of the partnership therefore depended on Dave Ebbutt undertaking this very substantial task of being a consultant, trainer and critical friend for all the schools. For example, when central government initiated its Best Practice Research Scholarship scheme, most of the TRCs found the scheme helpful for encouraging individual teachers in their schools to undertake inquiries; thereafter much of Dave's time was devoted to supporting participant teachers in planning and conducting their inquiries. He undertook such work with real commitment but also with some reluctance, since it seriously distracted him from his primary research role. This problem was exacerbated by the fact that it fell to him to do most of the planning for the regular TRC meetings and for other meetings of the whole partnership.

Partnership meetings

SUPER project team meetings took place for half a day once a month during school term time. Initially it was hoped that TRCs would take turns to host these meetings in their schools, and indeed be responsible for the agenda when their turn came round. Such arrangements did not happen because TRCs said that they valued the atmosphere and the resources of the School of Education. As the project evolved, team meetings came to involve 'housekeeping', planning for attendance and papers at conferences such as those of BERA and the European Conference on Educational Research (ECER), discussion of key research method-ology papers selected by Dave Ebbutt, discussion of important developments within the project (e.g. 'student voice' and 'thinking skills') and requests for help in the schools with data collection and other kinds of research support.

The attendance of TRCs at these regular partnership meetings was highly impressive. This was evidence not only of the commitment of the schools to the partnership, and of the individual TRCs to their roles, but also of the value that they placed on these meetings. It took some time for the university staff who attended these meetings to recognise that the motivation of the TRCs was not to plan joint research projects, and especially not to plan research with a view to generating educational knowledge for the benefit of the world at large. Instead, the motivation was to learn things that they could take back and use in and for their own schools. While full of goodwill, none of them had much energy or resources to spare to think about the needs of the wider world. Initially, the emphasis was heavily on what the schools could learn from the university; but, while this empha-sis continued, increasingly it came to be complemented by a recognition of the value of the meetings for networking purposes, with the schools learning from one another.

In addition to these team meetings, there were other meetings involving partnership headteachers or active teacher researchers. There were also research training meetings, usually in the schools, and usually with Dave Ebbutt as trainer. For example, training for potential student researchers was provided in three of the schools.

Various lessons were learned from this phase of the partnership, the most immediate and explicit of these being practical lessons about the different demanding roles to be played in the university's contribution to the partnership. Other lessons were implicitly learned and made explicit only through later reflection. One of these was that there were profound differences between and within institutions in the meanings given to 'research' or 'inquiry', but also significant difficulties in articulating these meanings and the aspirations and criteria associated with them. As partners, we were finding it difficult to communicate effectively about our varying visions. Another lesson implicitly learned, and reflected in the partnership's changing practice, was that the initial idea of a partnership that would meet both university and schools' needs was probably unrealistic. There was a gradual recognition that the partnership, if it were to be about anything, had to be about helping individual schools become, in their own terms and for their own purposes, 'researching schools'; other purposes were implicitly abandoned.

Phase 3: shifting conceptualisations of SUPER 2002–2005

The lessons learnt and the modifications that occurred throughout phase 2 of the partnership also helped to shape the subsequent period from 2002 to 2005. During this third phase of SUPER a number of additional changes took place which not only reflected these shifts in the conceptualisation of the partnership but also further influenced them. Three key developments are examined in the final section of this chapter. These are:

- effects and consequences of becoming a Networked Learning Community
- role of the faculty research critical friends
- processes supporting research in the schools and across the partnership.

During phase 3, the research interests of those university members who were actively involved in SUPER increasingly lay in understanding what might be meant by the concept of a 'researching school' and what could be done, practically, by the partner schools and the faculty, to support the development of such organisations. In particular, the schools wished to explore the nature of the relationship between practitioner research, the learning experiences of students and general school improvement. While all three elements had their place in the original aims of SUPER, over time they began to supersede the project's initial concern regarding the development of a research partnership between university staff and colleagues in schools. Implicit in this was an acceptance that a symmetrical partnership, based on collaborative research between the schools and the faculty, was not really achievable. For individual members of the faculty it seemed unlikely that SUPER was able to support their research interests. For the schools, the major attraction of the partnership was the access it provided to resources available in the university: most notably, the faculty research critical friends and other research training and related opportunities. Therefore, by 2005, members' understandings of the primary purposes of the partnership had shifted considerably from those that shaped the earlier conceptualisation of SUPER in 1997.

Against this background, meanwhile, there had been a change in the project staffing at the faculty. In 2001, as already noted, the researcher to the project, Dave Ebbutt, retired. He was replaced by Colleen McLaughlin, who took on the role of partnership coordinator and researcher, and by Kristine Black-Hawkins, who became the research officer to the project. The decision to appoint two people rather than only one was in recognition of the high demands that had been made of Dave Ebbutt as he set about conducting his own research into the work-ings of the partnership while also supporting the teachers in the SUPER schools who wished to engage in practitioner research. However, Colleen had to manage her new role in SUPER within the existing demands of being a full-time lecturer and Kristine's commitment to the project was funded part-time only (50 per cent), because the Wallenberg grant was due to end shortly.

As newly appointed partnership coordinator and research officer, Colleen and Kristine were in a position to reconsider how SUPER might be organised in the future. Furthermore, if the project were to continue beyond 2002, it was impera-tive that they sought further funding. Coincidently, a national initiative, Net-worked Learning Communities, was being launched by the government, under the auspices of the National College for School Leadership (2002). Groups of schools were invited to put forward proposals to become networks. Those that were successful would receive funding for three years, from 2002 to 2005. It was decided that SUPER would apply to become a NLC.

Effects and consequences of becoming a Networked Learning Community

The decision to put forward a proposal to become an NLC was a pragmatic one: without sufficient resources, especially to protect the time of the TRCs and the research officer, the partnership seemed unlikely to be able to continue. Those members most closely involved with the work (TRCs and headteachers in the schools, the project coordinator, the research officer and Professor Donald McIntyre at the faculty) were keen to maintain the partnership. Constructing a proposal that was agreeable to colleagues across the partnership provided a valu-able opportunity to reassess the purposes for and structures of SUPER, as well as to examine the expectations and needs of its members. Through this internal process, the conceptualisation of the partnership was redefined in ways that shaped the following three years of its existence.

In the literature produced to support the NLC initiative there was a strong emphasis on the inherent power of schools working together. David Jackson, director of the programme, noted that 'a key mantra ... [is] working smarter together, rather than harder alone' (Jackson 2002: 4). He argued that, groups of schools are able to 'provide a supportive context for risk-taking and creativity';

potentially useful conditions for practitioner research. Certainly, the scheme proved to be popular with schools in England. In 2002, the first cohort of networks were established, one of which was SUPER. By 2003, a second cohort had been established, bringing the total of networks to 110, comprising over 1,020 schools. For SUPER being part of this much larger concern led to certain advantages but also some more ambiguous consequences. For example, from the start there was tension between the primary emphasis of the NLC group on networks and networking between schools, and the existing emphasis of SUPER on research and the role of the university working in partnership with the schools.

As a result of writing the proposal to become an NLC, a number of collective decisions were made by key members of the partnership, regarding the strengthening of existing, and the development of new, structures and roles. How each was interpreted and made use of over the following three years, inevitably varied from school to school and details of these differences can be found in the case study chapters. An important decision was that the role of TRCs should be maintained and that the funding from the NLC group should primarily be used to continue their work. Another decision made at this time was the establishment of a student voice coordinator in each school to support the work of the TRCs. In the university, a new role of critical friend for each school was formulated, to share out and to develop work done largely by the university researcher up until that point. Five members of the faculty formed a critical friends' group, researching and working with either one or two schools each.

A major requirement of the NLC group was that teachers in networking schools should engage in practitioner research and, therefore, the proposal to become a NLC was expected to outline which structures were to be put into place to support this. For SUPER this provided a clear consistency with its existing purposes. However, it also contributed to the gradual shift away from a research partnership *between* the schools and the university and towards *practice-based* research and a research *schools* partnership, with the university more clearly in a supporting role only. Such changes are evident in the proposal put to the NLC group in the spring of 2002, in which neither the university nor the faculty is mentioned by name in the section outlining the aims of SUPER (see extract from proposal below).

The SUPER partnership had the following aims:
- observe, describe and document, analyse, interpret, conceptualise, understand and report on the processes, outcomes and effects of the practice-based research work undertaken within the evolving partnership
- concentrate, as a priority, on questions about understanding how a systemic research culture might be created within and across the Research Schools Partnership
- compare issues that arise from within the Research Schools Partnership with those being reported from partnership projects elsewhere
- use developing understandings of the processes and outcomes of the work

undertaken within the Research Schools Partnership to facilitate its constructive development

- disseminate the outcomes of the practice-based research work of the Research Schools Partnership as widely as possible by appropriate means.

Looking back, it is likely that this shift of emphasis was partly pragmatic. The proposal would probably be more successful in acquiring funding from the NLC if teacher and school research was highlighted rather than academic research in the university. However, it also reflected what the TRCs and headteachers generally wanted at that stage and subsequently. That is, their primary concern was with how practitioner research might support the improvement of teaching and learning in their individual schools.

The demands of the proposal also led to a rethinking of how school-based research might be organised across the partnership. Three interconnected research themes were chosen by the TRCs, headteachers and members of the faculty. These were:

- independence in learning, for students and staff
- the development of student voice in learning and the use of evidence
- learning about leadership

During phase 2 of SUPER efforts to engage the partnership as a whole in more focused collaborative research had generally not been successful. Therefore these research themes were constructed to be deliberately broad, providing teachers, students and schools with opportunities to research specific areas which were relevant to their particular contexts. The intention was that this degree of flexibility would allowed scope for connections to be made across the partnership but without constraining research choices. For example, the theme of student voice was developed in one school so as to gather students' feedback on teaching and learning across the curriculum; in another school it became a key process by which to gather evidence in any research undertaken there; in yet another, it informed the reasoning behind the introduction of a programme of students as researchers.

Such flexibility in the research themes not only took into account the different contexts of the schools but also provided some opportunities for learning across the partnership. For example, the varied approaches to student voice (already noted) were discussed in cross-partnership meetings in terms of the substantive issues with which they engaged and also the research processes involved. The open nature of the themes, however, also brought some disadvantages. Because the schools were generally involved in such disparate research activities and ones which were so firmly related to their specific contexts, there was little evidence of research from one school affecting the policies and practices taking place in others. That is, it was clearly more straightforward for individuals to learn from each other's research than to transfer such learning from one institution to another (Fielding *et al.* 2005). Furthermore, the expectation that the flexibility of the research themes would encourage joint research to take place across the partnership proved not to be realistic.

Thus, becoming a NLC and part of a national project was advantageous for the partnership for two main reasons: first, doing so secured some funding for the partnership for a further three years, and second, it offered an important opportunity to reassess the purposes and structural organisation of SUPER. However, both of these were concerned with the partnership's internal arrangements only. Joining a national network inevitably brought other advantages and responsibilities on a broader scale. For example, the NLC group provided a substantial amount of resources specifically related to practitioner research as well as to school improvement more generally, including a range of training opportunities, publications and support materials. Various members of SUPER, from the schools and the faculty, made use of these.

A more ambitious but nevertheless central aim of the NLC group was to promote learning not only within individual networks but also between them on a national scale. There was an expectation that teachers in NLCs would have access to, and benefit from, the work of teachers in other NLCs across England. This necessarily required that all teachers made their work similarly accessible. The work of writers such as David Hargreaves was influential, around this time, in shaping these aspirations. He suggested that national networks offered highly effective large-scale opportunities for engaging both with and in school-based research. He argued that their primary purpose, however, should not be to support the work of individual teachers, schools or even networks, but rather to provide a critical means by which radical innovation could take place, thereby eventually bringing about a systemic transformation of UK education (Hargreaves 2003). However, these large-scale and longer term aims did not directly influence the work of SUPER. The concerns of members were shaped by the specific context of their individual schools and when they chose to engage in collaborative learning with colleagues from other institutions this took place almost entirely within the local domain of the partnership rather than across the national structures provided by the NLC group. Even then, as noted earlier, such learning was generally between individuals and groups rather than institutions.

As part of the NLC group's strategy every network, including SUPER, was expected to contribute to its national programme of research. This entailed activities such as attending conferences, completing questionnaires and providing substantial archived evidence of the success of work undertaken as a network. There was a strong element of compulsion in many of these activities. They formed part of the NLC contract agreed by networks and the continuation of funding over the three years was conditional on their proper completion. However, these external demands caused resentment among some members of SUPER who considered some of the tasks to be time consuming and an unnecessary distraction from the research that they wanted to do.

Role of the faculty research critical friends

The formation of a group of five research critical friends, in the autumn of 2002, was an important development for the partnership. The reasons for this decision are described in Chapter 10, the case study of the faculty. It is, of course, not unusual for academics in education faculties to work with schools as institutions, particularly when teachers are engaged in practitioner research; see, for example, the Coalition of Knowledge Building Schools in Australia (Groundwater-Smith and Mockler 2002) and the TTA supported research consortia in England (Cordingley and Bell 2002). In both these projects, and like SUPER, the role of members from the universities has been a dual one: to be *supporters* of the research taking place in the schools as well as to be *researchers* of the processes and effects of that research on the schools. Both aspects of the role have been beneficial to the schools and to the critical friends, although maintaining a balance between them has also brought some tensions to the relationships.

As discussed earlier, prior to 2002, efforts to increase the numbers of faculty staff involved in SUPER had met with mixed success. Therefore, one of the intentions of forming a research critical friends' group was to provide a structure by which this could more easily happen. The function of individual critical friends was considered, with each partnership school being allocated a single named person from the faculty rather than the project coordinator and the research officer working generally across all the schools. However, an unintended consequence of this decision was a further shift in SUPER away from the idea of members of the schools and the faculty researching together in partnership, and towards members of the faculty exploring how schools develop as researching institutions. From 2002, the research role of a critical friend was described in terms of developing a case study of each school, plus providing some research support to colleagues in the school; that is, the role of critical friend was more clearly focused on the school than on the partnership as a whole. The following notes from the first critical friends' meeting (December 2002) illustrate this.

> The role of a critical friend is primarily a research one. It is intended to support/shape the research activities of Faculty members who might choose to make a systematic case study of a single school in terms of understanding what it means to attempt to be a 'researching' school ... At the same time the Faculty member should also take on a supportive role: asking helpful questions, channelling Faculty resources, etc.

This interpretation of the role was strengthened further because, although critical friends were welcomed, they were not expected to attend most partnership meetings and activities. Although this pragmatic decision was entirely justifiable because of pressures of time on critical friends, its effect was to sharpen the focus of their research onto the case studies of the schools as individual institutions. In this way the majority of the research undertaken examined the research taking place in each school and much less on understanding the significance of the research partnership as a whole. Only the roles of the partnership coordinator and researcher continued to have this broader scope.

Describing how the role of research critical friend has been made use of in SUPER is further complicated because each of the five faculty staff have, understandably, undertaken their responsibilities in slightly different ways, drawing on their own research strengths and interests. Similarly, the specific contexts, expectations and needs of the individual schools have necessarily make their own demands. Even those critical friends who have worked with two schools rather than only one have undertaken their roles somewhat differently in each of their schools. Furthermore, these variations have been perceived among the group of critical friends as an opportunity to examine understandings and purposes of the role itself (see, for example, Black-Hawkins 2003). The case studies of the schools in Chapters 2 to 9 help to illustrate the range of interpretations of the role.

Despite these differences it has been possible to identify key characteristics of the work of critical friends within SUPER. Indeed, these are comparable to findings made by others examining similar roles in schools (see Costa and Killick 1993; MacBeath *et al.* 2000; Doherty *et al.* 2001; Swaffield 2002). They argue that critical friends should be trustworthy; ask demanding and pertinent questions; find out about the school; actively support its development; provide an outsider's perspective. Even though these authors do not refer specifically to *research* critical friends there are clear correlations. Critical friends in SUPER have aimed to be 'trustworthy' (an expectation of any *researcher*); they have set out to ask 'demanding and pertinent questions' about the school's *research*; they have endeavoured to 'find out about' the *research* taking place; they have 'actively supported' the 'development' of such *research*; and by the nature of their position they have 'provided an outsider's perspective' on that *research*. These various aspects of the role are illustrated in the following comment by the headteacher of Sharnbrook School when reflecting on the work of the research critical friend.

> You're getting into the school, you get to meet the people ..., you're asking the right questions, you're coming to the steering group meetings, you're supporting the research and I think you're gaining an awareness of what we're actually about and what we're doing ... You're a link with other schools ... and because you're in a different position, you are able to watch us and see how we work.

There is little doubt, among members of the partnership, that the development of the research critical friend role during the third phase of its history has been highly beneficial for members of the schools and the critical friends themselves. The description of the role in the case study of Sharnbrook School, illustrates the potential of these mutual advantages. Most notably, the schools have welcomed the research support they have received and the critical friends have valued the access they have had to the everyday workings of a school.

There has also been evidence of tensions in the role. Indeed, it is implicit in the name itself: just how critical do we actually want our friends to be? Other key questions that have arisen over the last three years concern the nature of the relationship between members of the school and the critical friend. In her own research with schools, Baumfield (2001) describes a situation which corresponds to SUPER in some ways, in which critical friends may be assigned roles with which they feel uncomfortable; for example, when those from universities are ascribed the status of research '*experts*' by teachers when they would rather be perceived of as research partners. A practical difficulty for critical friends has been finding a balance which is acceptable to the school, between supporting the schools' research and undertaking their own. Particularly, in the earlier stages of the relationship there was a need for the critical friend to be supportive of the school, so as to build the trust and commitment required in the relationship.

Finally, another tension has been that the critical friends were, in effect, researching the impact of themselves, across the project as well as within individual schools, although the work of Vivienne Baumfield (see Chapter 10) was deliberately set up to provide an outsider's perspective. Nevertheless, as relationships developed it may have become more difficult for members of schools to comment impartially about the role of their faculty colleagues. Similarly, it may have been less straightforward for critical friends to maintain their critical stance as researchers, as they became increasingly committed to the work in their schools.

Processes supporting research in the schools and across the partnership

From its inception, a clear purpose of SUPER has been to support research to take place within individual member schools as well as across the partnership between schools and the university. To fulfil this aim a number of processes, structures and activities had been established which were further developed during the period of 2002 to 2005. Two particular contributions during these three years have already been discussed: first, the national support provided by the NLC group, and second, the expansion and restructuring of the role of research critical friend. However, a range of other research opportunities was also provided.

The TRCs were central to this work within the individual schools. They continued to develop their roles during this time and were increasingly able to provide research coaching and advice to colleagues in their schools, although the extent of this support varied from school to school. It was partly dependent on individual TRC's level of skills and partly on the time made available to them to work with colleagues. These differences were exacerbated in those schools where TRCs left and new ones understandably took time to develop their research expertise. As already discussed, research skills training was also provided by critical friends within their allocated schools. This took a number of forms: for example, supporting newly appointed TRCs and SVCs, training students as researchers, presenting research at staff development days, offering advice at school steering group meetings, and supporting the work of TRCs and SVCs.

All critical friends also acted as research mentors to those teachers who had been successfully awarded Best Practice Research Scholarships through the DfES's national scheme. Indeed, the role of the BPRS became increasingly important to the partnership as it provided additional funding directly to the schools which teachers could use to buy time and/or resources for individual research. The faculty also gained financially as the costs of mentoring were covered and this money helped to maintain the post of the research officer. For the last cohort of BPRS holders, in SUPER schools, research support was developed further. Teachers continued to receive mentoring from their critical friend in their own school but in addition they were invited to join a research training group at the faculty, which met half-termly. Not only did this provide a more efficient use of faculty's staff time; it also offered teachers the opportunity to work collaboratively with colleagues from their own school as well as others in the partnership. Unfortunately for SUPER, the BPRS scheme came to an end in 2004. In its final year, thirty-four teachers in the partnership were awarded scholarships amounting to some £68,000 in total. The loss of this funding was important to schools and the faculty, illustrating the recurring link between resources and the development of practitioner research.

Finally, existing structures and arrangements were revised and new ones introduced during this third phase of SUPER, all of which were intended to encourage colleagues from across the schools and the faculty to work together in more collaborative ways. A series of meetings were established and details of these can be found in Chapter 1. For example, TRCs continued to meet each half-term and the partnership's external steering group met on a termly basis. Various opportunities for SVCs to work together as a group were introduced but these efforts were less successful largely because, unlike their TRC colleagues, SVCs were not funded by their schools to have regular non-contact time. Eventually it was decided to invite SVCs to attend TRC meetings and, for a variety of reasons, this seemed to work well. If a SVC was unable to be present s/he could find out from the TRC what had taken place. Also, in some schools (for example, Arthur Mellows) the two roles were fulfilled by one person anyway. Furthermore, joint meetings encouraged TRCs and SVCs to work more closely together.

During this third phase of SUPER three key additions were made to the programme of meetings. Although all quite different in terms of their substantive purposes, together they helped to develop further a sense of community across the partnership, primarily in terms of strengthening communication, trust and collaboration among those who attended. First, a twenty-four-hour conference took place at the end of each summer term, attended by all TRCs, SVCs, headteachers and critical friends. The overall aim of these was to evaluate the progress of research within each school and across the partnership, as well as to discuss future aspirations and intentions, thus providing important opportunities for both celebration and reflection. Second, a number of Teaching and Learning Days were set up to give opportunities for all members of SUPER (teachers, students and faculty members) to present and discuss their research findings and concerns. Although the numbers attending from each school varied, mainly because of individual schools' timetabling constraints, the demand for these meetings was consistently high. Finally, a series of termly meetings for headteachers were introduced. Attendance at these was also mixed: some headteachers were nearly always present while others rarely came. However, for those who were regular attenders, the meetings seemed to both reflect and sustain their commitment to the partnership work.

Reflecting on phase 3 and the future of SUPER

In some ways, the period between 2002 and 2005 could be regarded as a particularly successful period for the partnership. During these three years, SUPER flourished in terms of developing structures and processes that successfully supported practitioner research in the schools. Most of the schools, in diverse ways and to varying degrees, had strengthened their research or inquiry cultures. This book reflects the university team's sustained efforts to document and to understand the various problems and opportunities the schools encountered when seeking to become researching schools. It is true that there had been a significant change in, at least, the faculty's aspirations since the partnership was initiated in 1997. By 2002 the earlier efforts to plan consensual research projects, that would meet the faculty's research productivity criteria as well of those of the schools, had been implicitly abandoned.

Thus, the relationship of the faculty with the schools had shifted from attempting to research in partnership with them towards providing a research support service. While this had been highly valued by the teacher researchers, it had not contributed greatly to the research agendas of the faculty members involved and far less to other members of the faculty. Furthermore, the individual schools had understandably been more concerned with their own particular research needs than with those of others and therefore had not really been motivated to undertake collaborative research of any significance across the schools. None of this, however, should be seen as indicative of any kind of failure. Instead, it can more helpfully be understood as reflecting the partnership's learning about the kind of research partnership that, in present circumstances, can most usefully be developed between a university faculty of education and a group of schools.

In this case study chapter and indeed, throughout the book, a number of reasons are given for why this shift had occurred. Further explanation is also provided by considering more recent developments in SUPER. From October 2005 a new Masters degree has been established as a joint initiative between the faculty and the SUPER schools, with the overall aim of developing and sustaining the use and generation of practitioner research. Its first cohort comprises two teachers from each of the SUPER schools. Like many other Masters degrees in education, the course is designed to support the development of each teacher's research expertise and knowledge. However, it also sets out to develop their skills to become 'research coaches' so that they are able to help a group of teachers in their school to undertake a collaborative research project. Furthermore, there is a clear expectation that any such research must contribute to the development of the school as an institution and not only support the individual professional needs and interests of the teacher researchers. Therefore decisions about what research should take place in each school are to be negotiated with its senior management team. In addition, the schools have decided to maintain the role of the TRC and the faculty has agreed to continue to provide a critical friend to each school, who will also act as the supervisor to teachers on the Masters course.

It has been clear from the start that the SUPER project is unsustainable without some funding; however, it has never been obvious from what source such funding might best be derived. In contrast, the Masters course has provided a straight-forward set of arrangements which is understood by both the schools and the faculty in terms of its financial and organisational structures. Put simply, the schools pay the fees for teachers to attend the course and in return the faculty provides the teaching. An undoubted strength of this current phase of SUPER is that the partnership is now no longer forced to seek external funding. And, while the Masters course signals an acceptance of the established role of the university as a provider of continuing professional development services, it also offers a innovative structure which will allow the partnership schools to continue to develop as researching institutions.

Chapter 12

Learning from stories of researching schools

Colleen McLaughlin and Keith S. Taber

This chapter will focus on one of the primary purposes of the partnership, which was to develop and sustain research activities in the schools. It will explore the question, 'What have we learned about schools' attempts to go beyond individual teacher research and to engage in generating research-based knowledge to inform practice?' This purpose cannot be neatly distinguished from the other purposes for the work which took place within the partnership; however, we will aim to maintain a focus in this chapter on the schools and in the next on the partnership. The chapter begins with an exploration of motivations and conceptions of research, then it explores what kinds of research and research knowledge were found to be useful and valued, what the issues were around knowledge creation and dissemination, how the activity was developed and sustained, and the claims made for the impact on teachers and pupils; finally, it ends with the achievements of and challenges faced by the schools.

Why engage in research? Why in this particular partnership?

Within the partner schools the participants held different views and hopes. Equally many of them changed their minds as the enterprise progressed. For some there was a hope that engaging in research would easily answer questions or quickly clarify matters of practice. There was initially some frustration at the pace of the work and awareness of complexity was a necessary part of the process. The pressure of modern policy makers and timescales meant that there was some small hope that evidence-based practice might provide quick fixes. This was dispelled for many in the case study schools and in schools, such as Soham Village College, there was an adjustment of time scales.

Others adopted a Stenhousian position (Stenhouse 1975), arguing for a research model of curriculum development and one that had teachers as researchers at its centre. This was also connected to a view of teacher professionalism and teachers as learners that Stenhouse (1975) had also articulated. Many teachers and headteachers emphasised the professional development capacity of engaging in research; in fact many saw it as the prime purpose. Others conceived of the enterprise as Hargreaves (1999) had done, that is, they wanted the school to create knowledge that could inform policy and practice. They aimed to go beyond individual teachers as researchers to whole school engagement and use of knowledge created in the school.

All were clear that it had to be focused on teaching, learning and school improvement. They were not interested in knowledge creation per se but in making a difference to the classrooms and students in their schools. It is exemplified in this quotation from the headteacher of St Ivo School:

> I'm not here just to be a research department. I'm not in that business, these kids are too important. I want to be certain that they get direct benefit in a learning sense that values them and makes them feel part of it all.

Although all were agreed that research should improve and inform practice, there were differences of view on how it related to school policy and in their view of the school's role and responsibility in disseminating the school generated knowledge more widely; this will be returned to in a later section. There is also some movement visible in many of the schools. A movement from individual teachers researching their practice to a more orchestrated enterprise connected to departmental or school agendas. There was also in two of the schools a decision not to continue within the partnership, although in both cases the espoused support of teacher research continued.

In all of the case study schools, joining the partnership was part of a history of engagement with the Faculty of Education and this will be explored further in this chapter, but the reasons for engaging in research within this particular partnership were connected to the perceived benefits of working with the faculty and the other schools.

How was 'research' conceived?

Of course, as discussed in Chapter 1, there are different notions both of what research is in a school context, and the type of research or knowledge-creation that it is appropriate for schools to aspire to (e.g. McIntyre 2005). There is an ongoing national debate on this topic (cf. Brown 2005; Furlong and Oancea 2005) and while the debate is far from crystallised, three credible positions seem to be visible. One is that the same standards (constantly under debate as they properly are) for valid research-based knowledge generated in an academic context should be applied to any such knowledge, irrespective of whoever generates it or in whatever context. A second is that taken by Stenhouse (1975), suggesting that teachers can and should do research to examine ideas critically for their own practice, without any necessary aspiration or obligation to provide evidence to persuade others of the validity of their research conclusions. The third and less adequately formulated as yet, is that described by Hargreaves (1999) as Mode 2 knowledge creation, which needs to meet many practical standards as well as academic standards, which can be legitimately and effectively disseminated only in local contexts, but which therefore perhaps does not need to meet criteria of external validity or relevance to non-local contexts.

In the SUPER schools the understandings of what research is range over a wide territory. Some activities perceived as 'research' in some of the case study schools may well have been considered as something else – development, sharing practice, consultation etc. – in other schools, and even in other schools within the partnership. This is an important issue, as there are clearly a range of standpoints that might lead to different views as to what counts as legitimate 'research': those of the individual practitioners, the school as an institution, the higher education partner, the funding agency or some other person or organisation. All the stakeholders have a legitimate view and may have different professional priorities and interests.

There is a very real debate about the role of the teacher as researcher, and some of the SUPER schools aspired to be Researching Schools (Soham Village College); for others it was enough to be a Thinking or an Inquiring School (Arthur Mellows Village College) or 'a school of collaborative reflective practitioners' (Queen Elizabeth's Girls' School). What could be said is that all the active partners, such as the TRCs, the headteachers and the critical friends, would probably support this statement of Nisbet's:

> research has become part of every professional role today, and in education one task of professional development is to weave a research element into the expertise of teachers, leading them to adopt at a personal level the self-questioning approach which leads to reflection and understanding, and from there into action.
>
> (Nisbet 2005: 43)

How the schools engaged with the notion of weaving 'a research element into the expertise of teachers' varied. Some conceived of this as letting individual practitioners engage in inquiry into aspects of classroom practice according to their own agenda along the BPRS model (and this was by far the most common); some saw it as positively encouraging individuals to engage in research and inquiry; some saw it as integrating an element of evidence collection into the evaluative aspects of teaching and learning; some saw it as groups of teachers, often within departments, working to increase subject-based knowledge; and some saw it as inquiry into a whole school theme, for example recall or thinking skills.

What we do see in the stories of many of the schools that have been longstanding members of the partnership is that as they engage with this issue, there is a movement from individual teachers as researchers to some form of collaboration on and orchestration of the research effort. So for example in Arthur Mellows, Chesterton and Comberton there is a move to work on themes or in departments and to coordinate the efforts more. This will be discussed more fully in the section on development and sustainability. It does seem to suggest a shift in the perception of the role and purpose of research activity in the school.

The other possible generalisation to make here is that in all the schools the key drivers of the activity saw a connection between teachers engaging in research, teachers as learners and classroom and school improvement. This connection is one which current and past research shows to be an important one. Stenhouse (1975) argued that teachers would only engage *with* research by engaging *in* research and this seems to be case in many of the stories here. The findings from the Teacher Training Agency's School-based Research Consortium Initiative (Simons *et al.* 2003) and ESRC Teaching and Learning Research Project both show that

> Many teachers did find that engaging in research themselves was a prerequisite for engaging in a meaningful way *with* research carried out by other people.
>
> (Simons *et al.* 2003: 353)

> the improvement of pupil learning often implies that there will be changes in classroom practice, and such changes only occur where teacher have learned.
>
> (Brown 2005: 389)

Just as there were variations in terms of how research was conceived between the schools, so there was variation within the schools. Not all teachers saw undertaking research as part of their role, which is not surprising. There are certainly many examples in the case study chapters where teachers not only embrace research, but also consider it to be either an essential part of their professional work, or a desirable extra, special activity that keeps them engaged in the job. However, these voices represent some of those who have already become engaged, and there are many other inaudible voices in the SUPER schools – inaudible because they had little to say about research and are not directly represented in the chapters. Where the schools have been successful at involving many teachers (such as at Sharnbrook, St Ivo, Chesterton and at Queen Elizabeth's Girls' School) and keeping them involved (less true at QEGS), they have persuaded them by one means or another that research *is*, or at least *could be*, a core activity for a schoolteacher. Other teachers have been happy to undertake research for a while, perhaps through the BPRS scheme, but see this as a special, 'one-off' activity rather than a part of developing professionalism.

There are also many examples of teachers lacking confidence in applying the term 'research' to what they are doing. The case of Diane at St Ivo is an example of a teacher who does not initially incorporate the notion of researcher into her identity and is very reluctant to give her inquiry work that label. But this changes: her identity as a teacher researcher changes as she engages with her own research, although this is not the case for all who engage in research activity. Nor is it necessarily the case that this is connected to the conditions created for the teachers in the school. However, there is some evidence that the climate created in the school impacts on whether the teachers do come to see inquiry, reflection and research as part of their identify and part of the legitimate work of a teacher.

What kinds of research knowledge were found to be useful and valued?

The relationship between research and practice is the subject of much debate (see Brown 2005) and in the SUPER partnership this is also the case. In engaging with this question, McIntyre (2005: 361) offers a continuum 'along which several different kinds of knowledge, each with its own distinctive purposes and discipline, may be ordered'. His continuum is this:

1   Craft knowledge for classroom teaching
2   Articulation of craft knowledge
3   Deliberative or reflective thinking for classroom teaching
4   Classroom action research
5   Knowledge generated by research schools and networks
6   Practical suggestions for teaching based on research
7   Reviews of research on particular themes
8   Research findings and conclusions.

McIntyre emphasises that this is a continuum, that 'a good deal of knowledge and thinking will fall between the points identified on the continuum' and 'more is understood about the more extreme points than is yet understood about the middle points' (McIntyre 2005: 362). In the SUPER schools we see that the schools are operating largely within the first four points of the continuum with some attempts to go into the realm of knowledge creation by a school and a network, although this is limited and found to be much more challenging.

In the SUPER schools, classroom action research is the form of knowledge creation that seems to be the most common and the easiest to achieve. It is where many of the schools focused their early efforts. The teachers involved saw this form of research as profitable and relevant. This work had the characteristics of Stenhouse's teacher-as-researcher approach to curriculum development. He argued that it involved teachers taking a research stance: 'By a research stance I mean a disposition to examine one's own practice critically and systematically' (1975: 156). As McIntyre (2005: 368) reminds us, this does not mean that 'the teacher needs to achieve the objectivity of an external observer, since the teacher is first and foremost an interested actor. What is needed is "a sensitive and self-critical subjective perspective" which is difficult enough' (Stenhouse 1975: 157). The teachers in the SUPER schools who engaged in research can be said to fulfil these criteria.

Although many of the schools now aspire to knowledge generation as a school and network, two of the schools (Soham Village College and Sharnbrook School) set out with this as an explicit aim. Sharnbrook had developed a method of engaging all staff in research when David Jackson was the headteacher. This had had a range of effects and has since been modified but continues to be seen as a central school improvement strategy. Soham in particular drew on the notion of

Hargreaves' (1999) 'knowledge-creating school' and therefore they approach the task of 'weaving a research element into the expertise of teachers' (Nisbet 2005) in a different way. Howard Gilbert, headteacher of Soham Village College, had had experience in his previous school of the individual teacher-as-researcher model, had seen it as very powerful, and wished to develop it by moving to a new model of departments generating knowledge on teaching and learning to be used by the whole school. This had necessitated a different approach and will be explored further later on. A shift from classroom action research to generating knowledge as a school does in these cases involve thinking differently about the processes of knowledge creation and dissemination.

So we see in these cases research being used to assist the reflection on and decision-making at different levels of the schools: individual teachers making decisions in their own classrooms; departments reflecting upon practice and making decisions at departmental level; and in some cases research being used to inform whole school policy on aspects of teaching and learning.

Collaborative research

There were some, albeit few, examples of collaborative research in the partnership. In the early stages of SUPER the schools did collaborate on a 'thinking skills' project but this came to be seen as limiting to the schools' particular agendas, and so wider themes were adopted as umbrellas for the research being undertaken, i.e. the themes of the development of independence in teaching and learning and the development of the student voice. There were also examples of collaborative research projects with university colleagues, e.g. the Technology Integrated Pedagogic Strategies (TIPS) project (referred to in the Chesterton case study in Chapter 3). Currently in SUPER there is an attempt to harness the collective learning and move on from that, but this is in its very early stages. This book is an example of research at the 'research findings and conclusions' end of the spectrum, but overall the work in the schools has largely been confined to individual teachers or schools.

Valuing and accessing the knowledge of students

Across most of the case study schools, the engagement with students' knowledge is seen as very powerful and useful. In two of the schools this came to be viewed as the most important form of research work and took precedence over teacher research. It often involved the development of students as researchers. There were different reasons for it being viewed as valuable. It was connected to principles of democratic rights and inclusion, it was seen as a powerful tool to aid teacher research and it was seen as a potent force for curriculum reform and teacher reflection. However, it was also seen as a controversial activity in some of the schools and one that might engender fear of scrutiny in some teachers. In another case it appears to have been seen as a safer alternative than teachers engaging in research. It is deeply connected to the history, values and context of each particular school.

Using others' research findings

The last three kinds of activity in McIntyre's (2005) continuum are largely concerned with engaging with research undertaken by others or accessing what is already 'known' or speculated upon by others. Within the partnership there are examples of university-based researchers working with the teachers in the schools in very profitable ways, such as the TIPS project, which was conducted in all but one of the partnership schools. Some schools had engaged in similar projects with members of the faculty prior to SUPER, e.g. the ARTE project in St Ivo. In some cases these collaborative ventures seem to have been a catalyst for the schools to develop teachers as researchers. There were few examples of this sort of collaboration being initiated by the schools; rather these were mostly university-initiated projects and the majority of these examples were prior to 2002, although in some of the schools the early work continues. There are also examples of the writings of others or research findings being highly influential in shaping the beginning or form of a project undertaken by the school or teacher. The work of Mike Hughes (1999) on brain research and teaching and learning was very influential for example in Soham Village College. In Sharnbrook the Cognitive Acceleration in Science Education project, which continues there, drew on the work of Adey and Shayer (1994). There have been examples of the schools asking for and receiving the findings of research reviews at SUPER conferences. For example, Mary James reported on the results of the TLRP Learning How to Learn project at the 2005 annual residential conference of SUPER. The critical friends were also a conduit and a resource in providing schools with examples of research or reviews of in relevant areas. However, overall the SUPER schools did not see themselves as operating at this end of McIntyre's continuum.

Knowledge creation and dissemination

The majority of the teachers did not usually see their primary purpose as contributing to more than their own knowledge and understanding of their own practice in their own classrooms. They were not driven to write for the wider public audience, although many did and found it professionally interesting and confidence building: BPRS required that teachers wrote up their work to a set framework. It is possible to speculate on the reasons for this. First, the teachers were interested in creating 'local knowledge' (Cochran-Smith and Lytle 2001: 51) or as Stenhouse put it, they saw the audience as 'the village' not 'the world' (Stenhouse 1981). It is also debatable as to whether many of the teachers saw their purpose as sharing it with the 'village' of the school community at all; many saw only themselves as the audience for the research. In the schools where dissemination and working with departmental or other colleagues was built into the model, they often found the shift from working for themselves, with the support of a critical friend, to working with colleagues a challenging one.

As stated in Chapter 1, Stenhouse (1975) saw the social and psychological climate of teaching as a barrier to teacher research since close examination of practice is threatening and therefore requires support. He saw these as major issues in the development of research in schools. 'I conclude that the main barriers to teachers assuming the role of researchers studying their own teaching in order to improve it are psychological and social' (1975: 159). This is borne out here. The teachers often found that collaborative critical dialogue was not a usual feature of the school life, although this is one of the reported changes as the culture around research changed in many of the schools. However, the initial engagement with colleagues was challenging, as well as extremely exciting and profitable. Teachers feared that they would be perceived as setting themselves up as experts and some were nervous when they went wider in sharing their findings with colleagues, as is reported in the Soham case study. This is not at all surprising since, as many have found, this type of collaboration is not necessarily a normal feature of life in schools. The culture of performance and accountability that is so prevalent in the English educational system (cf. Jeffrey 2002; Watkins 2005) is currently a barrier to the open exploration of complexity and ideas surrounding any research enterprise.

Does it matter that teachers did not feel compelled to write up and share their research findings? Stenhouse's (1979) definition of research as 'systematic enquiry made public' is widely used as a definition of research. However, in his later work he reviewed the public element. Stenhouse (1981: 103) defined research as 'systematic self-critical enquiry'. In reviewing his 'simple earlier definition of research', he argued that it was not the publication of the work that was important but the critical scrutiny that the work undergoes. 'Unpublished work does not profit by criticism. What seems to me most important is that research becomes part of a community of critical discourse' (Stenhouse 1981: 111). He argued that research work should be subject to critical scrutiny, for this would enhance its quality, and that it should be disseminated to the village or the critical community of which the researcher is a member, not necessarily to the world. The degree to which the teachers could be said to be a member of a community of critical discourse varied considerably and there were a range of settings in which teachers worked. Some were members of research groups who, often with the support of the critical friend from the university, debated the processes and outcomes of their research work. Others worked on their own with the critical friend and TRCs supporting them. Some worked completely alone. The teachers valued the opportunity to work in groups and to share the findings with other interested colleagues, although the opportunity to do this varied among the schools.

Dissemination

There were limited opportunities created across the partnership to share the findings of work being undertaken in the schools. There was an annual Teaching and Learning conference where all those engaged in research in the schools were invited to share and hear of each other's projects. However to release all these staff was very demanding of schools' resources. The partnership had a website on which accounts of the research, known as SUPER sheets, were posted but this was not an easy process and one which the partnership struggled with. A framework for writing up these projects, which was developed by Kristine Black-Hawkins, was found to be useful. This framework appears in Box 12.1.

Box 12.1 Template for SUPER sheets

Each sheet to be no more than four sides of A4 or approximately 2,000 words.

Its purpose is to address the What?, Why? and How? of research plus a summary of findings.

You may have more to say under some headings than others.

General information
- Research question(s) or title of project.
- Name of school.
- Name of contact person (plus telephone number).

The aims of the research
- What did you want to find out?
- And why?
- What was the main focus in terms of student groups, curriculum area, etc.?

The methods you used to gather evidence
- What information did you need to address your research question(s)?
- How did you collect it?
- Who did you involve and how?
- What was the timeline for your research?

The outcomes of the research
- What did you find out about the substantive issues of the research?
- What impact has the research had on practice in your school?
- What did you learn about the methods you used?

Dissemination of research findings
- With whom did you share your findings?

Within the schools various strategies were employed to disseminate the research. In some of the case study schools there was a harnessing of the existing forms of communication and the development of new ones to this end. The range of strategies included regular research sections in staff bulletins, specific research reports, the development of research sections on school websites, e.g. www.soham college.org.uk/knowledgecreation. Many of the schools have latterly used staff development occasions to share and debate the research being undertaken in the schools, although this has not been as developed as fully as it might have been.

Engaging with the issues of research quality

The idea of critical discourse is that through such debates the quality of the work will be examined and the quality enhanced. This debate about the quality of research work, including teacher research, is currently of great interest. Furlong and Oancea (2005) comment:

> While there may be great interest in them, there is an even greater disagreement as to how they should be defined and therefore how they might be assessed. Any quality standards for applied and practice-based research must therefore take into account the multitude of forms and aims that they can serve.
>
> (Furlong and Oancea 2005: 8)

Within the partnership schools there were some limited examples of practitioners wrestling with this question. In Soham Village College they engaged with it over time and proposed three criteria for their research: 'The validation of the knowledge was seen as coming from three sources. It was a triangle of teacher experience and reflection; data on pupil outcomes; and data on the pupils' experience and attitudes. This was seen as giving it credibility' (Soham case study). These criteria are different from the conventional ones used to validate academic knowledge. They are criteria for judging and learning about the effectiveness of teaching practices. They are persuasive to this end but they indicate a shift from validating knowledge to validating practices of teaching. In other schools there is not such a visible debate. In the Sharnbrook case study, the conclusion reached is:

> At Sharnbrook, the balance between the *act* of engaging in research (how *being* a researcher is a form of professional development) and the pursuit and establishment of robust *findings* (evidence-based practice) fluctuates depending on the intentions and needs of the researcher(s) and the school. This is partly, but not always, related to whether the research is primarily concerned with the improvement of *individual teachers* or across the *wider school*. If the latter, however, it is probably even more critical that research is of a robust nature.

So there is some evidence that some of the schools have begun to differentiate purposes and to apply different criteria according to the primary purposes. Accessibility, relevance to practice, manageability and usefulness were key criteria for the teachers' judgements about their own and others' research. It is also clear that for many of the schools, the engagement with colleagues from the university was seen as part of the process of making the research more rigorous.

How was it developed and sustained?

This section will explore how the schools developed and sustained their research activity in collaboration with the university. Three key concepts are put forward as helpful in understanding the development and sustainability of teacher research in this section: alignment; critical mass; structures and support.

First, it is important to say that there is a development visible in many of the stories. Developments in thinking as well as developments in practice. It is dynamic. The principle of gradualism is also visible. Many of the leaders of the activity within the schools saw that they needed to move slowly to develop a research culture (Ebbutt 2002) and that this often began with the involvement of a few enthusiastic volunteers and then moved to a more sustained engagement with research either through departments or through themes. In some schools the process materialised more quickly than in others. However, it is also true to say that the process of acquiring knowledge through research and disseminating or translating that into action is a longer one than the school research leaders anticipated. It is necessarily slow, although some schools have harnessed their efforts more effectively to work efficiently. It is also important to recognise the different histories of engagement with research to be found in these schools. Two of the schools that have been involved with SUPER since the beginning have now been engaged in teacher research in some form or another for over thirteen years.

Dave Ebbutt (2002) in the first stage of the analysis of this question in relation to the partnership argued that there were four different research cultures which were: no culture of research, emergent research culture, established research culture and established-embedded research culture. He offered this conclusion

> One way of seeing the differences between the research cultures of the schools that I have described is to view them as a series of developmental stages along an evolutionary path. The implication of this observation is that should schools wish to develop to the point of embracing an embedded research culture, they will need to evolve through the prior stages: 'no culture of research', 'emergent research culture', 'established research culture,' to 'established-embedded research culture'.
>
> (Ebbutt 2002: 138)

We need to acknowledge also that these cultures are fragile and that they can change rapidly, as is evident in these case studies. The leadership of these cultures is important and when key players leave and move on it can take a long time for a culture to recover. There is now awareness within the SUPER partnership that they need to plan for sustainability and continuity.

Alignment

In the GoodWork Project, Gardner *et al.* (2006) investigated the following question.

> How do individuals who desire to do 'good work' – work that is at once excellent in quality and socially responsible – succeed or fail at a time when unmodulated market forces are extremely powerful and the search for ever greater profits pervades the society, there are few if any comparable controlling forces, or and our whole sense of time and space is being altered in our technologically oriented global society?
>
> (Gardner *et al.* 2006: 20)

One of the central concepts that emerged was that of the extent to which activities within a profession and a workplace were aligned:

> a major factor in facilitating 'good work' is the extent to which a profession is well aligned. In alignment, all of the various interest groups basically call for the same kinds of performances ... 'Good work' is most likely to occur when four forces all point in the same direction. When professional standards, peer behavior, internal values and social values all tell us to do the same thing, there is no problem.
>
> (Gardner *et al.* 2006: 19)

This concept seems to apply also to the work of developing and sustaining good work in teacher research. First, it seems important in these case studies that the initiators of the work, in this case the headteachers, and the key leaders of research in the school (the teacher research coordinators) share a belief in and valuing of the activity. This needs to go beyond the superficial for as Gardner *et al.* (2006: 25) comment 'apparent (or superficial) alignment may desensitize individuals to potential problems.' Second is the notion of harnessing forces to support the processes: not allowing major forces to inhibit is a key factor in these cases. In Soham Village College the structures and processes of management and communication were all shifted to support the process of teacher research. So there was a flow to the activity and those engaged in it had to battle with the impressive enough problems of research rather than battle the problems of actually engaging in the research process. BPRS was cited as a significant element in many of the cases. It could be seen as a force for alignment providing status, structure, and finance to buy time and resources and a time boundary. (These structures and supports will be explored more fully in the following section.) In the absence of

BPRS many of the schools in these cases have now gone on to provide these listed elements from their own resources.

Judith Warren Little (2002) has also suggested that the subject department may be an undervalued force for reform and, in Gardner's terms, it may be a way of aligning agendas and interests.

> Findings point both to the potential contribution of professional communities situated in subject departments and the challenge of capitalizing on such communities to advance whole-school reform. The study suggests complex relationships among organizational context, teacher community, teacher development, and institutional reform.
>
> (Little 2002: 2)

So one of the concepts that might help us to understand the development in a school and its culture is how well the school's structures and processes are aligned to the research process from the perspective of the teacher researchers. This requires a shift in the organisation and in the conditions of those undertaking research. Gardner *et al.* (2006: 24) warn us that 'all alignments and misalignments are temporary' and they say that 'while, on the average, "good work" is easier to carry out when the sector is well aligned, some individuals are actually motivated by misalignment'.

Structures and support

It is clear from the case study schools that even when school management favours a research culture and encourages teacher research, *and* makes resources available to teachers to support research, this does not ensure widespread research activity. Part of establishing and maintaining a research culture is providing structures that support staff in their research. These structures go beyond rhetoric and even the availability of funding. All case study schools had an apparent commitment to developing research cultures, and had funding available for staff to undertake research. The level of research activity has however been very variable, both across schools, and within some schools across time.

The structures developed in the Networked Learning Community Phase of the partnership were not necessarily helpful to all the schools. The steering groups worked well in some schools but not in others and the leadership for learning strand is almost invisible in the case studies. However, three roles emerge as important over time. They are the roles of the teacher research coordinator, the critical friend and the student voice coordinator. The pivotal role of the teacher research coordinator is clear in most of the case study chapters, and several TRCs co-author these accounts.

Generally, the role of the student voice coordinator was seen as more suited for an enthusiast than a senior manager. However, where at St Ivo it was decided to make student voice part of a senior management role, this was seen as an important and effective commitment to this work in the school. The appointment of a member of non-teaching staff at Sharnbrook was also considered to be successful – giving a point of reference that was accessible to students. Elsewhere, for example at Netherhall, junior members of teaching staff found that enthusiasm was not enough when there was little perceived support from structures within the school, and time to undertake the role was not forthcoming. In Queen Elizabeth's Girls' School a less senior member of staff had great impact in developing the work. The critical friend role is constantly cited as important in bringing resources from beyond the school, supporting the individuals or groups, providing research training and expertise and bringing an external dispassionate and different perspective on the work. The role of giving critical constructive feedback to the school is also highly valued.

Perhaps the key idea here is the permeability of research structures. Netherhall seems to offer a prime example of impermeable structures in this regard: not only did the existing action research group not evolve into required new structures when the school joined SUPER, but also a distinct group with similar interests carried on working in parallel with the SUPER initiatives, based in the lower school. Although there was some mutual acknowledgement, and interaction, there was no imperative in the school to unify the different traditions.

The move in many of the schools to the subject department as an organising structure is interesting in the case studies. Little (2002) has written and researched the issues around the place of and use of the department in secondary school reform. She makes two interesting observation that illuminate aspects of the SUPER case studies

> We have persuasive evidence in this and related studies that abandoning departments – or more accurately, failing to attend systematically to the subject-specific aspects of teacher development and school reform – seriously constrains efforts to transform secondary schooling.
> We have yet to uncover an instance of a comprehensive high school in which reform leaders have sought to strengthen professional community both within and across subject departments.
>
> (Little 2002: 27)

What is clear is that the move from individual teachers researching their own practice to the creation of knowledge by a school demands much more of the school's organisational and leadership structures.

Critical mass

When does a school shift from becoming a group of individual researchers to a researching school? The metaphor of 'critical mass' may be useful – the notion that at some point enough staff are involved to switch the school into becoming a 'researching' institution. This is not to suggest that this is solely about numbers of staff involved, whether taken in absolute terms or as some proportion of the establishment. Clearly there is something more than this: the distribution of staff among school structures, the levels of involvement and engagement, the suitability of individuals as catalysts (to borrow another scientific metaphor) or change agents (in terms of formal responsibilities, and the power of the personalities) are, inter alia, as important as the number of people involved.

However, the critical mass analogy does offer some potentially useful insights. The reason a small mass of radioactive material does not 'go critical' is because there is too little interaction between its components – most of the energy released by its activity is lost from the system without triggering anything further. For a chain reaction to occur each event has to trigger at least one more event, and this is not possible if either there are too few active centres, or the density of active centres is so low that energy released is absorbed by the inactive centres. Similarly, in a school context, enthusiasts need colleagues to provide feedback and encouragement, and to help trigger and sustain innovations.

Researching schools are, like nuclear piles, complex systems, and it takes careful experimentation and planning to get them to 'go critical'. Resources (in the form of fuel rods) are fed into the core of a nuclear power plant, at an appropriate rate to initiate a sustainable nuclear chain reaction. This resourcing leads to radiation being released into the core to trigger further activity. The core also contains material that will absorb energy, dissipating the effects of the resources and preventing them from setting off more productive events. Without any mediation, the valuable resources cannot sustain a chain reaction in the presence of the absorbers. However, 'moderating' materials are added, which are able to utilise the resources to build up the sustainable nuclear furnace. We would not want to wish to push this analogy too far, but a workable nuclear core needs sufficient resources, enough moderators (in relation to the absorbers), and a design that allows the moderators to do their work effectively. It took physicists and nuclear engineers many years to design effective and efficient nuclear power plants. Schools are many orders of magnitude more complex, and the moderators and absorbers are unique – so that optimum design cannot be readily transferred between them. Perhaps then it is not surprising that there is no simple blueprint for a researching school. However, there is enough evidence in the SUPER project to offer indications that if research is given a high enough priority, schools can 'go critical' – at least for a period. With a strong research culture in place, absorbers can even become moderators in time. This can be compared this to a fast-breeder reactor, one that generates more nuclear fuel than it uses, but that may be just a little too much physics.

Impact on teachers and students

In the case study on Queen Elizabeth's Girls' School, James and Worrall (2000) were quoted thus:

claims for the impact of these developments over the impact of other interventions, such as the introduction of academic review and target setting, cannot be made with absolute confidence. However, in that so much of the school's resources had been put into this developmental programme, it would be reasonable to assume that improvements must at least be partly attributable to it.

(James and Worrall 2000: 110)

This is true for all the schools. A direct causal link cannot be established. However, it is equally true that many of the case study schools did see the research activity as contributing directly to pupil achievement and school improvement. It could be argued that schools leaving the partnership may not be so convinced but, again, there is no direct evidence for that.

The teacher researchers speak strongly of the impact on their sense of professional identity, sense of autonomy, motivation and professional regeneration. Many of the school leaders support and underline this. One headteacher saw teacher research as a key retention strategy. The power of engaging in research to impact on teachers' learning is shown in these case studies. It also supports the view that by engaging *in* research, teachers will engage more easily *with* research and, as Mary James (2005) has argued, without teacher learning there can be no improvements in pupil learning.

There are examples within the schools of major and minor changes in practice as a result of teacher research. The degree to which the schools embed the changed practices varied from making it a central plank of school policy on teaching and learning to listening to the outcomes of the research work but not necessarily supporting its institutionalisation, which may or may not be appropriate.

Achievements and challenges

How did the schools in the SUPER partnership face the challenges detailed in Chapter 1 and are these the challenges that schools in this partnership saw as the central ones? What have we learned about schools' attempts to go beyond individual teacher research and to engage in generating research-based knowledge to inform practice? The first challenge is one of commitment and perseverance. Stenhouse (1975) had suggested that it would take a long time to realise the notion of teaching as a research-based profession. The case studies suggest that the process of becoming a researching school is a long one, that it requires stamina and resources and that it has great benefits for teachers and pupils. So the challenge of time and perseverance is a real one and one that the majority of the schools here have faced. The achievement is to hold the line in the face of multiple initiatives and contrasting agendas. Maintaining and sustaining the activity when the key players are not there still remains a challenge.

The second key challenge was one of organisational change and adaptation. The schools here in their different ways shifted their organisational arrangements to fit the purpose of becoming a researching school. Gardner *et al.*'s (2001) notion of alignment is very helpful here and to varying degrees do we see authentic alignment in these case studies. There were some great achievements in this area where the research leaders in the school managed to harness the natural resources and focus them on becoming a researching school. This is still a challenge and how deep the changes need to be is one key area for debate.

The third key area identified as a challenge was the psychological and social climate of teaching, which is similar to the notion of a research culture. How far did this appear as a barrier and did the schools see shifts here? It was a barrier at the beginning of the process of engaging in becoming a researching school: teachers talked of how difficult it was to engage in a reflective discourse and to engage in learning with colleagues. There was also evidence that the culture and the discourse shifted as the activity increased and was valued. There was some evidence that the culture of accountability and performance is still a potential barrier but that engaging in research has a considerable impact on teachers' learning and sense of professional identify and reward. There was also some evidence that engaging students in these processes impacts on teaching and learning as well as on teachers' perspectives in the classroom.

The fourth debate relates to one detailed in Chapter 1, which was in the field of research methodology and the implications for school-based research, in particular the issues of knowledge validation and dissemination. These are very important issues in the production of education knowledge and they proved to be ones that engaged those in the SUPER partnership. The extent to which the participants were aware of them as a challenge varied. Those who had been engaged in the activity for a long time and who had high aspirations to become a knowledge creating school saw these as very important and complex. The audience, the language and style of the dissemination were all key issues. The schools valued necessarily knowledge dissemination that was manageable and accessible. How to achieve manageability without losing complexity is a challenge still faced.

Finally, one of the achievements has been the collaboration within the partnership, certainly between the school and the university, and between the schools – at least as far as maintaining and developing SUPER as an initiative. Like most partnerships it requires the individual partners to be somewhat self-sustaining and not depend totally on the interaction between partners: like most partnerships it is bound to have challenges of power, durability and conflict. It is also dynamic. What these case studies show is that becoming a researching school is a possibility – at least according to particular notions of what the researching school could and should be – and that it requires resources and internal reorganisation, external help and most importantly clarity of purpose and values. If the purposes are clear, then the daunting, but worthwhile, challenge of fitting the processes and structures to the purposes is made a little easier.

Chapter 13

Reflections on schools–university research partnerships

Donald McIntyre and Kristine Black-Hawkins

When the SUPER partnership was formed in 1997, there were some things that we were clear about and other things about which we knew we were ignorant. Among the things that we thought we knew was that we had a common interest in educational research, and that that common interest stemmed from a shared belief that the primary purpose of educational research is to inform practice. We shared, and still share, the view that if educational research does not lead to educational practice that is in some sense better – more thoughtful, more just, more effective, more rewarding for pupils or teachers – then there is not much point to it. We also shared the view that there was 'room for improvement' in what educational research was achieving, and therefore in how it was done. And, although there was much less clarity or consensus among us about how it could be done better, we shared sufficient confidence in the idea of a schools–university research partnership to be willing to invest a good deal of effort in exploring the possibilities of such a partnership.

We were also confident in knowing that schools and the university could make complementary contributions to the work of the partnership. It was in the schools that the findings of research would have to be interpreted and translated into useful and practicable practice, relevant to different contexts. It was therefore school staff who were best placed to judge how to use research findings and, more fundamentally, to determine the kinds of research questions that it would be most useful to answer. In addition, it was of course in the schools that the research would have to be conducted. Faculty staff, on the other hand, were likely to have more research expertise and resources, an institutional climate already developed to support research and, crucially, a remit to spend a substantial proportion of their working time engaged in educational research. An optimistic view was that partners with a common interest in educational research, and bringing such complementary contributions to the partnership, would find themselves able quite easily to develop complementary roles through which they could fruitfully pursue joint research enterprises.

It is of course in the nature of ignorance that we were much less clear about our areas of ignorance. But we were at least aware that we did not know how best the partnership would work. And, indeed, it is appropriate to re-emphasise here that initial funding for SUPER was obtained for the purpose of investigating the implications of such a partnership and in particular with the remit, quoted in Chapter 1, of seeking

> to understand how [university] staff and school staff within the partnership find ways and means of working together on research issues and questions of mutual interest in order to create a systemic research culture within and across the partnership schools. One problem (of perhaps many) posed by this challenge will be to find ways in which the research process and outcomes can have utility for teachers in terms of their front-line accountabilities, at the same time as meeting the different accountability pressures upon [university] personnel.

In Chapter 12, we have sought to synthesise evidence relevant to questions about the development of research cultures within the schools. In this final chapter, we must reflect on what kinds of partnership between the schools and the university have been most helpful in facilitating our common purpose of doing educational research to inform practice. 'Partnership' is of course a conveniently flexible concept, but that puts us under an even greater obligation to clarify whatever kinds of partnership we have had that have worked. Minimally, partnership would seem to involve collaboration, and an effective partnership would seem to be one in which the benefits of collaboration outweigh the costs from the perspectives of both partners. So in what ways has SUPER been an effective partnership? What benefits and what costs have there been, from school and from university perspectives? And, have the benefits outweighed the costs from either perspectives?

To examine these questions, we shall look in turn at three interconnected themes. First, focusing on the purpose of the partnership, has 'research' indeed been the primary concern for both sets of partners? Has 'research' meant the same conceptually to both? And in what sense have both been helped by the partnership to achieve their own research purposes? These questions direct our attention to the kinds of knowledge or learning generated by the partnership's activities, and to the terms in which these kinds of knowledge or learning have been valued by the different partners.

Our second theme is concerned with the economics of schools-university research partnerships. Given the increasing autonomy and financial accountability of both schools and university departments, what are the real financial costs and benefits associated with such partnerships? How are these influenced by constantly changing national arrangements? Under what circumstances, therefore, are effective schools-university research partnerships likely to be financially viable.

Third, what have we found out about the conditions, structures and organisational arrangements that are necessary to make such research partnerships work? Given the diversity of arrangements and developments in the SUPER schools, are there any useful lessons to be learned? And, in particular, are there processes and activities which are likely to affect opportunities for collaborative working across institutions, including the development and utilisation of research?

In the concluding section of this chapter, we shall allow ourselves to speculate about the future prospects for schools–university research partnerships. In particular, we shall suggest that, despite the difficulties encountered by SUPER and the complexity of its work, these kinds of partnerships may well become increasingly important as the nature of schools and of teachers' work evolves.

Generating research-based knowledge to inform practice

Divergent concerns

The partnership was set up with a commitment to active involvement of the schools in research, but without any preconceptions about how or whether it would contribute to, or change the nature of, the university's conduct of research. It was assumed at the start that the different partners would make the complementary contributions that they were best placed to make. One approach that was initially anticipated, as outlined in Chapter 11, was that the partners would collaborate on agreed research projects of mutual interest. And, especially during the 1999–2002 period, that was done. Yet there were real difficulties in pursuing such collaborative projects. For a start, the university might not be the most appropriate partner for particular research projects in the schools. For example, at least two of the schools were strongly committed to the CASE research project, run over a long period from King's College London, not from Cambridge. Similarly, when the Learning without Limits project, run from the Cambridge Faculty of Education, advertised for teachers who did not rely on concepts of 'ability' in their teaching, only one of the teacher respondents was from a SUPER school. But even when research projects were agreed upon as SUPER projects, and even when such projects passed the further hurdle of attracting the necessary funding, they were not always experienced as meeting the interests of all the partners. It is important that we should understand why this was so.

As is clear from the case studies, one major reason is that, while the schools and the university can indeed make complementary contributions, the knowledge that they want from the research in which they engage has tended to differ in the following respects:

- *The population to be served*: all the schools are in no doubt that their primary obligation is to their own present students, not to a wider and more abstractly defined population.
- *The context of knowledge use*: it follows that the schools' interest have been overwhelmingly in knowledge that is useful in their own specific and distinctive context, and much less in more generally useful knowledge.
- *The process of dissemination*: whereas the university researchers are obliged to

disseminate their findings and conclusions primarily through written publications (which also fulfils a critically important quality control function), the schools have relied much more on internal dissemination through face-to-face meetings and sharing of practice.

- *Criteria for quality control*: whereas the university researchers know that their work is judged first in terms of its academic rigour and only thereafter in terms of wider criteria, the schools judge their research primarily in terms of professional credibility and demonstrable relevance to current practices rather than conventional academic methodological criteria.

- *Process rather than product*: whereas the value of research for the university researchers is almost entirely in the contribution that the research findings make to educational knowledge, the value of the research for the schools tends to be at least as much in its process: as one headteacher put it, the major benefit of teachers and students engaging in educational research has been in its contribution to developing 'a thinking school'.

- *Time-scale*: while the usefulness of the knowledge generated by research depends for the schools on the immediacy of its availability, in order to maintain the momentum of teachers' or students' personal engagement with the project, for university researchers the speed with which knowledge becomes available is much less important than the transparent rigour of the evidence-based conclusions.

The effects of these contrasts in the nature of the knowledge sought by the schools and by the faculty are further exacerbated by several characteristics of the way academic educational research is organised and evaluated within the university faculty and also nationally. The contrast in the concerns with time-scale, for example, can be sharpened by the pressure on those bidding for research projects to budget less time than is actually needed for contract research staff to complete the analysis of evidence as quickly as possible. Such time-scale tensions can also be increased as a result of the strong tradition within universities for staff to have a high degree of autonomy in the research that they undertake: some staff can commit themselves to too many research projects while others can give too much priority to their teaching and administrative roles, with the consequence in either case that the research work is done only when time becomes available.

More generally, however, it is the lack of connection between the systems of accountability for university lecturers' two main kinds of work, teaching and research, that exacerbates the contrasts. It constrains lecturers from adopting, however much they might like to, the more open stance adopted by schools towards what counts as research, including both the valuing of process as much as product and the use of a wide range of criteria for evaluating outcomes. The national research assessment exercise, a major determinant of faculty income, ensures that this division is quite inflexible, through its emphasis on publications as products, through the criteria by which it evaluates these products and in its focus on members of staff individually. None of these characteristics need be significant problems for academic educational research itself, but they do exacerbate considerably the contrasting aspirations within a research partnership. As such, they reflect the policy vacuum within which SUPER has worked, and which it was created to explore, the absence of any faculty or national policy for supporting researching schools.

Nonetheless, despite these exacerbating factors and the quite widely and consistently differing emphases placed by the schools and the faculty on these contrasting criteria, no sense of conflict has been apparent. On the contrary, there has been consistent recognition of the appropriateness of each other's concerns, a readiness to be helpful wherever possible in helping the other, and a recognition that each side has things to learn from the concerns and criteria of the other. Nonetheless, while a project might be judged to be highly successful from the perspective of one partner, it might at the same time be seen as not very fruitful from the other's perspective. It certainly has not been impossible to design research projects that have met both sets of criteria but, quite simply, it has been much more difficult to meet simultaneously both sets of criteria than to meet only one or other of the two sets.

Reflection on one of the most successful of the collaborative research projects, the TIPS project, suggests that a number of key conditions made this rewarding both to academic researchers and to researching schools:

- The focus of the research was on the already established practice of a number of teachers.
- This established practice was seen as good practice by the teachers concerned.
- The research was aimed in the first instance at documenting the practice, elucidating it from the teachers' perspectives, and explaining its claimed merits.
- Furthermore, the research involved the collection of relevant evidence by the academic researchers to test the claimed merits of the practices.
- It was not too difficult for the practices that were thus documented and 'warranted' to be effectively learned by other teachers in the same schools.

This is a type of research that we believe to be highly desirable, but of course many very useful research projects will not necessarily meet one or more of these conditions. Other kinds of research that have been considered to be simultaneously rewarding to both academic researchers and to researching schools are those where schools and university researchers share a concern about a particular issue or problem and are willing to co-operate, to various degrees, on the process of research and the development of practice. Two examples of this are first, the project on knowledge transfer, at Soham Village College, with Susan Barnet and second, the bystander project, at Chesterton Community College and Arthur Mellows Village College, which has researched into students' responses as bystanders to bullying.

We may briefly note here that the divergence of concerns that have complicated the working of the partnership between the schools and the university have also complicated the working of the partnership among the schools. The SUPER partnership had originally been conceived as primarily between the schools on one hand and the university on the other, but from an early stage it was obvious both that the working of SUPER depended on collaboration among the schools and also that the schools could benefit considerably from learning from each other. Yet, while such mutual learning, especially among the TRCs, has been a sustained feature of the partnership, the frequently voiced aspirations by schools to engage in joint across-school research projects have not been realised. This cannot of course be explained in terms of the contrasting criteria emphasised by the schools and the university, since all the schools have tended to emphasise broadly similar criteria. But the schools' shared prioritisation of the use and dissemination of research-based knowledge, each within their own boundaries, does seem to have militated powerfully against any adequate investment in cross-school collaboration.

An asymmetric partnership

The contrast we have outlined above, between the knowledge sought from research by the schools and that sought by the university, is – we have belatedly recognised – quite close to Hargreaves' (1999) contrast between academic educational research and the work of 'knowledge-creating schools'. In articulating this contrast, Hargreaves drew strongly on the distinction made by Gibbons *et al.* (1994) in the technological context between traditional academic 'Mode 1' knowledge production and the new 'Mode 2' knowledge production 'in the context of application'. This contrast is important, we have suggested, for understanding the ways in which the SUPER partnership has *not* worked. We now go on to ask whether Hargreaves' (1999) account helps us to understand how the SUPER partnership *has* worked.

The school case studies presented in Chapters 2 to 9 of this book show, we believe, that the SUPER partnership has with one possible exception been found to be helpful and successful from the perspective of the schools. This success, as articulated in Chapter 12, has lain in the development, in various ways and to varying degrees, of 'researching schools'. But in what ways has their partnership with the university been a success? In Hargreaves' (1999) model, university staff play a service role, supporting research that is done primarily by the schools for the schools; and in general terms, that has certainly been the nature of the SUPER partnership. Given that schools are not much interested in the production of abstract academic knowledge, but rather in research to foster the development of their own well-founded, contextualised practice, the function of university involvement in the partnership is to help schools generate the kind of knowledge and practical development that they value. Instead of a symmetric partnership in which each partner helps the other to pursue its own distinctive goals, this is an asymmetric partnership, with the school partners in the front-line role and the university faculty in a crucial support role.

The basis of such a partnership is one of mutual respect for contrasting kinds of expertise and of *shared* goals, including the common ultimate goal of providing high-quality education, and the intermediate goal of the development of researching schools. It depends equally on the university's acceptance of the appropriateness of the distinctive kind of research that schools aspire to do, and on the schools' recognition that academics have considerable expertise that is relevant to the development of such research. (It is a kind of partnership that both partners should recognise well, since it is quite similar in its asymmetry to the kind of partnerships for initial teacher education to which we are now, in England, well accustomed. In these partnerships too, the target situation is the school: the purpose is to prepare competent and thinking schoolteachers, not to prepare educational scholars. There too, university involvement is fruitful only if it influences how people learn to think and act in schools. There too, the partnership is asymmetric.)

Of what, more specifically, has the university's service or support role in the partnership consisted? Hargreaves (1999: 137) suggested four ways in which 'university researchers can lead the way into an expansion of Mode 2 educational research' and we shall consider in turn these four kinds of contribution, but first one other:

Being the hub of the wheel

Perhaps the most basic distinctive part played by the university in the partnership is that it has been the centre around which the partnership has functioned. It was the university that took the lead in forming SUPER (although the idea was suggested by two of the headteachers). Also, on the three successive occasions when the need arose, in 1999, 2002 and 2005, it was the university that conceived and developed successful proposals for how the partnership was to be funded in the next phase of its existence, and therefore for the organisational and financial procedures that would be necessary. Most crucially, it has been the university that has taken the major responsibility for the management, coordination and administration of the partnership. While the partners have frequently discussed, using the analogy of a wheel, the importance of contacts around the rim as well as those through the hub, in practice most communication has been through the latter. It is not that the university has played a strong leadership role, far less that it has sought to do so. It has been more the case that – as with ITE partnerships – it was very much more convenient from the point of view of all the partners for the university to adapt existing apparatus to manage and coordinate this new kind of partnership. If that sometimes made the university seem *primus inter pares* among the partners, that did not seem to upset anyone, and it was certainly far less diplomatically problematic than the adoption of such a role by one of the schools would have been.

Training and supporting teachers in research skills

This is the first of the four ways in which Hargreaves (1999) suggests that university researchers can play an important part in the expansion of 'Mode 2' educational research. It is also probably the most important and most valued way in which the university has contributed to the SUPER partnership. This has taken a wide variety of forms, of which the following five have probably been the most significant:

- playing a major part in setting agendas for, and contributing to, the regular and frequent deliberations of the teacher research coordinators
- contributing to seminars, conferences, workshops and training days both at the university and in partner schools
- acting as mentors to individual teacher researchers, including those who have had BPRS scholarships
- acting as critical friends to partner schools, helping them to develop their research policies and programmes
- contributing to the training of students as researchers in the partner schools.

It has been very striking to the university staff involved in SUPER that although the research that teachers in the partner schools have wanted to do has been different in important respects from 'Mode 1' educational research, these teachers have nonetheless seen themselves as needing to learn many of the skills that are used in such academic research.

Seeking opportunities to contribute to the externalisation and combination mode in school-led professional knowledge creation

For Hargreaves (1999), an especially important kind of research to inform practice is that which starts from practice and 'externalises', or makes explicit, the thinking that is implicit in it. Such research necessarily depends on the committed engagement of the teachers whose expertise is being elucidated, but also involves highly disciplined and skilled research, and therefore can benefit substantially from the involvement of experienced academic researchers. Such 'externalised' professional craft knowledge can be especially useful when combined with other (similar or different) professional knowledge. Hargreaves (1999: 137) also emphasises the *validation* of such knowledge and comments that 'Unless higher education staff serve as consultants in the design of teacher-led research, validation among teachers will remain "soft"'.

Many of the experiences of SUPER support Hargreaves' view on this also. It is with just such research into the externalisation, validation and combination of teachers' professional craft knowledge that the TIPS project was concerned; and, it will be remembered, this was one of the research project which best met both the schools' and university researchers' criteria for usefulness.

Making the study of the networked creation, validation and dissemination of professional knowledge a focus of university-led research

and

Reconceptualising both professional knowledge creation and its dissemination

These were the last two of Hargreaves' four suggestions for how 'university researchers can lead the way into an expansion of Mode 2 educational research'. Again, we find ourselves in agreement with these suggestions. Seeking to understand the nature and implications of researching schools and of a schools-university-research partnership has been a central purpose of SUPER from the beginning, and this book and several other publications (e.g. Ebbutt *et al.* 2000; Ebbutt 2001, 2002; McLaughlin and Black-Hawkins 2004; McLaughlin *et al.* 2004; McIntyre 2005) have sought to contribute to that purpose. It has furthermore tended to be a purpose particularly espoused by the university side of the partnership. Creating and disseminating professional knowledge has been of equal importance to school and university members of the partnership, but *studying* and *conceptualising* the creation and dissemination of professional knowledge is understandably a distinctive interest, and perhaps a distinctive obligation, of academic researchers. We are in no doubt, however, that studying and understanding the realities of researching schools and of schools-university research partnerships are important ways of contributing to clearer thinking about what such organisations can fruitfully do and how to provide more effective support for them.

These then seem to us to have been the main ways in which the university has learned to play a helpful support role within the framework of an asymmetric schools-university partnership. Of course, as we hope has been clear from the case studies, the schools with which the university has been in partnership are all different, in their contexts, their histories, their aspirations and their practices. In acting as a partner to these different schools, however, the university has at no stage sought to take any systematic account of these differences. On the contrary, we have assumed – and still believe we can assume – that the differences among the schools do not imply any systematic differences in the kind of partnership that they need from the university. For all schools, three principles seem to have been of paramount importance:

- that the shared goal should be the provision of the best possible educational experience for the school's own students
- that the university should not expect the school to want to engage in academic educational research, but should instead be sensitive to the school's perceptions of how it sees 'research' or 'inquiry' as likely to be conducive to the attainment of its educational goals
- that the university should be ready to contribute its research expertise, including its capacity for critical research thinking, in ways that seem likely to help the school to engage effectively in research.

The economics of research partnership

As we were forced to realise fairly early in the life of SUPER, the financial viability of schools–university partnerships is an important issue. For SUPER's first eighteen months, we had no dedicated income for it and so, although we had some very interesting discussions, nothing much happened. The first thing that we had to recognise, therefore, was that research partnerships carry significant costs.

Quite apart from the costs involved in conducting particular research projects, the development of research activity is always dependent on significant prior expenditure. Even able and motivated individual researchers need to invest a significant amount of time and energy in the careful planning of research projects before they can expect to attract funding for these specific projects. In the field of education, furthermore, they also generally need to work hard to identify potential sponsors and to shape their proposals to meet the sponsors' interests and criteria. When the planners are not individuals but rather institutions such as schools, and even more when several institutions are involved in partnership, the amount and costs of such preparations increase. And when most of the institutions involved do not have an established research history, culture, infrastructure or body of expertise, the necessary costs involved in developing and supporting purposeful research activity grow. One of the great merits of partnership is that it allows a sharing of the costs of, for example, training and planning as well as computer, library and administrative support. Partnership, however, has its own distinctive kinds of expenses in that it depends much more heavily on formally arranged meetings, on travel between institutions and on highly explicit communication.

As we discovered in SUPER, then, a schools–university research partnership is quite an expensive undertaking even before particular research projects are undertaken. But from what source is it appropriate to seek the funds to meet such expenses? We have identified and indeed tried several possible answers to that question, all of them with some attractions, but none of them ideal. Each of them merits attention.

Surely, one might say, there is money available for educational research and it is from such research budgets that the costs of research partnerships should be met. Currently in the United Kingdom, there are broadly two types of sources for research funding. One of these is the research grant or contract that a researcher can attract, from a research council, a charitable body, a national or local government body, or indeed any other group or individual prepared to finance the specific research project. Specificity is the key idea here: the researchers are accountable for undertaking effectively the specific research project that they have contracted to undertake. Such research grants are not given to meet the costs of, for example, research infrastructure or training. Nonetheless, most of the considerable costs of the SUPER project from 1999 to 2002 were met from such a grant, from the Wallenberg Research Centre, on the (perhaps questionable) grounds that the main purpose of the project was to undertake research into the nature and implications of such a research partnership. It is not the working existence of the partnership that justifies such a grant, but attempts – such as this book – to answer research questions about the partnership.

The other source of research funding is that of grants from higher education research councils to universities to give their staff time and resources to conduct research. These grants are given differentially to universities on the basis of regular assessments of the quality of the research that they do. Staff generally have considerable freedom to engage in research of their own choosing, but they are highly accountable to their university for the production of highly rated research publications: without such publications, this large and crucial stream of a successful university's income would dry up. The cost of most of the time devoted by four of the authors of this book to the SUPER project (and much of that of the fifth), together with the very extensive university support services on which they have drawn, have come from this source. We hope that the book and other SUPER-related publications will be assessed as being of sufficient quality to justify our research in this area. There is no way, however, that we can justify expenditure from this source on consultancy or training for our school partners.

Other sources of funding on which such a partnership can draw are those to support professional education and training courses for teachers. Courses such as MEd degree courses provided by universities are financially supported in England partly by fees and partly by specific grants from the Teacher Development Agency. It is only in so far as a main purpose of SUPER is seen as providing professional education for teachers, that these are appropriate sources from which to fund the partnership. Because, until 2005, that was not viewed as one of the partnership's primary purposes, these sources were not drawn upon. But, as explained in Chapter 11, a SUPER MEd degree was initiated in September 2005, to foster research leadership in the partnership schools, with fees being paid by the schools. Again, this is an entirely satisfactory arrangement for one important element of the partnership's work, but it does not provide either adequate or appropriate funding for other important aspects, most notably the research activities of the partnership.

The most fundamental problem for the funding of research partnerships is of course that there is no established element of schools' own budgets for research. Therefore any research costs met from schools' budgets are necessarily at the expense of what are understandably seen by many teachers and governors as more immediate needs, such as increased staffing or mended roofs.

There is then no framework, within established ways of funding for either school or university activities, that is very suitable for funding research partnerships. There have, however, been a number of government initiatives that have been of some help for research partnerships such as SUPER, although unreliably so. Three of these are worthy of particular mention, and illustrate both the strengths and the weaknesses of such initiatives very well. During the 2002–2005 period, SUPER was able to depend primarily on a three-year grant from the Networked Learning Groups initiative, set up by the National College for School Leadership, on condition that the partnership met the quite demanding bureaucratic conditions stemming from the distinctive ideological enthusiasms of this initiative. Such enthusiasms are of little consequence if the opportunity is taken to learn from experience, or even – dare we say? – from research. That was not to be allowed, however, since the initiative was summarily terminated after four years.

Another helpful initiative was the Best Practice Research Scholarships, directly funded by the DfES from 2000 to 2004. Although it too had some limitations, these were mostly associated with the short-term, isolated, individual nature of the scholarships; and, supplementing other sources of funding, the BPRS scheme was very helpful in allowing and encouraging individual teachers in schools to take advantage of the partnership's work. The early termination of this scheme too was, however, almost as demoralising for teacher research coordinators as the scheme itself had been helpful for individual practitioner researchers. A third example of the government's helpful but unreliable schemes is the Training Schools initiative. Several of the partnership schools, having been awarded Training School status, are able to use the extra funds they gain from this to foster their research activities. But whether or not schools gain such status seems to be unrelated to whether or not they adopt a researching approach.

It may well be many years before we can expect all schools to be researching schools, or before we can expect all university departments of education to work in research partnerships with schools. How quickly we move in that direction, and how well we learn along the way, will depend crucially on the availability of appropriate and adequate funding to make it possible for willing pioneers to do the extra work necessary to develop the expertise and understanding that is needed.

Conditions, structures and organisational arrangements to support schools–university research partnerships

From our experiences of SUPER we have been able to highlight a number of organisational and practical arrangements which we consider likely to affect the quality of work within schools–university research partnerships. Our findings draw on the case studies in this book as well as earlier research we have carried out (McLaughlin and Black-Hawkins 2004; McLaughlin *et al.* 2004). They also accord with findings of others who have undertaken similar research (see, for example, Lieberman and Grolnick 1996; Cordingley *et al.* 2002; Groundwater-Smith and Mockler 2002).

Determining clarity of key purpose(s)

As noted in the introduction to this chapter, all members of SUPER, the schools and the university, share a core belief that the primary purpose of educational research must be to inform and improve practice in schools. This commonality has continued as a unifying principle of the partnership throughout the various forms it has taken over the years. However, as has also been noted in this chapter, there has not been the same unanimity about the nature of such research, or what these differences in understanding might mean in practice for the work of the partnership. In particular, resolving the distinctions between notions of academic research and that undertaken by practitioners remains problematic.

Developing and sustaining supportive and invigorating relationships

SUPER, like any partnership, whether professional or personal in nature, has been fundamentally reliant on the people that comprise it and the quality of the relationships between them. The time required to build open and trusting relationships should not be underestimated. For collaboration to be successful it seems there must a balance between respect for the diverse range of perceptions and interests held by members and as a willingness to share and take risks together. In SUPER the responsibility for nurturing these relationships, and supporting them when they have occasionally broken down, has largely been taken by the university project manager. This has made some high demands on her time. Part of this responsibility has included maintaining the continuity of relationships when key people have left, such as TRCs and/or headteachers. A similar role within each of the individual schools has be taken by the TRCs and sufficient time for them to do so is important.

Building a range of effective and flexible communication strategies across the partnership

Communication seems to be essential if a partnership and the relationships between its members are to flourish. Over the years, much effort has been made in SUPER to develop effective communication strategies which provide real opportunities for learning to take place. Across the partnership much of this work has been undertaken by university staff, while in the schools it has mainly been the responsibility of the TRCs. Such activities have required much time and effort on the part of these people. Face-to-face meetings have been particularly important, largely because they have also supported partnership relationships, referred to above. Certainly, various attempts to develop electronic forms of communication have proved less successful. Generally, the most rewarding meetings have been those which have focused on the sharing of research interests and concerns rather than on the 'business' of maintaining the partnership. The specific communication requirement of disseminating research findings in ways which are useful for members working in a range of different contexts, but who do not attend the regular meetings, remains problematic for SUPER.

Engaging and maintaining the commitment of schools leaders

Those headteachers and other school leaders of SUPER schools who have been strongly committed to the work of the partnership have had a positive effect on both the research activities taking place in their own schools as well as on the wider work of SUPER. Particularly valuable are those headteachers who have been explicit advocates for practitioner research and who have also encouraged colla-borative working practices among the teacher-researchers in their schools. While this has clearly required more than providing just time and money to support research and partnership activities, the importance of doing so should not be underestimated (see also *Resources* below).

Learning from the perspectives of other institutions

A clear strength of SUPER is that it has provided many opportunities for members to draw on the knowledge and experiences of people from other institutions. Teachers have found it stimulating to learn about research and other practices taking place in partnership schools. Similarly, university critical friends have gained from developing a relationship with their particular SUPER schools, which has involved everyday contact with staff and students. Furthermore, the schools have constantly requested to maintain their links with the university, both in terms of the specific focus of the critical friend but also more generally by drawing on the resources of the university. They have especially valued the provision of research training as well opportunities to discuss with university colleagues the substantive topics of their school-based research.

Sufficient resources in terms of time and money

For SUPER the issue of resources has been a constant concern, and a clear theme within this chapter and the book overall. It does not seem possible to maintain a schools–university research partnership without sufficient funding. In some schools, headteachers have been creative about how they have deployed resources so as to support practitioner research and other partnership activities. It also seems that the allocation of extra funding is seen as a marker of the status and value ascribed to such work in the schools. From the perspective of the university, as discussed earlier in this chapter, the partnership can only continue if sufficient, regular and appropriate funding is made available.

Of course, none of these organisational and practical arrangements to support a schools–university research partnership exists separately from the others. For example, our current funding arrangements for SUPER have been partly deter-mined by the level of commitment from the headteachers and the university. Also, establishing clarity of purpose across the partnership has been dependent on the quality of the relationships among key members and these in turn have been shaped by the communications strategies that have been developed. Finally, much of the work is made possible through the willingness of individuals in the schools and the university to give generously of their time, because of their commitment to the partnership's core values. However, it is not easy to judge how far such support can be sustainable.

Research partnerships: an important idea for the future

We have found that the ideas of researching schools and research partnerships have sustained their attractiveness to most of the school leaders with whom we have worked, and to many teachers, over a number of years. It has become clear that the Mode 2 kind of research that we have described can not only be seen by school leaders as an intelligent and responsible way of approaching school development but can also be experienced by teachers as an element of their work that is especially intellectually rewarding and professionally motivating. Support from a university for such research does furthermore seem to have been an important facilitating condition for schools' sustained engagement in it.

The partnership schools were of course only a small number of self-selecting schools; and even in most of these schools, only a minority of teachers have been actively involved in the research activity. So it cannot plausibly be claimed that in England the day of researching schools has arrived. The conditions are not yet in place for that day. We have already noted that the financial conditions are not conducive either to schools' investment in research activity or to universities' engagement in research partnerships with schools. It is even more evident that the policy climate in England in recent years has not been one to foster researching schools or partnerships: it is conformity that the national government has seemed to value in teachers more than thoughtful questioning and evidence-informed development.

Yet perhaps the day of researching schools is nor far off, even in England. At least the rhetoric of government in recent years has fairly consistently emphasised the importance of practice being informed by evidence. We have noted too the sporadic short-term initiatives taken by government bodies that have helped to finance research by schools and by teachers. Most fundamentally, a slow but very significant change is apparent, in government thinking (e.g. Morris 2001) as well as more widely, about the nature of teacher professionalism and the conditions that will be necessary for the effective operation of that new professionalism. Among the most important aspects of that new thinking about teacher profes-sionalism are:

Different kinds of teacher knowledge and decision-making

Classroom teaching has been virtually unchallenged as the way of working in our schools for almost the past two centuries. It is a pattern of working that has necessarily led to a kind of teacher expertise that prioritises tacit knowledge and intuitive decision-making. The complexity of the classroom teaching tasks that teachers have had to undertake has meant that teachers' work could be done fluently and effectively only if experienced teachers relied primarily on such intuitive decision-making. The isolation in which teachers have worked has meant that there has been very little need for communication about teachers' decision-making, nor therefore any problem about the tacit nature of their expertise. Increasingly, however, the limitations of such classroom teaching are becoming apparent; and awareness is slowly growing that substantial improvement in the effectiveness of schooling may not be possible by the introduction of various specific pedagogical 'methods' or 'strategies', but only through more fundamental changes to the established system (see McIntyre 2000). Hence the increasingly consensual demands for an end to teachers' classroom isolation and an increasing dependence on collaborative problem-solving among teachers, and between teachers and parents, other professionals and the students themselves. Hence also demands for 'personalised learning plans' for students. These changes all imply increased explicitness, discussion and rational consideration in teachers' decision-making, and therefore much slower decision-making. Such developments will be possible if, and only if, substantially increased resources are available. But since it can certainly not be taken for granted that any such changes will necessarily lead to improvement, they will need to be introduced slowly and critically.

Different kinds of workloads for teachers

For most of the past two hundred years, teachers' workloads have been dominated by the time they have spent in classrooms with their classes. In addition, there has always been a lot of time required for preparation for classroom teaching and for marking pupils' work. In addition in recent decades, a steadily increasing amount of time has been required for planning and consultation meetings, but as yet with only very modest decreases in the amount of student contact time. It is not surprising that most classroom teachers see research (or other suggested extensions to their workloads) as an unreasonable additional demand. But it is now being suggested that school students may not always need to be supervised by a qualified teacher in order for them to be engaged in fruitful learning activities. And if that premise were to become generally accepted, it would be possible to conceive of both the time and the space of schooling becoming structured in radically different ways.

Perhaps the most concrete alternative vision that can be offered is of schools becoming similar in these respects to universities, with the work of a schoolteacher being similar to that of a university lecturer. Significantly less of the working week than is currently normal for schoolteachers would be spent in face-to-face contact with students, and the size of the student groups taught would commonly vary for each teacher from one to over a hundred. Much more of the teacher's week would be spent in planning and preparation, much of it of a collaborative nature, and a significant proportion of his or her time would commonly be spent in research. If, but only if, teacher workloads were to become much more like this, one might expect researching schools to become the norm.

If, in such circumstances, many teachers in schools were devoting substantial amounts of time to research, it could make a great deal of sense for university staff to devote significant amounts of time to supporting them. It might even, in these circumstances, be appropriate for a significant proportion of the funding currently allocated to the Mode 1 educational research activity in universities to be reallocated to university staff to support school staff to undertake Mode 2 research. That would depend, however, on evidence about the greater usefulness of such Mode 2 research. Finding such evidence, and understanding its implications for schools-university partnerships, remains our challenge for the future.

Glossary

ARTE	Action Research in Teacher Education
Beacon school	Beacon schools were schools which had been identified as among the best performing in England and represented examples of successful practice which were to be brought to the attention of the rest of the education service with a view to sharing and spreading that effective practice to others. The scheme ran from 1998 to August 2005. (www.standards.dfes.gov.uk/beaconschools, accessed May 2006)
BERA	British Educational Research Association
BPRS	Best Practice Research Scholarship
CARN	Collaborative Action Research Network
CASE	Cognitive Acceleration in Science Education
CATs	Cognitive Ability Tests
CPD	continuing professional development
DfES	Department for Education and Skills
ESRC	Economic and Social Research Council
GCSE	General Certificate of Secondary Education
ICT	information and communication technology
IQEA	Improving the Quality of Education for All
ITET	initial teacher education and training
ITT	initial teacher training
LEA	local education authority
LSDA	Learning Skills and Development Agency
Midyis	Middle Years Information System
NCSL	National College of School Leadership
NLC	Networked Learning Community
NQT	newly qualified teacher
Ofsted	Office for Standards in Education
PE	physical education
PGCE	Postgraduate Certificate in Education
PSHE	personal, social and health education
RAE	research assessment exercise
RE	religious education

SAR	students as researchers
SATs	Standard Assessment Tasks
SDP	school development plan
SIP	school improvement plan
SMT	senior management team
SUPER	Schools–University Partnership in Educational Research
SVC	student voice coordinator
TIPS	Technology Integrated Pedagogic Strategies
TRC	teacher research coordinator
TTA	Teacher Training Agency
VAK	visual, auditory and kinaesthetic learning styles
Yellis	Year 11 Information System

References

Action Research in Teacher Education (ARTE) (2005) www.educ.cam.ac.uk/arte/int.
html (accessed May 2006).

Adey, P. and Shayer, M. (1994) *Really Raising Standards: Cognitive Intervention and Academic Achievement*. London: Routledge.

Adey, P., Shayer, M. and Yates, C. (2001) *Thinking Science: The Materials of the Cognitive Acceleration through Science Programme*. Cheltenham: Nelson Thornes.

Arnot, M., McIntyre, D., Pedder, D. and Reay, D. (2004) *Consultation in the Classroom*. Cambridge: Pearson.

Barnett, S.M. and Ceci, S.J. (2002) 'When and where do we apply what we learn? A taxonomy for far transfer'. *Psychological Bulletin*, 128(4): 612–637.

Baumfield, V. (2001) 'The north east school based research consortium: an overview of the changing nature of the roles and relationships between the universities, schools and LEAs'. Conference paper. British Educational Research Association Conference, University of Leeds, September.

Black, P. (2003) *Promoting the Development of a Learning Organisation*. BPRS report. Available at: www.teachernet.gov.uk/professionaldevelopment/resources andresearch/ bprs/search/index.cfm?report = 1073

Black-Hawkins, K. (2003) 'Are school–university friendships critical? Developing professional and institutional research relationships'. Conference paper. British Educational Research Association Conference, Heriot-Watt University, Edinburgh, September.

Bradley, H., Connor, C. and Southworth, G. (1994) *Developing Teachers, Developing Schools*. London: David Fulton.

Brown, S. (2005) 'How can research inform ideas of good practice in teaching? The contributions of some official initiatives in the UK', *Cambridge Journal of Education*, 35(3): 383–405.

Cochran-Smith, M. and Lytle, S.L. (eds) (1993) *Inside/Outside: Teacher Research and Knowledge*. New York: Teachers College Press.

——(2001) 'Beyond certainty: taking an inquiry stance on practice', in A. Lieberman and L. Miller (eds) *Teachers Caught in the Action: Professional Development that Matters*. New York: Teachers College Press.

Coffield, F., Moseley, D., Hall, E. and Ecclestone, K. (2004) *Should We Be Using Learning Styles? What Research Has to Say to Practice*. London: Learning and Skills Development Agency.

Cordingley, P. and Bell, M. (2002) 'School-based research consortium initiative: an overview report'. Conference paper. Teacher Training Agency Conference: Working and Learning in Partnership, London, March.

Cordingley, P., Baumfield, V., Butterworth, M., McNamara, O. and Elkins, T. (2002) *Lessons from the School-Based Research Consortia*. Exeter: British Education Research Association, University of Exeter.

Costa, A.L. and Killick, B. (1993) 'Through the lens of a critical friend'. *Educational Leadership*, 51(2): 49–51.

Dadds, M. (1995) *Passionate Enquiry and School Development: A Story about Teacher Action Research*. London: Falmer Press.

Dadds, M. and Hart, S. (eds) (2001) *Doing Practitioner Research Differently*. London: RoutledgeFalmer.

Darling-Hammond, L. (ed.) (1994) *Professional Development Schools*. New York: Teachers College Press.

Deaney, R. and Hennessy, S. (in press) 'Sustainability, evolution and dissemination of ICT-supported classroom practice'. *Research Papers in Education*.

Deaney, R., Ruthven, K. and Hennessy, S. (2003) 'Pupil perspectives on the contribution of information and communication technology in teaching and learning in the secondary school'. *Research Papers in Education*, 18(2): 141–165.

Department for Education and Skills (DfES) (2005) *Leading and Co-ordinating CPD in the Secondary School*. London: DfES.

Desforges, C. (1992) 'Children's learning: has it improved?' Conference paper. Association for the Study of Primary Education (ASPE) Annual Conference.

Dewey, J. (1929) *The Sources of the Science of Education*. New York: Liveright.

Doherty, J., MacBeath, J., Jardine, S., Smith, I. and McCall, J. (2001) 'Do schools need critical friends?', in J. MacBeath and P. Mortimer (eds) *Improving School Effectiveness*. Buckingham: Open University Press.

Ebbutt, D. (2001) 'Teachers' purposes for and sources of knowledge about educational research'. Cambridge: University of Cambridge Faculty of Education.

——(2002) 'The development of a research culture in secondary schools'. *Journal of Educational Action Research*, 10(1): 123–140.

Ebbutt, D., Robson, R. and Worrall, N. (2000) 'Educational research partnership: differences and tensions between the professional cultures of practitioners in schools and researchers in higher education'. *Teacher Development*, 4(3): 319–337.

Elliott, J. (1991) *Action Research for Educational Change*. Buckingham: Open University Press.

EPPI-Centre (2002) *A Systematic Review of the Effectiveness of School-level Actions for Promoting Participation by All Students, Review Summary*. London: Evidence for Policy and Practice Information and Coordinating Centre.

Fielding, M. *et al.* (2005) *Factors Influencing the Transfer of Good Practice*. London: DfES.

Frost, D., Cullen, J. and Cunningham, H. (2003) 'Making a difference: building a research community of practice'. *Professional Development Today*, 6(2): 13–22.

Fullan, M. (1991) *The New Meaning of Educational Change*. New York: Teachers' College Press.

Furlong, J. and Oancea, A. (2005) *Assessing Quality in Applied and Practice-based Educational Research: A Framework for Discussion*. Oxford: Oxford University Department of Educational Studies.

Gardner, H., Csikszentmihalyi, M. and Damon, W. (2001) *Good Work: When Excellence and Ethics Meet*. New York: Basic Books.

——(2006) *The Good Work Project: An Overview*. Available at: www.goodworkproject.org (accessed May 2006).

Gibbons, M., Limoges, C., Nowotny, H., Schwartzman, S., Scott, P. and Trow, M. (1994) *The New Production of Knowledge*. London: Sage.

Groundwater-Smith, S. and Mockler, N. (2002) 'Building knowledge, building professionalism: the coalition of knowledge building schools and teacher professionalism'. Conference paper. Australian Association for Educational Research Conference, University of Queensland, Australia, December.

Hannon, V. (2005) *Establishing a Network of Schools*. Cranfield, UK: National College of School Leadership, Networked Learning Group.

Hargreaves, D.H. (1996) 'Teaching as a research-based profession: possibilities and prospects'. Teacher Training Agency (TTA) Annual Lecture, London.

——(1999) 'The knowledge creating school'. *British Journal of Educational Studies*, 47(2): 122–144.

——(2003) *Education Epidemic: Transforming Secondary Schools through Innovative Networks*. London: Demos.

Harris, A. and Lambert, L. (2003) 'What is leadership capacity?', in A. Harris and L. Lambert, *Building Capacity for School Improvement*. Maidenhead: Open University Press.

Harris, S. and Rudduck, J. (1993) 'Establishing the seriousness of learning in the early years of secondary schooling'. *British Journal of Educational Psychology*, 63: 322–336.

Hennessy, S. and Deaney, R. (2005) 'T-MEDIA: exploring teacher mediation of subject learning with ICT: A multi-media approach'. Available at: www.educ.cam.ac.uk/istl/ pub.html (accessed May 2006).

Hennessy, S., Deaney, R. and Ruthven, K. (2005a) 'Emerging teacher strategies for mediating technology-integrated instructional conversations: a socio-cultural perspective'. *The Curriculum Journal*, 16(3): 265–292.

Hennessy, S., Ruthven, K. and Brindley, S. (2005b) 'Teacher perspectives on integrating ICT into subject teaching: commitment, constraints, caution and change'. *Journal of Curriculum Studies*, 37(2): 155–192.

Hiebert, J., Gallimore, R. and Stigler, J.W. (2002) 'A knowledge base for the teaching profession: what would it look like and how can we get one?' *Educational Researcher*, 31(2): 3–15.

Hillage, J., Pearson, R., Anderson, A. and Tamkin, P. (1998) *Excellence in Research on Schools*. London: Institute for Employment Studies/DfEE/HMSO.

Hopkins, D. (2000) 'Schooling for tomorrow: innovations and networks'. Rapporteur's report. OECD/CERI Seminar, Lisbon, September.

——(2002) *Improving the Quality of Education for All*, 2nd edn. London: David Fulton.

Hopkins, D. and Jackson, D. (n.d.) *Networked Learning Communities – Capacity Building, Networking and Leadership for Learning*. Nottingham: National College for School Leadership, www.ncsl.org.uk/nlc (accessed May 2006).

Hopkins, D., Ainscow, M. and West, M. (1994) *School Improvement in an Era of Change*. London: Cassell.

Hord, S.M. (1997) *Professional Learning Communities: Communities of Continuous Inquiry and Improvement*. Austin, TX: Southwest Educational Development Laboratory (SEDL), www.sedl.org (accessed May 2006).

Hughes, M. (1999) *Closing the Learning Gap*. Stafford, UK: Network Educational Press.

Jackson, D. (2002) 'Networks and networked learning: knowledge management and collaborative enquiry for school and system improvement'. Conference paper. Standing Committee for the Education and Training of Teachers (SCETT) Annual Conference, Grantham, October.

Jackson, D. and Payne, G. (n.d.) *The Headteacher – Guardian of Leverage for School Improvement*. Discussion paper. Nottingham: National College for School Leadership. Available at: www.ncsl.org.uk/nlc (accessed May 2006).

Jackson, D. and West, M. (1999) 'Learning through leading: leading through learning: leadership for sustained school improvement'. Conference paper. International Congress for School Effectiveness and Improvement, San Antonio, TX, January.

James, M. (2005) Editorial. *The Curriculum Journal*, 16(1): 83–96.

James, M. and Worrall, N. (2000) 'Building a reflective community: development through collaboration between a higher education institution and one school over ten years'. *Educational Action Research*, 8(1): 93–114.

Jeffrey, B. (2002) 'Performativity and primary teacher relations'. *Journal of Education Policy*, 17(5): 531–546.

Jones, D. (2002) 'The role of teacher research coordinator in the SUPER project: a teacher's perspective'. Paper presented to the Schools–University Partnership for Educational Research, Cambridge.

——(2003) 'Reflections of a teacher research coordinator'. Conference paper. British Educational Research Association Conference, Heriot-Watt University, Edinburgh, September.

Lieberman, A. (1999) 'Networks'. *Journal of Staff Development*, 20(3): 43–44.

Lieberman, A. and Grolnick, M. (1996) 'Networks and reform in American education'. *Teachers College Record*, 98(1): 7–45.

Little, J.W. (2002) *Professional Community and the Problem of High School Reform*. Berkeley, CA: Graduate School of Education University of California, Berkeley.

Lowndes, V. and Skelcher, C. (1998) 'The dynamics of multi-organizational partnerships: an analysis of changing modes of governance'. *Public Administration*, 76 (summer): 313–333.

MacBeath, J. (1998) '"I didn't know he was ill": the role and value of the critical friend', in L. Stoll and K. Myers (eds) *No Quick Fixes: Perspectives on Schools in Difficulties*. London: RoutledgeFalmer.

MacBeath, J., Schratz, M., Meuret, D. and Jakobsen, L. (2000) *Self-evaluation in European Schools: A Story of Change*. London: Routledge Falmer.

McIntyre, D. (1997) 'The profession of educational research: 1996 BERA presidential lecture'. *British Educational Research Journal*, 23(2): 127–140.

——(1998) 'The usefulness of educational research: an agenda for consideration and action', in J. Rudduck and D. McIntyre (eds) *Challenges for Educational Research New BERA Dialogues*. London: Paul Chapman.

——(2000) 'Has classroom teaching served its day?', in B. Moon, M. Ben-Peretz and S. Brown (eds) *Routledge International Companion to Education*. London: Routledge.

——(2004) 'Schools as research institutions', in C. McLaughlin, K. Black-Hawkins and D. McIntyre, *Researching Teachers, Researching Schools, Researching Networks: A Review of the Literature*. Cambridge: University of Cambridge Faculty of Education for the National College of School Leadership Networked Learning Communities.

——(2005) 'Bridging the gap between research and practice'. *Cambridge Journal of Education*, 35(3): 357–383.

McIntyre, D. and McIntyre, A. (1999) *Capacity for Research into Teaching and Learning*.

Final Report ESRC Teaching and Learning Research Programme, Swindon. Available at: www.tlrp.org/acadpub/Mcintyre1999.pdf (accessed May 2006).

McIntyre, D., Pedder, D. and Rudduck, J. (2005) 'Pupil voice: comfortable and uncomfortable learnings for teachers'. *Research Papers in Education*, 20(2): 149–168.

McLaughlin, C. and Black-Hawkins, K. (2004) 'A school–university research partnership: understandings, models and complexities'. *British Journal of In-Service Education*, 30(2): 265–283.

McLaughlin, C., Black-Hawkins, K. and McIntyre, D. (2004) *Researching Teachers, Researching Schools, Researching Networks: A Review of the Literature.* Cambridge: University of Cambridge Faculty of Education for the National College of School Leadership Networked Learning Communities.

Miller, L. (2001) 'School–university partnership as a venue for professional development', in A. Lieberman and L. Miller (eds) *Teachers Caught in the Action: Professional Development that Matters.* New York: Teachers College Press.

Morgan, B. (2000) 'How teachers respond to and use pupil perspectives to improve teaching and learning'. Unpublished MPhil thesis, University of Cambridge.

Morris, E. (2001) *Professionalism and Trust: The Future of Teachers and Teaching.* London: DfES.

National College for School Leadership (NCSL) (2002) *Networked Learning Communities: Learning from Each Other . . . Learning with Each Other.* Nottingham: NCSL.

——(n.d.) *Why Networked Learning Communities?* Nottingham: NCSL. Available at: www.ncsl.org.uk/nlc (accessed May 2006). www.teachernet.gov.uk/professional development/resourcesandresearch/bprs/report= 2225 (accessed April 2006).

Naylor, A. (2004) *What Effect was There on Students' Learning Once They were Trained as Students as Researchers?* BPRS report. London.

Nisbet, J. (2005) 'What is educational research? Changing perspectives through the 20th century'. *Research Papers in Education*, 20(1): 25–44.

Nonaka, I. and Takeuchi, H. (1995) *The Knowledge Creating Company.* Oxford: Oxford University Press.

Ofsted (2003a) *Report of the Inspection of Arthur Mellows Village College.* Unique reference number 110875. London: Ofsted.

——(2003b) *Report of Short Inspection of Queen Elizabeth's Girls' School.* Unique reference number 249560. London: Ofsted.

——(2003c) *Report of the Inspection of St Ivo School.* Unique reference number 110874. London: Ofsted.

——(2003d) *Report of Short Inspection of Soham Village College.* Unique reference number 110909. London: Ofsted.

Pedder, D. and McIntyre, D. (2006) 'Pupil consultation: the importance of social capital'. *Educational Review* (special issue edited by J. Rudduck), 58(2): 145–157.

Putnam, R. (2000) *Bowling Alone.* New York: Simon and Schuster.

Raymond, L. (2001) 'Student involvement in school improvement: from data source to significant voice'. *Forum*, 43(2): 58–61.

Richards, J. (2003) 'A case study of a researching school: Sharnbrook Upper School'. Conference paper. British Educational Research Association Conference, Heriot-Watt University, Edinburgh, September.

Richert, A.E., Stoddard, P. and Kass, M. (2001) 'The promise of partnership for promoting reform', in F. Rust and H. Freidus (eds) *Guiding School Change: The Role and Work of Change Agents.* New York: Teachers College Press.

Richmond, G. (1996) 'University/school partnerships: bridging the culture gap'. *Theory into Practice*, 35(3): 214–218.

Ruthven, K. (1999) 'Reconstructing professional judgement in mathematics education: from good practice to warranted practice', in C. Hoyles, C. Morgan and G. Woodhouse (eds) *Rethinking the Mathematics Curriculum*. London: Falmer.

——(2002) 'Linking researching with teaching: towards synergy of scholarly and craft knowledge', in L. English (ed.) *Handbook of International Research in Mathematics Education*. Mahwah, NJ: Lawrence Erlbaum.

Ruthven, K., Hennessy, S. and Brindley, S. (2004) 'Teacher representations of the successful use of computer-based tools and resources in secondary school English, Mathematics and science'. *Teaching and Teacher Education*, 20(3): 259–275.

Ruthven, K., Hennessy, S. and Deaney, R. (2005) 'Incorporating Internet resources into classroom practice: pedagogical perspectives and strategies of secondary-school subject teachers'. *Computers and Education*, 44(1): 1–34.

Simons, H., Kushner, S., Jones, K. and James, D. (2003) 'From evidence-based practice to practice-based evidence: the idea of situated generalisation'. *Research Papers in Education*, 18(4): 347–364.

Somekh, B. (1994) 'Inhabiting each others' castles: towards knowledge and mutual growth through collaboration'. *Educational Action Research*, 2(3): 357–381.

Stenhouse, L. (1975) *An Introduction to Curriculum Research and Development*. London: Heinemann.

——(1979) 'Research as a basis for teaching'. Inaugural lecture, University of East Anglia.

——(1981) 'What counts as research?' *British Journal of Educational Studies*, 29(2): 103–114.

Stronach, I. and McNamara, O. (2002) 'Working together: the long spoons and short straws of collaboration', in O. McNamara (ed.) *Becoming an Evidence-based Practitioner: A Framework for Teacher-Researchers*. London: RoutledgeFalmer.

Swaffield, S. (2002) 'Better than the sum of our parts: a study of local educational authority inspectors as critical friends of headteachers'. Unpublished MEd thesis, University of Cambridge.

Watkins, C. (2005) *Classrooms as Learning Communities: What's in it for Schools?* London: Routledge.

Wells, A. (2002) *To Evaluate the Use of Online Learning to Develop Students Understanding*. BPRS report. Available at: www.teachernet.gov.uk/professionaldevelopment/resources andresearch/bprs/search/index.cfm?report = 364

Wilson, G. (2003) 'The birthdate effect'. *Communicating … Consulting Pupils Project Newsletter* 10(July), Cambridge: ESRC Consulting Pupils Project.

Worrall, N. (1994) '"Oh, good, it's Wednesday!" – reflections on teacher and pupil perceptions of a curriculum initiative'. Unpublished MEd thesis, University of Cambridge.

——(2002) 'Teaching as a research-led profession: nothing but a pipe dream?' Conference paper. British Educational Research Association Conference, University of Exeter, September.

——(2003) 'Oiling the wheels *and* cleaning the plates? Reflections on the first year of being a co-leader of a Networked Learning Community'. Conference paper presented as part of SUPER symposium, British Educational Research Association, Heriot-Watt University, Edinburgh, September.

——(2005) 'Trying to build a research culture in a school – trying to find the right questions to ask: "You have to listen to the river if you want to catch a trout"'. *Journal of Teacher Development*, 8(2–3): 137–149.

Zajano, N.C. and Edelsberg, C.M. (1993) 'Living and writing the researcher–researched relationship'. *International Journal of Qualitative Studies in Education*, 6(2): 143–157.

Zeichner, K.M. and Noffke, S.M. (2001) 'Practitioner research', in V. Richardson (ed.) *Handbook of Research on Teaching*, 4th edn. Washington, DC: American Educational Research Association.

Index

Page references **bold** indicate figures, tables or boxes